SIMULATION IN HIGHER EDUCATION

SIMULATION IN HIGHER EDUCATION

Papers from the Denison Simulation Center
Denison University, Granville, Ohio

EDITED BY
ESTHER THORSON

An Exposition-University Book

EXPOSITION PRESS   HICKSVILLE, NEW YORK

54411

COPYRIGHT ACKNOWLEDGMENTS

Grateful acknowledgment is made for permission to use the following material:

For chapter 9: Excerpts from *Stages in the Development of Moral Thought and Action* by Lawrence Kohlberg (New York: Holt, 1969). Used by permission of the author.

For chapter 10: Excerpts from "Developmental Hierarchy in Preference and Comprehension of Moral Judgment" by James Rest (unpublished doctoral dissertation, University of Chicago, 1968). Used by permission of the author.

For chapter 12: Illustrations from *Living Maps of the Field Plotter* by Robert E. Nunley (Washington, D.C.: American Geographers, Commission on College Geography, Technical Paper No. 4, 1971). Used by permission.

Chapter 15 first appeared in *Computer Science in Social and Behavioral Education,* ed. Daniel Bailey (Englewood Cliffs, N.J.: Educational Technology Press, 1978).

For chapter 16: Illustrations of Melzack and Casey models which appeared in *Science,* vol. 150, fig. 4, 19 November 1965 (copyright 1965 by American Association for the Advancement of Science) and in *The Skin Senses,* ed. Dan R. Kenshalo, 1968. Courtesy of Charles C. Thomas, Publishers, Springfield, Illinois.

FIRST EDITION

© 1979 by Denison University

LIBRARY OF CONGRESS CATALOG CARD NUMBER: 78-72489

ISBN 0-682-49122-5

Printed in the United States of America

CONTENTS

ACKNOWLEDGMENTS

With a few exceptions, the authors of the papers in this volume are Denison faculty. Many of these persons have been working with simulation research or teaching projects for years, having been instrumental in creating the institution-wide project. Two authors deserve special credit for their efforts within the project. One, Louis F. Brakeman, as Dean of the College, and later as Provost, brought together and stimulated the original simulation group, guiding the conceptualizing and writing of proposals. He has been the continual guide, protector, and champion of the project throughout its work. The second individual is Larry C. Ledebur, an economist who worked on the original simulation committee and who directed the project during its first year. Without his enthusiasm and perception of how simulation could be broadly used, many fewer than the current fifty percent of the Denison faculty would now be involved. Other faculty who have long been involved in the growth of the project and who deserve special thanks are Bruce E. Bigelow, Stanley Huff, Paul G. King, Donald G. Schilling, Lee Scott, and Donald Valdes.

Esther Thorson

INTRODUCTION

ESTHER THORSON

"Simulation" is a word used frequently and with a variety of different meanings. In its broadest sense, a simulation can be a model, theory, or, in general, any representation of a system. Although researchers disagree about defining "system," it can, in simplest form, be thought of as a set of elements and a set of relationships among these elements. There can be philosophical, psychological, biological, physical, artistic, and many other kinds of systems; and simulation is often used as a form of investigation in the study of these systems.

Simulation can be formulated in a role-playing, gaming, or mathematical model format, and it can either partially or completely rely on interaction with computerized material. These forms of simulation can be considered to fall on a continuum of detail to which the simulation system is specified. Points along the continuum could be characterized in the following way:

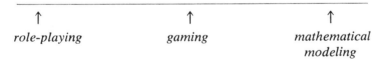

| role-playing | gaming | mathematical modeling |

Role-playing is an activity in which participants assume the responsibility of a particular role but are free within that general constraint to respond as they wish to situations that require choices or decisions to be made. For example, a group, following preparation in ethical theory, might act as a committee charged with the responsibility of allocating the use of a life-saving medical device to three of ten individuals. The only constraints operating on the individuals in this case would be that they respond in terms of the case histories of the ten individuals. An example wherein the role is more extensively defined might be a city planning game where each participant is assigned a more particular role such as "environmentalist" or "Black activist" or "mayor." In this case the participant can still simulate from his own preferences and conceptions of the world, but he may also have to work from a list of statements constraining his behavior to certain outcomes, given certain situations. Nevertheless, the total interaction of all the participants is not specified in advance, and the system that comes to operate in the role-playing would be virtually impossible to predict in detail.

Gaming is an activity in which participants, as groups, compete with each other, or against specified conditions, to attempt to reach particular objectives. For example, games may replicate complex situations in educational administration, labor-management disputes, urban politics, the tradeoffs of environmental regulation, the legislative process, or international affairs. Unlike role-playing, we would be able to predict, at least generally, what the set of occurrences will look like because certain rules must be followed. Role-playing may occur as part of a game, as for example, in "Internation Simulation" (Guetzkow, 1959), where groups of participants act as "countries" but also where there are both competition and rules.

Modeling is the activity of building a highly specified schema or some other kind of representation of a system. Possible formats of models include (1) a series of mathematical equations, (2) a computer program, or (3) a physical "mockup." Examples would include a physical model of a gene, a computer simulation of a city (e.g., Forrester, 1959), or a series of mathematical expressions representing the propagation of disease through a community.

Much of the three simulation areas have been used in research or counseling approaches, and simulation is often characterized as a useful heuristic approach (for example, there is a Simulation Special Interest Group of the American Educational Research Association). However, many simulations from commercial enterprises or from the research literature would prove useless to the teacher of undergraduates because they are either hopelessly simplistic, or simply too complex. For that reason, in 1971, a group of faculty at Denison University began meeting to search for faculty development funding that would allow them to create new materials or revamp old, and bring them to a point of having a "fair" chance as heuristic tools. In July, 1974, the Denison Simulation Project became established with funding of $292,000 for three years from the Lilly Endowment. Just as might be expected, the major goals of the Project were to provide the opportunity for faculty, first, to inventory existing simulations in their areas and determine which ones were appropriate for their classroom use; second, to redesign existing simulations or design their simulations for their own particular teaching needs; third, to implement these simulations in their classrooms, and, fourth, to evaluate their teaching effectiveness.

The hypothesis under which the Simulation Project has operated is that "to represent a system," in any of the forms described above, is to take an important step toward producing a student who can successfully solve problems—an activity that many argued to be at the heart of the liberal arts approach. An accompanying hypothesis is that the active student will be more effective, will "learn more" than the passive one. Whether simulation actually produces active problem solvers, however, remains an open question. Therefore, in addition to developing and/or using simulations, the Denison faculty are becoming increasingly involved in attempts to evaluate the teaching effectiveness of simulation. Such evaluation, in fact, was the major goal of the third year of the project, and five articles exemplifying much of the evaluation work are contained in this volume.

In the main, however, the present set of papers is aimed at cataloging and evaluating what is available in simulation, and appropriate for college curricula. Additionally, many of the papers introduce simulations developed at Denison, both to serve particular heuristic needs, and to overcome major deficiencies in the simulation literature currently available. Much of the reported work was carried out with grants from the Project to individuals at Denison. Some of the papers resulted from a workshop held for faculty from colleges throughout the United States during June, 1976. Three of the papers were authored or co-authored by persons outside Denison and who served as consultants to the workshop. The present series of papers was authored by a wide variety of faculty, including fields such as chemistry, economics, psychology, history, political science, anthropology, education, geology, and college administration. The common threads in these papers are that they all involved simulation, were aimed at heuristic goals, and there was generally a concern for evaluating whether those goals had been accomplished.

Much of the simulation material referred to here is available commercially; some of it appears in the educational and scientific literature, and some is available from the Denison Simulation Center. Wherever it was possible, it has been the aim of the authors to point out sources. If some of the sources are not made clear, requests for information would be welcomed by the Center.

It should be noted that, in addition to providing a teaching tool, many of the Denison faculty are finding simulation to be useful research tool. Of course, modeling has long been accepted as an investigatory approach in such disciplines as economics, physics, chemistry, and psychology, among others. At Denison, however, the research applications appear to be spreading into the humanities, philosophy, and additional social science areas. When research and teaching strategies can be successfully integrated, it is clear that the faculty person involved is in a fortunate and exciting situation indeed, in that the "laboratory" and the classroom no longer are in opposition. The reader is asked to take special note, therefore, of those "integrative" approaches described in some of the papers.

An additional advantage of simulation, at least at Denison, has been the encouragement of cross-disciplinary interests and courses. If an individual wants to model a social or a biological system, for example, he generally is forced to take account of variables that cut across disciplinary lines. Two excellent examples of this kind of activity can be found in the chapters on urban studies (Potter), and on values (Straumanis and Auge). Many other approaches, cross-disciplinary in nature or in scope, are also being developed, but are not yet ready to be cast into a form publicly available. To give but a few examples, a course on women in history was taught with simulations relating to psychological, sociological, and biological principles. A values clarification course using resource allocation simulations was taught Spring Semester, 1977. There is being offered an industrial psychology course that integrates economic, sociological, and group dynamics principles, as well as those more typically used by experimental psychologists. The cross-disciplinary approach, then, is one infinitely compatible with simulation, and one hopes to see more activity along these lines of endeavor.

One final point important to the Simulation Project must be mentioned. As anyone familiar with the educational simulation literature knows, there are many designs that can only be called educationally inferior. Some are based on faulty or unnecessarily simplistic assumptions about the phenomena in question; others require too little intellectual activity on the part of the participants; still others are simply not designed sufficiently well to accomplish their stated goals. The attempt at Denison has been to select carefully from what is available, weeding out inferior materials or using them only as starting points to develop more sophisticated designs. This, of course, is not to say that the present authors never have used poor materials, or that their own materials are faultless. It is to say, however, that the Project has put major emphasis upon moving simulation activities into clearly credible intellectual circles. "Playing games" in the derogatory sense is simply not applicable to the work reported here. For those who are cynical about whether simulation is an intellectually respectable enterprise, it is hoped that the present essays will at least lessen the cynicism. Simulation is surely no educational panacea, but, for some, its development at the highest levels can provide excitement, research challenges, and, best of all, active engagement of the student's perception of the world.

REFERENCES

Guetzkow, H. A use of simulation in the study of internation relations. *Behavioral Science,* 1959, *4*(3), 183-191.
Forrester, Jay. *Urban dynamics.* Cambridge: The M.I.T. Press, 1969.

Part I

SIMULATION IN A LIBERAL ARTS CURRICULUM

The first paper in this volume serves as an overview of how simulation can be justified as a technique that forms an integral part of course curricula. In formulating the justification, the paper outlines many of the original conceptions the Denison faculty had about the Simulation Project, and summarizes how simulation came to be a set of actively used heuristic approaches at Denison. The paper discusses how simulation has been broadly defined by the Simulation Project so as to include a wide variety of applications, and how this definition of simulation can be linked to an "inquiry" or "problem-solving" approach to learning. And, finally, the paper overviews a number of ways simulation has been incorporated into the curriculum, and what some of the attempts to evaluate the teaching effectiveness of the approach have been.

1

THE DENISON SIMULATION PROJECT: FORMULATING, INTRODUCING, AND EVALUATING, CURRICULAR CHANGES[1]

ESTHER THORSON

ABSTRACT

A number of faculty at Denison University have been making heuristic use of gaming and simulation for several years. In the fall of 1974, the college was awarded nearly $300,000 from the Lilly Endowment to continue and expand that heuristic use. Three years later, forms of simulation are being used by fifty percent of the Denison faculty, and the college is becoming a center for the study of college-level applications of simulation.

This paper will discuss four major topics related to the Simulation Project: first, how the simulation concept has been defined so as to be of widest interest and applicability; second, how simulation can be linked to a problem-solving approach to learning; third, a short case history of how the previous two formulations were integrated in an extensive way into a traditional college curriculum; and, fourth, a discussion of some of the attempts to evaluate these simulation efforts.

In July, 1974, Denison University was awarded a grant of $292,000 from the Lilly Endowment to establish a faculty development program aimed at introducing gaming and simulation into the college curriculum. Although ten or fifteen members of the Denison faculty were previously familiar with simulation methodologies, the concept of integrating the methodologies into one programmatic effort was an activity new to all involved. To illustrate the orientation toward simulation, I quote from the original proposal to the Lilly Endowment:

> It is a basic objective of liberal education that there must be a working relationship between learning and the quality of an individual's life. We are committed to that objective at Denison; and because we are, we want, again and again, to stimulate students to perceive the practical value of what they are learning. We also want to enhance their personal confidence—and their competence—to use that learning with integrity and wisdom.
>
> We are impressed with simulation because it works directly on those objectives. It provides intensive training in problem-solving and decision making. It creates contexts in which complex questions of values and ethics may be addressed more effectively. It forces attention toward reality.
>
> Thus, simulation promises to help to close a gap too long neglected by liberal education. This is the gap between abstract learning and the application of what is learned. We are determined, according to the highest standards, to close that gap—to stress the application of learning as well as abstract or theoretical understanding.
>
> Simulation helps to do that because it emphasizes the relationship between knowledge, principles and values and real situations, so that knowledge, principles and values are translated into understanding, decisions and solutions. In summary, then, simulation is a mode of education which demands that knowledge be integrated with reality and with behavior. It helps students to perceive values and ideas not as the material for arm-chair rhetoric, but rather as the bases of practical decisions and the touchstones of responsible action.
>
> From "Simulation and Learning at Denison University,"
> Granville, Ohio, 1974

As can be seen, the major assumption in this approach is that simulation, in all its various forms, engenders or encourages problem solving. Is simulation consistent with a problem-solving approach? The present paper will attempt to respond to this question, both at a theoretical level, and in terms of the empirical outcomes of attempts to use simulation in such a way. I shall first discuss the problem of defining simulation, arguing that the various areas within simulation actually involve the same process, rather than many different ones. Second, I shall be concerned with the problem of defining problem solving, and linking that process with simulation. At that point, I shall briefly overview ways in which the preceding work with concepts of simulation and problem solving was integrated into much of the heuristic and research activity of a large percentage of the Denison faculty. Lastly, I shall ask about evaluating the validity of simulations, about their teaching effectiveness at the classroom level, as well as about the programmatic success of simulation used in a college-wide effort.

I. *Defining Simulation*

For present purposes, role-playing, gaming, and simulation will be subsumed under the most general term of the three, simulation. All three activities involve building and/or manipulating *models of systems.* Because both "model" and "system" carry large numbers of connotations, both concepts must be examined carefully.

The term "system" is used in numbers of jargon-filled analyses of phenomena of the social and physical sciences. Many of these uses are derived either from the literature in *systems analysis* (e.g., White & Tauber, 1969) or from *general systems theory* (e.g., Laszlo, 1975). The concept of system in both these endeavors can be argued to be quite similar. In its simplest form, a system can be described as a set of structures, a set of relations among those structures, and a set of attributes (or properties). Relations among the attributes compose functions of the system (Laszlo, 1975, p. 20). As Laszlo points out, there are several principal types of systems: (1) the physicochemical (e.g., atoms, molecules, etc.); (2) the biological; (3) organ systems; (4) socialecological (formed by "energy and mass transfers of organisms within a geographic region"); (5) sociocultural ("distinguished by . . . a symbolic communication system, extraskeletal memory stores, the . . . capacity to acquire, code and hand down empirically gathered information"); (6) organization (i.e., "formed by human beings . . . to carry out specific tasks"); and (7) technical systems ("made of suborganic components by organizations to carry out special purpose tasks within sociocultural systems"). Clearly then, any kind of phenomenon can be treated as a system. This fact, as will be seen, opens the way for simulation to become a tool usable in most all classical disciplines, and to become an important tool for cross-disciplinary investigation.

What then is a *model?* In its broadest sense, a model is any form of description of a system. This means that, just as systems require concern with the component *structures, relations among structures, attributes,* and *relations among attributes,* a model of a system requires some form of representation of each of the four components. These required representations may take the form of verbal descriptions, physical "imitations," mathematical formulae, or computer programs.

The distinction between role-playing, gaming, and computer simulation, then, can be said to occur largely as a function of the forms of models involved. An additional consideration, however, is that the level of specificity that characterizes the models may vary. That is, the degree to which information about the components of the system are known and described in the models may vary. For example, when one simulates a jury deliberating a case, the legal structures are generally specified completely, but the personalities and decision-making characteristics of the jury are frequently left entirely unspecified. On the other hand, Forrester's (1969) elaborate computer simulation of a city specifies all the structures, relations, and so on that its author considered relevant components of the urban system.

To simulate, then, is to model a system. Certainly, this is a broad definition, and, as such, it often brings the heuristic use of simulation under a peculiar form of fire. The criticism generally takes the form of "then nearly everything one does in the classroom is simulation." An example of this criticism that is worth describing involves an English instructor who once told me he resented the fact that a student putting himself into the position of an historic character and then doing creative writing as that character, could be considered to be simulating. My response was that, although the described activity did involve role-playing, there was probably only the most intuitive of attempts to identify and describe the components of any system. So, although one of the *forms* or *formats* of simulation was there, the necessary analytic process that true simulation requires was not.

Two additional points should be made before leaving the definition of simulation, the first of which is not unrelated to the "everything is simulation" notion. There is existent much criticism of the heuristic uses of simulation on the basis of claims that it is the "fun-and-games" approach to learning, something only for the poorest students, or, in general, a tool that encourages only the lowest caliber of intellectual activities. The Denison Simulation Center contains one of the largest collections of games and simulations at the high school or post-secondary level. Certainly, much of the material one would want to avoid. There exist in it inaccuracies, oversimplifications, and even some requirements for behavior that could only be termed offensive. This fact, however, ought not be allowed to discourage the instructor who is interested in treating complex problems in a sophisticated manner because, just as the heuristic simulation literature includes some of the worst materials and ideas, it clearly contains much of the best. Many social and physical scientists are finding simulation a powerful investigatory tool. The instructor working toward sophisticated conceptualizations of phenomena on the part of his students can, therefore, be expected to find simulation equally worthwhile.

An additional point that is important to note about the above discussion of what simulation is, concerns the fact that it is of broad applicability—to the physical sciences, the social sciences, the humanities, and, though perhaps to a lesser extent, the arts. What the fact implies is that simulation allows it to be said that what the scientist is doing is related to what the humanist is doing. What is the exact nature of that link? We shall argue here that the main linkage flows from the simulation methodology moving all participants toward *active problem solving*.

Unfortunately, although most of the faculty now using simulation at Denison would argue similarly, it is clear that close questioning of these faculty may uncover only vague concepts of what is meant by "problem solving." And, further, even these vague concepts are often inconsistent with each other. Before engaging in an attempt, therefore, to analyze simulation as a problem-solving technique, we must turn to the educational and psychological literature for more satisfactory clarification of problem solving.

II. *Algorithmic Approaches to Problem Solving*

A major difficulty in discussing problem solving concerns the fact that its usage varies so drastically from discipline to discipline, or even between research areas within a single discipline. In mathematics education, for example, the term generally refers to solutions of "word problems," enumeration problems, or problems from arithmetic, algebra, geometry, and so on. In these kinds of problems there are generally known solutions, or at least known algorithms to determine whether a solution exists, if not to determine the solution itself. An excellent example of an analysis of this kind of problem solving can be found in Wickelgren (1974). This psychologist and mathematician limits his theoretical treatment to solution of the above examples of "formal" problems, that is, those for which there are "ways of restricting thinking to a specified set of given information and operations" (p. 2). Wickelgren differentiates specific problem-solving methods from general ones on the basis that the latter involves generalizing the application of a method from one problem to a nonidentical other. For Wickelgren, solution of formal problems requires treatment of four major components: "givens," "operations for transforming givens," "goals," and "subgoals." Givens are a set of initial informational statements about whatever subject matter is being examined. Operations are the "actions" that can be taken to change or deduce from givens new informational statements. Goals are the final statements that the problem-solver wishes to obtain. Subgoals are, just as one might imagine, informational statements that serve as way-stations toward goals. Wickelgren points out that subgoals are generally used to decrease the possible number of operations that must be tested to determine which ones provide progress toward goals. Finally, Wickelgren defines "insight" problems as those in which the solver makes a "critical transformation of the givens that essentially solves the problem," and he suggests that the insight form of problem solving usually occurs in a small number of steps.

Another algorithmically based, but somewhat more general concept of problem solving is outlined by Glaser (1976). He uses Simon's (1969) distinction between "design" and "descriptive analysis" as an analogy for differentiating problem-solving and nonproblem-solving approaches to education. Glaser points out that "the essence of design is to devise courses of action aimed at changing existing situations into preferred ones." Examples would include "devising a sales plan for a company, constructing a new social welfare policy for a state, and designing a program of instruction for a school system." On the other hand, "descriptive analysis" would presumably involve material wherein a student's major task is to understand and remember solutions that have been arrived at previously by someone else. Simon refers to this process as describing "how things are and how they work."

The main way in which Glaser's and Simon's approach to problem solving is similar to Wickelgren's is that mathematical optimization theory is suggested as a possible approach to teaching "design" activities. Given a goal, a set of parameter values (values of the initial states of the system), and a set of constraints, optimization procedures allow determination of an "optimal" set of values for the variables in the system (or, in other words, determination of the goal). An example might involve a game in which the player received a particular number of points if, after a certain base was named, he could reach that base within thirty seconds. Given a set of points for each base, given the probability that any base is named, and given the relative spatial locations of each base, the optimization question would concern where the player would position himself for a maximum payoff in points (that is, the goal).

Another important approach to problem solving is one derived from theories about the psychological processes humans engage in when formulating the kind of algorithmic approach described above. Looking at numbers of these so-called "information-processing theories" of problem solving is beyond the scope of this paper, but one such model will be included because it adds much to our understanding of problem formulation. Suchman's Inquiry Training Model (1964) is based closely upon Piaget's (1926) model of intellectual development. A brief look at Suchman's work (a more elaborated introduction to his approach can be found in Joyce & Weil, 1972) indicates that he views problem solving as an operation carried out on concepts and schemas that are brought into conflict with occurrences in an individual's environment. The classic example of such conflict involves the child watching a strip made of two different metals laminated together. When turned in one direction over a flame, the strip bends upward. When turned in the opposite direction, it bends downward. The child must determine the series of events that would lead to such a "strange" outcome. To do so requires scientific problem solving, involving such steps as, first, determining what variables might be relevant to the problem (e.g., the length of the metal, its components, their response to heat); and, second, setting up experiments to test the effects of those variables. In the metal strip example, the child might set up an experiment in which he examined the effects of two values on the variable "length" (long and short) and of two values on the variable "type of metal." This arrangement would result in a simple 2 × 2 factorial experiment as shown in the diagram.

Variable I: Length

Short   Long

Variable 2:   Copper

Type of metal   Steel

The above description of inquiry training as a problem-solving approach looks, to this point, much like the algorithmic approaches discussed previously. Indeed, in a sense, it is somewhat algorithmic in nature. But its further assumption includes a stipulation that children at various stages of development go about using algorithms very differently. Only the child at the highest level of development (called "formal operations" by Piaget) would set up the appropriate experiment in the example of the metal blade. Younger children would not have the information-processing skills available for such an activity, and, therefore, would produce a developmental series of approaches, only when reaching "formal operations" coming to the proper experimental (or problem-solving) algorithm.

So, it is in this sense that inquiry training is an information-processing model of problem solving. The way, in fact, that it combines the algorithmic analysis of what problem *solutions* should look like, and the *thinking processes* through which one goes to reach those solutions is of major consequence to the present discussion. For surely the place where educators must eventually find themselves exists at a point where both the form of problem solutions (or algorithms) *and* the information-processing occurrences that lead to those forms are understood. And, if this claim is in fact true, then making the argument relating simulation and problem solving requires examining the effect simulation has both on algorithms, and the process of their creation.

Where do we stand at the end now of this overly brief comparison of approaches to problem solving? Probably the major outcome is that there is at least a passing acquaintance with one general model for describing the setting of and solutions to problems: To combine Wickelgren's, Glaser's, and Suchman's (or Piaget's) notions, it seems reasonable to say that problem setting and solving requires analysis of given states of affairs, knowledge about rules and constraints for possible manipulating of those states, and an analysis of what one wishes to accomplish. This process could be carried out by setting up a mathematical optimization problem, structuring a logical (deductive or inductive) argument, or formulating hypotheses and an experiment to test them. It should be noted, of course, that such an approach assumes that most problems can be treated as if they were, in Wickelgren's terms, formal ones.

III.   *Problem Solving and Simulation*

As can be seen in the above admittedly biased review of some approaches to problem solving, there is little theorizing about complex problem-solving processes that can be easily applied to the practical concerns of incorporating the process into one's teaching activities or into the learning processes of one's students. Where college instructors are claiming to use problem-solving approaches, their analyses of both the problem-solving algorithms and the problem-processing activities of their own systems and those of their students seem to remain largely at an intuitive level. What, then, the reader may well be asking himself, is the special merit of simulation as a problem-solving tool? The answer is straightforward in some respects. Simulation is the design and analysis of systems. Whatever the structure of problems and their solutions is, and whatever humans do when they set and solve problems, are identical to the structures and processing of simulation. Simulation *is* setting and solving problems—but to simulate, that is, to do it well, requires a reflective analysis of what one is doing. Casting this idea into other words, expert simulation requires self-knowledge about one's problem-processing activities. And, further, the argument will be made that this self-knowledge enhances the ability to transfer problem-processing from one domain to another.

I must now elaborate upon the notion that to simulate is to engage in problem solving. Under the assumption that simulation involves a model of structures, relations among structures, attributes, and relations among attributes, its relations to algorithmic analyses of problem solving like those of Wickelgren and Glaser become immediately clear. For example, assume it was desirable to create a simulation of pattern-recognition processes on the skin (Thorson, Snyder, Anderson, & Thorson, 1976). A reasonable first step would be to list the "givens" or rules about skin structure, and the limits of information handling by the cutaneous system (e.g., the receptors in the skin, the way information is sent into the spinal column, or the way in which the sensory cortex is arranged.) These givens would correspond to structures. Next, the relevant operations would have to be hypothesized (e.g., stimulation of one area of the skin will inhibit sensory registration at other areas). The hypothesized *operations* would here correspond to *relations* among the *structures*. (Whether it would be necessary to separate attributes from relations among structures is not clear, so in this case that distinction will not be made.) The *goal* might be stated in terms of a model of cutaneous processing for which, given any patterned input (e.g., a letter drawn on the skin), the system either recognizes it accurately or does not. Because the cutaneous literature does not yet provide empirical examples of all relevant inputs to the skin, a justifiable subgoal would be to ask the model to predict accurately examples of cutaneous input that are actually available for empirical verification.

This example, then, provides, it is hoped, a straightforward argument that the steps in setting and solving problems are, in important ways, identical to the steps in building a simulation. Unfortunately, the reader may now be commenting, the link between simulation and problem solving might be relevant for the research scientist, but surely one cannot expect the undergraduate student to build such a simulation. And, if he does not build the simulation himself, he is not participating in problem solving. Two responses to these comments seem appropriate. First, it does seem justifiable to claim that modeling a system is problem solving in one of its most sophisticated forms. But problem solving of what Wickelgren calls formal problems can be argued to be quite similar to working through predictions in an already-formulated simulation. The cutaneous model can again be used as an example. Assume that the model has already been formulated, and that, in fact, its structural and relational characteristics are all available in the form of an interactive computer program. In that case, of course, the student does not have to formulate all of the givens or operations, although he does have to come to understand them. What he does have to do, if his instructor is wise in using the simulation, is set up goals and/or subgoals for (1) choosing inputs to the simulation that will allow him to understand better how it works; (2) predict how the simulation will respond to the inputs; and (3) as he carries out 1) and 2), actually rediscover additional relations existent in the model and that may not have been given to him in their entirety as he began. So, even though the cutaneous problem is a more formalized one (that is, having, more nearly, an enumerable set of alternative strategies), it is still not perfectly formal. In other words, the student working with a developed simulation still remains largely in the role of the original problem-solver. A major advantage, however, is that he can be given varying amounts of prior information, so that, at the beginning of his endeavors, his problem-solving skills are not required to emerge fully developed.

IV. *Introducing Simulation in the College Curriculum*

The preceding sections of this paper have attempted to formulate fairly specifically just what simulation is, and how it relates to problem-solving approaches to higher education. Once the justification and defining stages of curricular developments are completed, the next step, of course, is to introduce changes into the work and research of faculty and students. The experience at Denison seems especially interesting in that it involves more extensive integration of simulation into all portions of college life than has been accomplished elsewhere.

To discuss activities of introducing change, two kinds of occurrence are relevant. The first concerns how to communicate enough information to others for them to become willing to make some personal attempts at the necessary reeducation processes. Such communication is partially an intellectual process, but more extensively it is political. A well-elaborated description of that process at Denison is available in an article by Ledebur (1975).

The second kind of occurrence relating to introductory processes concerns what programmatic structures come into existence. Because these have not been discussed previously, they will be treated briefly here. Five primary occurrences are included in the group of programmatic structures: (*a*) consultants, (*b*) workshops, (*c*) faculty development programs for developing classroom and research applications of simulations, (*d*) stimulation of production of written papers and materials, and (*e*) a system of classroom and program evaluation.

The initial decision about encouraging faculty to take advantage of the opportunity to learn about simulation involved the presumption that the most exciting approaches in the field are those wherein sophisticated research applications are being made. It was decided, therefore, to create a program of visiting consultants, including primarily prestigious researchers and authors who happened to use simulation as a major methodology, but who were not necessarily schooled in heuristic applications. Consistent with this approach was the assumption that Denison faculty, once excited by the possibilities of simulation as a problem-solving tool, would be able to formulate their own heuristic applications.

Although there is no way to compare the success of the resultant program of visiting simulation experts to other possible structures, many of the now-involved Denison faculty report their interactions with consultants to have been pivotal in their decisions toward experimentation with the approach. To mention but a few of the more than fifty simulation experts who proved so effective, there were representatives from psychology such as William Bewley (Minnesota Educational Computing Consortium), Philip Spelt (Wabash College), and Dana Main (West Virginia College of Graduate Studies); from sociology, Cathy Greenblat (Rutgers College): from geology, John Harbaugh (Stanford University); from mathematics and engineering, Maynard Thompson (Indiana University); from international relations, Margaret and Charles Hermann (The Ohio State University), and Karen Feste (University of Denver);

history, Robert Hauser (Pennsylvania State University at McKeesport); from education, Charles Plummer (University of Illinois) and Donald Cruickshank (The Ohio State University); from chemistry, Norman Craig (Oberlin) and William Child (Carleton College), and from Women's Studies, Rosabeth Kanter (Brandeis University).

All of these individuals have made significant contributions to their field, and their expertise and sophistication in using simulation were responded to strongly by Denison faculty.

A second form of simulation activity that seemed to have major impact upon introduction of change into the curriculum was workshops. For the most part, these workshops were organized around special topics related directly or as helping tools to simulation approaches. In most cases, the workshops were organized by a single Denison faculty person, who invited consultants and/or used resource persons from the campus. Many of the workshops involved faculty participants from other schools; some were only for the local constituency. A few directly involved students. Examples of these workshops include such topics as "Simulation in Chemistry," "Simulation of Reasoning Processes in Children," "Cognitive Styles and Simulation," "Simulation in Assertiveness Training," "Simulations and the Roles of Professional Women," "Simulation and Racial Relations," as well as many others. In addition to these special topic activities, the Simulation Center presented wide-ranging summer workshops in 1976 and 1977, including all the areas of application that had been developed.

There are two major payoffs for investing in these forms and varieties of workshops. The first is that they create a rich source of information dissemination. Because simulation as an heuristic tool is a fairly new endeavor, it is an area that often requires direct communication, rather than filtering through journal articles. Further, the area is so diverse that only individuals gathered from a variety of areas and representing many backgrounds can assure inclusion into one's own repertoire of all the myriad examples and ideas. And, second, organization of workshops requires organization of one's own resources, as well as expansion of these resources. The requirement to "produce" for others, then, serves as a strong motivating force. Overall, workshops uniquely allow both expansion and integration of activities in simulation.

A third activity aimed at introducing simulation into the curriculum involved summer and semester released-time grants for individual faculty work in simulation. Nearly seventy such grants have been made at Denison, thereby allowing a large number of faculty to experiment with simulation activities in their own fields, and to recast these activities into a form usable in their classrooms. The faculty development program involves, then, incentives and provides the time that is necessary for creating sophisticated applications.

Coordinate with the faculty development program has been the assumption that those who were provided the opportunities would share the proceeds, in terms of papers, articles, essays, computer programs, and games, with others. To date, the Denison Simulation Center has available more than a hundred such products. Denison faculty are actively reporting their work both within disciplinary forums and to educational groups. A sampling of the projects is contained in the chapters that follow.

The final introduction format to be discussed here is the notion that, whatever is developed, be it computer simulations, a game, an integration of course materials with a set of games, or an interdisciplinary course formed around a complex simulation, it must be evaluated, at least in some manner. Educational and curricular evaluation are always difficult. Nevertheless, the difficulty has not seemed sufficient to warrant ignoring evaluation, and at least one-fourth of the simulation activities at Denison have been subjected to evaluational scrutiny. Because Morris's (1977) paper analyzes much of the classroom evaluation occurring at Denison, the remarks herein about evaluation will remain fairly general. An elaboration of the philosophy formulated in the Project to guide the evaluation of simulations and their heuristic use is contained in the final section of this paper.

V.   *Evaluation of Simulations and Their Heuristic Use*

As I have argued previously (Thorson, 1977), evaluation of a simulation and evaluation of its effectiveness when used in the classroom are two very different enterprises. For that reason, they will be treated separately, though briefly, in the following paragraphs. The goal here is to outline what we have attempted to accomplish in "evaluating" simulation activities at Denison.

EVALUATION LEVEL I: VALIDATION OF SIMULATIONS AND GAMES

Surprisingly little research has been aimed directly at the problem of validating simulations and games. One of the most extensive logical analyses of the simulation validation techniques was done by Hermann (1967). He was concerned with defining rules for establishing the scientific validity of simulations and games, applying his analysis to some of the early models of international politics. According to Hermann, two initial kinds of specification of simulation must be made before it can be validated. First, what type of simulation is it: man, man-machine, or machine? Second, to what purpose will it be put to use: (*a*) as an instrument for discovering and defining alternatives for processing activities, for policy, etc.; (*b*) as a model that produces accurate predictions about further events; (*c*) as an instructive device; (*d*) as a mechanism for formalizing theories and hypotheses, and perhaps "pretesting" them, or (*e*) [presumably] for some combination of these purposes. It is important to note that Hermann made two suggestions for validation of simulations used as instructive devices. First, he suggested they should not "transmit systematic misperceptions . . . of the reference system involved in the instructional program" and, second, they should "provide the student with greater empathy for those persons who operate in the reference system being simulated" (Hermann, 1967, p. 218).

Once the type and purpose(s) of the simulation or game have been established, the degree of validity exhibited by the simulation can be ascertained. Hermann emphasized three kinds of validity: face, internal, and event. Face validity involves the "intuitive convincingness" of the simulation, or how "realistic" it appears to be. Internal validity involves having the rules contained in the simulation or game fit together in a logically consistent way. Event validity is defined similarly to Campbell's (1957) notion of external validity; that is, that "natural" events occur in the same relations to each other as do the events in the simulation. Hermann's work in analyzing validity-establishment procedures for simulations, though not the only such approach, does provide a reasonable overview of questions to ask of the structures and functions of simulations and games. (For a similar treatment of the validity problem, with an emphasis upon economics, see Naylor, Blintfy, Burdick, and Chu, 1966.)

Hermann's approach, however, is not totally appropriate for establishment of validity for simulations still in developmental stages. Further, validation or at least partial validation of simulations that are not fully formulated is important, because these simulations are often used for heuristic purposes, and because it is important for further investigation that a researcher be able to evaluate the simulation or game as it progresses toward final formulation. Although in some ways an even more complicated issue, some suggestions for validating in-progress simulations were made by Thorson, Anderson, and Thorson (1975). Two of these suggestions will be mentioned here. First, ideally, each variable in the simulation should be provided with more than one operational definition, and these definitions should converge in the sense that relations between other variables and the two or more operational definitions indexing the one variable should be consistent. For example, if the number of persons per bathroom and the number of persons per housing unit both serve as operational definitions for "crowding," then measures on "psychosis levels," if related to one operational definition of crowding, must in a like manner be related to the other one. The second criterion for establishment of the validity of in-progress simulations requires that not only the inputs and outputs of the simulation or game be accurately reflective of actual occurrences, but that the structures and functions intervening to connect certain inputs with certain outputs also be accurate.

For example, in an international relations simulation, two countries, one highly industrialized and having a large bureaucracy, and the other having neither characteristic, may both exhibit the same response to a particular international crisis, but to claim the two responses were mediated by the same internal system would clearly be unsatisfactory.

Other analyses have been written on the topic of validating simulations, and, although time is not sufficient to discuss those works here, some of the more notable examples include Kress (1965), Coplin (1966), and Guetzkow (1968), all of whom worked in the area of international relations. A more recent, though abbreviated, discussion is available in Greenblat (1975).

EVALUATION LEVEL II: THE TEACHING EFFECTIVENESS OF
SIMULATIONS AND GAMES

Once some indication has been established regarding the validation of a simulation or game, the next level of educational evaluation concerns how well the devices "teach." The question of "teaching effectiveness" is, at Denison, as in most teaching institutions, a controversial one. Parlett and Hamilton (1972) characterize quite well the general nature of the controversy. (Although these authors are referring to program evaluations, their suggestions apply equally well to evaluations of teaching effectiveness.) Many educators, they suggest, advocate the experimental/psychometric approach, in which pretest measures are compared statistically with posttest measures to determine whether an intervening "treatment" (such as the use of simulations) has had an effect. A position polarized against this one is the "humanistic" approach, which generally claims that processes occurring in educational environments are simply too "complex" for scientific study (at least with techniques currently available), or that the educational processes are *a priori* not amenable to scientific investigation. The position intermediate to the humanistic and psychometric ones is that orientation referred to by Parlett and Hamilton as the social-anthropological approach. This approach would claim that educational outcomes *can* be investigated, but that the psychometric approach is unsatisfactory for a number of reasons. First, in educational research the number of relevant variables seems to be quite large. In psychometrics, there are two techniques for handling these numerous variables. First, it can be assumed that, by using large samples, many of the variables' effects will be randomized so as to have essentially an equal effect in every experimental group. Large-sample techniques are, however, difficult to set up satisfactorily, and often impossible to use in the setting of one particular class, several classes, or even in the entire institution. A second way to treat the "number of variables" problem involves maintaining strict experimental control over all the relevant variables. Here again, however, the problems are great. First, the researcher must be able to identify all the relevant variables—which is certainly a difficult, if not impossible task. Second, he must manipulate students and educational personnel in ways that may prove ethically unacceptable to many. Finally, the strong possibility exists for creating "artificial" environments where the results are not generalizable to the educational situation in which the researcher was originally interested.

Another criticism of the psychometric approach is that it requires that there be no changes in the "treatment" (e.g., the simulation procedure) while the experiment is in progress. In an educational environment, however, it can be argued that few, if any, procedures are developed to the stage where the instructor can or is willing to forgo occasional changes.

Perhaps the most important of Parlett and Hamilton's criticisms of the psychometric method concerns the fact that, by emphasizing scientific methodology too strongly, the researcher is led to ignore many occurrences or kinds of variables that, because of their "subjective" nature, are difficult to study. In examining the educational research literature, one does frequently receive the impression that many studies are well controlled, but have omitted so many possibly pertinent variables that the studies are simply uninteresting and unconvincing. Other studies attempt to ask difficult questions, but their methodology includes so many confoundings that the results again are not useful.

The approach Parlett and Hamilton suggest as a replacement for psychometric evaluations involves three basic procedures. First, the initial analysis and description of the technique to be evaluated must be expanded to include both subjective and objective methods. For example, various kinds of interviews with major actors involved in the educational innovation should be extensively employed. Both unobtrusive (Webb, 1966) and participant (McCall & Simons, 1969) observation methods should be used. Generally, then, better identification of relevant variables can occur. Second, the researcher should make every attempt to find out into what kind of environment (or "learning milieu") the teaching device is being introduced. This environment, then, should be the one in which the treatment is tested, rather than testing it in a more easily handleable but, unfortunately, artificial environment. Finally, it is suggested that the kind of educational method being used determines how it is tested, rather than the methodology itself being the first concern.

Parlett and Hamilton's description of the humanistic and psychometric approaches to evaluation of teaching innovations is quite helpful, and their suggestions for an intermediate approach are interesting for the present problem of evaluating the teaching effectiveness of simulations and games. We argue here, however, that, after all their suggestions are taken into account, essentially the same psychometric approach is being advocated. What has been added are important considerations for making psychometric methodologies more sophisticated and, therefore, making their outcomes more intuitively convincing.

Such a "modified" psychometric approach is the one currently being used in all of the Denison projects evaluating the teaching effectiveness of simulation and gaming applications. Basically, pretest and posttest measures are being taken and compared, but for each project the kinds of measures being used vary considerably. In fact, Morris (1977) points out specifically, in this volume, that differences in both the purposes of using simulation and the form of simulation being used require variation in what measures are most appropriate.

Although, as pointed out above, evaluational activities have accompanied many of the Denison simulation projects, the present section of this paper would not be complete without providing at least one example of how the two levels of evaluation elaborated here can be and have been analyzed. The example to be used is especially informative because its purpose was to test whether working with simulations would allow the students' problem-solving skills to develop and transfer to new situations.

Paul King, a Denison economist, compared in two classes two differing approaches to teaching macroeconomics (King, in this volume). In one class, a textbook-plus-lecture method was used. In the other, students worked with the same text, but spent a significant portion of their class times working with computer simulations of various macroeconomic phenomena. The developmental emphasis in this class involved first understanding the models, then understanding their structures and *how the instructor had come to formulate those structures,* and, finally, it required the students to create their own models.

To determine whether the two groups would show differing degrees of change in their "general problem-solving skills," the pre- and posttests included questions requiring that just such generalizations occur, for the student to receive full credit. One of the instruments used to ask this question divided test questions into "simple applications" of principles and "complex applications." Both kinds of application essentially required the student to formulate and use models to suggest solutions to new, though related, economic problems. Compared with national norms for the test, both the control and the simulation classes performed fairly well on the complex applications but not as well as on the simple applications. Importantly, however, on the simple applications, the simulation class was significantly better. This outcome provides, then, at least one initial indication that work with models, together with analysis of the information-processing occurrences in formulating them, can lead to transfer of problem-solving skills. In addition, however, the result led King to question the validity of the set of simulations he had used, especially with regard to their lack of complexity. Therefore, after completion of his project, he rewrote the simulations, making them much more complex. He is now engaged in replicating his evaluational study, using what he believes to be "more valid" macroeconomic simulations.

What we see here, then, is an instance of work evaluating both the validity and the teaching-effectiveness aspects of a set of simulations. The outcomes in this example seem to us highly encouraging for the general orientation the Denison Simulation Project has taken toward evaluation.

VI. *Some Conclusions*

The present paper has outlined the essential assumptions and structures involved in conceptualizing, implementing, and evaluating a wide-ranging program of simulation at the college level. Can we talk yet about the overall outcome or success of such an enterprise? Certainly, in a short-term sense, some characteristics of success are present. Nearly half of the teaching staff is using or has used simulation. Most of the faculty have created their own simulations, or improved considerably upon existent simulations. There have been major efforts to monitor, through evaluation of their validity and teaching effectiveness, many of the simulations used. New courses and interdisciplinary courses have been created. Clearly, then, the short-term or immediate response about the Project would be positive.

But what of the long-term consequences? Will Denison students prove themselves better problem-solvers after graduation? Will the faculty continue to create and use simulation? Will the impetus toward evaluation continue? These questions seem of primary importance, and, of course, they cannot yet be answered. Given our present state, we think the prognosis looks encouraging. We hope to be able to continue a basically analytic approach to simulation in the years to come, and thereby eventually to find and report some answers to these long-term questions.

NOTE

1. This paper was presented at the Annual Meeting of the American Educational Research Association, New York, April 4-8, 1977.

REFERENCES

Campbell, D. T. Factors relevant to the validity of experiments in social settings. *Psychological Bulletin,* 1957, *54*(4), 297-312.

Coplin, W. Inter-nation simulation and contemporary theories of inter-nation relations. *American Political Science Review,* 1966, *60,* 562-578.

Forrester, J. *Urban dynamics.* Cambridge: The M.I.T. Press, 1969.

Glaser, R. Components of a psychology of instruction: Toward a science of design. *Review of Educational Research,* 1976, *46*(1), 1-24.

Greenblat, C. S. From theory to model to gaming-simulation: A case study and validity test. In (Eds.) E. S. Greenblat and R. D. Duke, *Gaming-simulation: Rationale, design, and applications.* New York: Halstead Press, 1975.

Guetzkow, H. Some correspondences between simulations and "realities." In (Ed.) M. Kaplan, *New approaches to international relations.* New York: St. Martin's Press, 1968.

Hermann, C. F. Validation problems in games and simulations with special reference to models of international politics. *Behavioral Science,* 1967, *12,* 216-231.

Joyce, B., and Weil, M. *Models of teaching.* Englewood Cliffs, New Jersey: Prentice-Hall, 1972.

King, P. G. Computer technology and the teaching of macroeconomics: An evaluation. In this volume, ch. 19.

Kress, P. F. On validating simulation: With special attention to simulations of international politics. Unpublished manuscript, Northwestern University, 1965.

Laszlo, E. The meaning and significance of general system theory. *Behavioral Science,* 1975, *20,* 9-24.

Ledebur, L. C. Simulation in the liberal arts college: A program of educational change. *Proceedings of the North American Simulation and Gaming Association.* San Diego: University of Southern California Press, 1975, 255-267.

McCall, G. J., and Simmons, J. L. *Issues in participant observation.* London: Addison-Wesley, 1969.

Morris, C. J. Simulation evaluation designs. In this volume, ch. 22.

Naylor, T. H., Blintfy, J. L., Burdick, D. S., and Chu, K. *Computer simulation techniques.* New York: John Wiley, 1966.

Parlett, M., and Hamilton, D. Evaluation as illumination: A new approach to the study of innovatory programs. Unpublished manuscript, Centre for Research in the Educational Sciences, University of Edinburgh, October, 1972.

Piaget, J. *The language and thought of the child.* Translated by Marjorie Worden. New York: Harcourt, Brace & World, Inc., 1926.

Simon, H. A. *The sciences of the artificial.* Cambridge, Massachusetts: The M.I.T. Press, 1969.

Simulation and Learning at Denison University. (A proposal to the Lilly Endowment, Inc.) Denison University, Granville, Ohio, 1974.

Suchman, J. R. The Illinois studies in inquiry training. *Journal of Research in Science Teaching,* 1964, *3,* 231-232.

Thorson, E. Gaming and computer simulation as problem-solving vehicles in higher education. In press, *Liberal Education,* 1977.

Thorson, E. Snyder, R., Anderson, P., and Thorson, S. J. Cutaneous pattern recognition: A computer simulation. *Proceedings of the Summer Computer Simulation Conference.* La Jolla, California: Simulation Councils, Inc., 1976, 523-527.

Thorson, S. J., Anderson, P., and Thorson, E. Governments as information processing systems. *Proceedings of the Summer Computer Simulation Conference.* La Jolla, California: Simulation Councils, Inc., 1975, 1088-1097.

Webb, E. J. *Unobtrusive measures: Non-reactive research in the social sciences.* Chicago: Rand McNally, 1966.

White, H. J., and Tauber, S. *Systems analysis.* Philadelphia: Saunders, 1969.

Wickelgren, W. A. *How to solve problems.* San Francisco: W. H. Freeman, 1974.

Part II

A FACULTY
DEVELOPMENT
APPLICATION

The second paper in this volume was written by the Provost of Denison University, Louis F. Brakeman, and an Associate Dean of Students, Susan R. Bowling. It describes a major effort to design a role-playing simulation for a particular problem of faculty development. In this case, the concern was to provide a format to allow faculty members to think originally, creatively, without all the constraints that seem to inhibit the growth of new ideas, about redesigning their own institution for its future. The paper describes how the "College For the Future" is carried out, documents its use in three very different faculty development situations, and outlines a critical evaluation of the simulation.

2

DESIGNING A LIBERAL ARTS COLLEGE FOR THE FUTURE: A SIMULATION EXAMINING FUTURE CHANGE AND EDUCATIONAL VALUES

SUSAN R. BOWLING
LOUIS F. BRAKEMAN

ABSTRACT

To facilitate faculty discussion on educational goals and change in higher education, faculty at Denison University constructed a simulation that focused upon designing a liberal arts college of the future. The structured discussion format involved participants in developing curricula, academic policies, and focusing on student learning in the future. The simulation has been used three times with different participant groups. Formal and informal feedback from participants showed the experience to be of value in highlighting discussion of significant issues and goals. While sometimes finding it tiring in length, participants have generally reacted favorably to the experience. General recommendations for modification of the simulation are included.

> In the ever-renewing society what matures is a system or framework within which continuous innovation, renewal and rebirth can occur. (Gardner, 1963)

Where will you be in the year 2000? How will your academic discipline have changed? What educational needs will students have in the twenty-first century and what educational system can best facilitate the necessary learning? Which of our current procedures, practices, and values will stand the test of time and which will need to become more flexible and able to change? Which of your personal educational values have stood unexamined but daily affect your students? Can you articulate your educational values?

These and many other questions intertwine to illustrate the merit in focusing on personal educational values. An examination of personal values, however, when conducted in the present, is often muddied by self-censoring comments like "I would never do that," "It would never work here," or "It would cost too much." In an effort to free faculty from these barriers and to help them focus upon defining personal educational values, several faculty and staff at Denison University (the authors and Larry C. Ledebur) designed a simulation constructed to focus upon the nature of liberal arts education in the future. The primary focus was on the participant's personal educational values and an examination of those values within Gardner's concepts of change and renewal. In addition to the benefits and stimulation of thinking of education in the future, the "future" was chosen consciously by the designers for increased effectiveness in the process and group dynamics of the simulation. By placing the simulation at a future date, constraints participants might react to in their work groups, budgets, equipment, and other barriers are reduced, thereby freeing the participants to be as creative and flexible as their own values.

Obviously, actually designing a liberal arts college in a twelve-hour workshop is an impossible task and was not a primary goal of the simulation. It was hoped, however, that the structured discussion mechanisms to facilitate this design (i.e., task forces, liaison communications, workshop facilitators, etc.) would lead to stimulating discussions with the focus of a real educational institution and real task concerns.

The simulation has been used on three different occasions. The simulation was originally used in the summer of 1975 with the Great Lakes Colleges Association faculty development program. It was modified slightly and used at Albion College during January, 1976. It was again used in the GLCA faculty development program during the summer of 1976.

I.   *Simulation Process*

The process used in the simulation involved six basic steps:

(1) Participants were asked to prepare prior to the experience in some manner like readings or seminars. At the start of the simulation a presentation by a guest speaker emphasized change in higher education through the examination of future educational values, change, organizational renewal, and new ways to conceptualize education.

(2) Participants also completed two rounds of a Delphi technique (Delbecq, Van de Ven, & Gustafson, 1975) to reach group consensus on educational goals and objectives for the future. The Delphi technique is

a process where participants read items, the group's responses are summarized, and participants are asked to again revise and rank items by considering the summary of other's rankings. Using this technique, participants were asked to rank fourteen goal statements (see Table 1). Group rankings were then compiled and participants were asked to respond again to these group rankings with their own revised preferences to refine group consensus.

TABLE 1
EDUCATIONAL GOALS FOR
A LIBERATED ARTS COLLEGE IN THE YEAR 2000

1. To learn to deal with the phenomena of increased leisure in a meaningful and creative manner.
2. To provide a solid base of information and skills to facilitate entry into graduate or professional school and success in obtaining professional goals.
3. To excite curiosity and enthusiasm for living a full and meaningful life, characterized by understanding, insight, accomplishment, and constructive contribution.
4. To obtain an integrated understanding of one's intellectual, ethical, and spiritual life.
5. To develop the ability to analyze, synthesize, and evaluate.
6. To pursue individual development and personal growth, develop a sense of self-worth, and achieve a significant level of self-understanding.
7. To prepare for competent and creative citizenship in contemporary society.
8. To learn and develop competence in the concepts, methodologies, and content of a particular academic discipline.
9. To develop social and interpersonal competence, that is, the ability to have open, trusting, meaningful relationships with others.
10. To develop a sense of competence, of confidence in one's ability to cope with what comes and to achieve successfully what one sets out to do.
11. To prepare for a career and for immediate entry into a vocation.
12. To enhance the ability to learn, with a goal of matriculating individuals capable of learning throughout their lifetimes.
13. To develop critical judgment and effective decision-making skills.
14. To develop the capacity to be creative, curious, and imaginative.

(3) Next, through varying techniques, participants were divided into smaller groupings (sixteen to twenty participants in each group) to design their colleges of the future. Participants were asked to assume that they were a planning team called upon as consultants to design the college specified. A background sheet defining college characteristics was distributed to establish boundaries that might prescribe some aspects of college planning. These characteristics included student body size and age range, faculty size, nature of institutional funding, locale, and other nearby institutions.

(4) Within these groupings, participants were given choices on the specific task areas on which they would focus. These task area choices were: *Task Force I*—Change and renewal mechanisms and the structure

and organization of the college; *Task Force II*—Academic affairs administration and academic personnel policies; *Task Force III*—Instruction and co-curricular student development; and *Task Force IV*—Curriculum development. (See Table 2 for specific definitions.)

(5) As the simulation began, participants met in the Task Force groupings within their college division. Liaison relationships with other task force groups were established and communication sessions were held periodically.

(6) Finally, groups compiled a concluding presentation by coordinating the work of each task force group. In a session involving all the participants, presentations were made by each college. Group discussion then highlighted differing educational values, differing effects on education of future events, assessments of feasibility on a here-and-now index, assessment of unique needs prescribed in the college characteristics, and a debriefing on workshop procedures.

The simulation has been modified slightly each time it has been used, to smooth out procedural detail or to make needed variations based upon the participant group, their needs and interests. The modifications and a limited report of outcomes and participant reactions follow.

TABLE 2
TASK FORCE CHOICES

Task Force I

A. *Change and Renewal*: Discuss creative and effective ideas, systems, mechanisms, and procedures for building in growth, evaluation, change, and renewal. Consider applications of this change and renewal philosophy to *individual* members of the academic community (faculty, students, and administrators), collections of individuals (i.e., departments, disciplines, governance groups, student organizations, etc.) and the total institution.

B. *Structure and Organization*: Continue discussion of Task Force A by focusing on the method of organizing the faculty (i.e., departments, disciplines, schools, interdisciplinary groupings, temporary systems, etc.), the students, and the administration to form an effective and functioning institution. Consider also the governance systems of faculty/students/administrators and their role. Consider how temporary or permanent these groups should be.

Task Force II

A. *Academic Affairs Administration*: Consider academic calendars, registration, and scheduling, interinstitutional cooperation, research, degrees, evaluation of administrators, internal and external institutional appraisal, and admission criteria for freshmen and transfers.

B. *Academic Personnel and Policies*: Consider faculty recruitment, selection, tenure, or other retention or promotion systems, work load, including method of determining faculty/student ratios, orientation to the college (of faculty), faculty rights and responsibilities.

Task Force III

A. *Instruction*: Discuss evaluation of instruction by students, peers, and self, developing and improving instruction, professional growth, academic counseling and student educational planning, evaluating and rewarding student academic progress (i.e., grading, etc.) and criteria for continuation as a student.

B. *Co-Curricular Student Development*: Student development in residence hall settings, student activities including social, recreational, and educational programs, orientation, counseling (including career counseling, growth and adjustment counseling, special needs, etc.), student publications, special interest groups and their needs and contributions (i.e., international students, blacks, women, veterans, mature-older-students, etc.), athletics, including intercollegiate and intramural programs, student health concerns including preventative programs, religious needs, evaluation of student growth and development, and opportunities and skills for developing interpersonal relationships.

Task Force IV

A. *Curriculum Development—Part I*: Structure for general or basic education (if any), course requirements for major or specialization, academic majors offered, senior year experiences, experiences for which credit will be given, and off-campus student opportunities.

B. *Curriculum Development—Part II*: Procedure for course and curriculum design and approval, course evaluation, major curriculum revision, use of faculty rewards for course and curriculum revision, learning resources such as the library and instructional resources.

II. *GLCA Fellows Faculty Development Summer Institute: Winona, Minnesota, 1975*

Workshop participants gathered for a two-week faculty development program. Approximately three faculty from each of eleven member institutions participated, along with several spouses. In preparation for this culminating experience, participants were asked to read *Self-Renewal* by John Gardner. Key points from Gardner's philosophy were incorporated into a keynote address stressing the need for growth and renewal in organizations.

EDUCATIONAL GOALS

Each participant was asked to rank in importance fourteen educational goals and objectives (see Table 1), adding any they chose. Workshop facilitators had previously evaluated each educational goal regarding its stress on cognitive emphasis, affective emphasis, or a mixture of both cognitive and affective emphases.

Participants were next clustered into two major groups to design competitively a liberal arts college of the future. Within each college grouping (College X comprised of those stressing cognitive learning and College Y stressing affective goals) participants completed another round of the Delphi process refining their goal rankings. It is important to note that several goals were shared by both groups. (See Table 3.) (*Note:* Grouping participants by shared priorities in goals is NOT recommended for at-home use. It can serve to magnify existing splits within faculty groups and reinforce existing educational values instead of constructively confronting differing values. It was tried at this workshop as a way to minimize dissonance and highlight different views of the future of education.) Referring to Table 1, it should be noted that College X's goals in rank order were 3, 12, 13, 6, 14, and 4 stressing affective learning. College Y's goals were 5, 8, 12, 13, 3, 10, and 2 stressing cognitive learning.

TABLE 3
GOALS SHARED BY COLLEGES X AND Y

| *Goals* | *Final Rank Order* | |
	College X	*College Y*
12. To enhance the ability to learn, with a goal of matriculating individuals capable of learning throughout their lifetime.	2	3
13. To develop critical judgment and effective decision-making skills.	3	4

BACKGROUND COLLEGE CHARACTERISTICS

Both participant groups were given the same background characteristics for the college to be designed. The college would have 100 faculty and 1,500 students, with no age range specified. Student tuition comprised 60% of the institution's budget. The college was located in a town of 26,000 with a nearby megauniversity but no competing liberal arts college.

GROUP PROCESS OBSERVATION

Very quickly, College X coined a name, SAVE U., illustrating their college's theme of "Society, Aesthetics, Values, Environment," and College Y became STRAIT College (Strait when you arrive . . . Strait when you leave!"). The facilitators noted a healthy and enjoyable sense of competition between college groups. Located in different rooms, participants would hide some materials from others wandering through their "territory" and took great pride and delight in clapping and cheering as their presentations were made. This sense of competition was created because both were working on the same background college characteristics and only their own educational values differed.

The mental effort needed to grind through the tasks was tiring for many who had participated in a full week's activity prior to the simulation. Individual task forces often got bogged down on one small task and lost sight of their larger charge. Liaison relationships were hurried, but continually pointed out the need for communication with other task groups as decisions cannot be made in a vacuum. More than one participant remarked, "No wonder some bad policies get made, we didn't offer the input we had and they didn't listen once we came to give it!" Several individuals learned a great deal about their personal effectiveness in a group, particularly if a more verbal member seemed to be in charge.

COLLEGES DEVELOPED

As the final presentations unfolded, SAVE U (College X) created a college with growth and renewal as their theme ("aspire" was their slogan). SAVE U adopted new terminology and established a College Renewal Council. The Council was made up of representatives from each of the four learning units and from each student living community. Persons serving as administrators flowed into that role from their positions as faculty (or Renewal Agents) and as students (Apprentice Renewal Agents). The calendar was year round, and growth contracts were required of everyone. Their campus community consisted of learner-scholars of all ages.

STRAIT College (College Y) also emphasized renewal, stressing the development of competency in the thinking process. Review of administrators would occur every five years. Tenure did not exist for faculty and they, too, were on five-year contracts. Growth contracts existed for faculty in STRAIT College as well as in SAVE U. A strong faculty development program existed in STRAIT as well, with an emphasis upon making personal assistance available on a professional basis. An internship experience was required of students directly related to the interface between the college and the "outside world." While more realistic and often more pragmatic than SAVE U, STRAIT College's flair for looking at new systems to create learning was also evident.

PARTICIPATION EVALUATION

Once they returned home, all participants were sent an evaluation form. All questions allowed for open-ended comments, and participants were asked to list the best and worst features of the workshop. Thirty out of forty participants returned their evaluations, for a 75% response rate. Fifteen of those returned were from STRAIT College (fourteen were usable), and fifteen were from SAVE U. Where there was no significant differences between the scores of the participants of the two college groups, the participants in College X were slightly more satisfied with their experience.

While the participants from SAVE U generally found the experience to be more valuable, it should be noted that the scores of all participants reflect a positive learning experience (even if some parts were not completely valuable).

TABLE 4
RESPONSES TO EVALUATION ITEMS: WINONA, 1975

Item		Response Choices			
		1	2	3	
		very valuable	somewhat valuable	not valuable	missing
1. Overall, how valuable was the workshop to you?	STRAIT	8	6	1	0
	SAVE U	11	4	0	0
2. What about the quality of the discussion in your task force? Was it vigorous and substantial? Overall, how valuable was the discussion in contributing to the total value of the workshop?	STRAIT	10	3	1	1
	SAVE U	11	4	0	0
3. What about the nature of the interaction among the participants? Was it even and relaxed, dominated by one or two, and tense? Did the interaction contribute to the value of the workshop?	STRAIT	7	6	1	1
	SAVE U	11	3	1	0
4. What about the results of the discussions in substantive terms? Many significant issues were discussed and resolutions were developed on several of these issues. How valuable were these results to you? That is, were some of the ideas discussed useful?	STRAIT	6	7	1	1
	SAVE U	8	6	1	0
5. One objective of the simulation was to help each participant to learn how he or she functions and how to be more effective in translating ideas into action. How valuable to you was the workshop in these terms?	STRAIT	4	7	2	2
	SAVE U	5	5	4	1

III. *Albion Workshop (January, 1976)*

Based upon their experience at Winona, faculty from one of the participant colleges asked the designers to assist them in presenting the simulation as a faculty development program at their institution. The basic workshop design was retained, while some modifications were made for the institution's particular goals.

WORKSHOP MODIFICATIONS

The competitive element was reduced by NOT dividing participants into groups based upon evaluating their goals on an affective-cognitive dimension. Some 60-70 faculty took part at Albion. Three colleges, rather than two, were established, because, given the number of task forces in the design, colleges of over 40 participants would not be effective in providing opportunity for discussion. No spouses participated and faculty went home to sleep. The schedule was shortened as well, to a total of about eleven hours. Two rounds of the Delphi technique were used and those goals so defined were assumed for all groups. Additionally, three different sets of characteristics were defined (yet, all *could* typify an "Albion" of the future). It was hoped that groups would respond differently to these three sets of characteristics, illustrating how institutions must meet needs differently.

BACKGROUND COLLEGE CHARACTERISTICS

Prior to the experience of the simulation, participants were asked to read "Prolegomena to Revision of the Curriculum" by John Gusted (1971), "The Ethical Crisis in Education" by Warren Martin (1974), and other articles from *Liberal Education* and *Change.* Albion faculty also participated in a discussion prior to the simulation, with a focus upon Albion's future. Task force groupings were similar to those in Table 2, although fewer task assignments were used.

College One was ascribed characteristics of an 1,800-size student body ranging in age from 17 to 70. There were 120 faculty members. College Two was given 900 in the student body with a faculty of 60. Students were predominately from the 18-21 year group. College Three had a student body of 1,800, with the traditional 18-21 year age group and with 120 faculty. All three colleges were set in the same locale with several surrounding universities and liberal arts colleges. Regional characteristics did not vary by college.

COLLEGES DESIGNED

Final presentations illustrated some interesting differences in perceptions of the future of Albion. College One emphasized change and renewal by requiring that faculty members were to have alternating joint appointments, one in the college and one in the "real world." Students were expected to return every ten or fifteen years as they developed new interests. The college had two schools, the School of Human Resources, and the School of Skill Development. The first had four divisions:

Pre-Career—students preparing for a career;

Mid-Career—adults wishing to expand beyond the limits of their profession;

Post-Career—for persons in retirement;

"Ageless" Studies—courses of interest to all ages.

The School of Skill Development had an off-campus division and an on-campus division that trained students in mathematical, manipulative, and language skills. The calendar had six eight-week terms with competency-based degrees.

College Two featured faculty and students living together in "living-learning" units, grouped according to student years in college. A Council made up of persons from four divisions constituted the governing board of the college. Problem-centered learning modules in each of these four divisions were required.

Like College One, the calendar was year round and the curriculum was competency-based. One-third of the faculty held rotating positions. All served on four-year renewable contracts. There were no academic ranks. Evaluation of students and faculty was ongoing.

College Three was the college with boundary conditions similar to the Albion of 1976. The focus of this college was the curriculum. Participants assumed that College Three was in a consortium in which each member specialized. The specialization of College Three was to help students learn to understand and use methodologies, not to impart skills or facts. Four levels existed: empirical analysis; conceptual and aesthetic analysis; synthesis based on specific areas of inquiry; and synthesis based upon all forms of analysis. Related to these areas were physical environment, social relations, and conceptual and esthetic modes of expression. Detailed routes through these levels were specified and much of the unique parts of College Three built on this particular foundation.

PARTICIPANT EVALUATION

An evaluation form, parallel to the one at Winona, was distributed to all sixty participants. Seventeen usable forms were returned, for a 28% response rate; hence, extreme caution should be used in interpreting these results. Albion participants responded on the same response scale as Winona with (1) illustrating a valuable experience, (2) somewhat valuable, and (3) not valuable.

Compared to the experience at Winona, participants at Albion who returned the questionnaire found some value in the experience, yet were less satisfied than those at Winona. Albion participants found less value in the usefulness of their discussions, a fact that could relate to the

TABLE 5
COMPARISON OF GROUP RESPONSES:
ALBION (1976) AND WINONA (1975)

Item*		Response Choices			
		1 *very valuable*	2† *somewhat valuable*	3‡ *not valuable*	*missing*
1. Overall value	ALBION‡	2	13	2	0
	WINONA	19	10	0	0
5. Quality of	ALBION	8	7	1	1
discussion	WINONA	21	7	1	0
6. Nature of	ALBION	12	3	1	1
interaction	WINONA	17	9	2	1
10. Usefulness of	ALBION‡	1	11	4	1
substantive	WINONA	14	13	2	0
discussion					

*Items summarized—for full wording see Table 4.

†These categories were collapsed for computation of statistics.

‡Significantly different at .01 level using chi square test incorporating Yates' correction for continuity (since $N < 40$).

different types of colleges being designed (hypothetical ones at Winona versus a redesign of Albion). While the quality of the conversations and nature of the interaction were similar and valuable, it is important to note, although with reservation, that the exercise seems less valuable in the redesign of an existing institution by its current faculty than as a hypothetical exercise.

IV. *GLCA Fellows Faculty Development Summer Institute, 1976*

After experiences at Winona during the summer of 1975 and at Albion, the simulation was again slightly revised for use with a second group of GLCA fellows at their summer program. Nearly all of the participants were new to the experience, although some might have heard what the fellows did in their program the previous summer. Two had participated in the Albion workshop. The thirty-seven faculty and twenty-three spouses had participated in several life-planning exercises prior to the beginning of the simulation. Earlier, they had read papers and discussed the nature of liberal education.

BACKGROUND COLLEGE CHARACTERISTICS

Participants were asked to choose one of the three kinds of college described below, and virtually all choices were honored.

The three colleges to be designed were given characteristics that, it was hoped, would illustrate different program design in the final presentations. College One was a liberal arts college stressing preprofessional and personal development; located in a small town with four or five other educational institutions. The 1,500 students ranged in age from 18-21, with 60% of the college's budget coming from tuition. There were 150 faculty. College Two was also described as a liberal arts college, historically preprofessional, with current heavy emphasis in vocational concerns. College Two was located in a medium-sized city with three other institutions in the same city. The 1,500 students ranged in age from 18-21, and their tuition supported 50% of the college budget. College Three was academic and vocational in emphasis, with additional emphasis on human development. The 1,500 students ranged in age from 18 to 70, with equal portions in the 18-21 group and the older-than-45 group. Fifty percent of the college budget was accounted for by student tuition.

EDUCATIONAL GOALS

The Delphi process was used within each college grouping to define goals for that college. Table 6 illustrates the goal rankings of each of the three college groupings. Groups were not told to have their goals reflect the nature of their institution.

TABLE 6
GOALS CHOSEN BY COLLEGE GROUPINGS
IN 1976 WINONA CONFERENCE

Goal *(refer to Table 1 for complete* *wording of the goal statement)*	*Rank Order Choices*		
	College One	*College Two*	*College Three*
1. Increased leisure time	—	—	—
2. Impart information and skills	—	—	—
3. Enthusiasm for a full life	4	5	1
4. Understanding of self	8	—	7
5. Analytical abilities	1	3	4
6. Pursue personal growth	—	—	6
7. Understand society	—	—	—
8. Competent in a discipline	3	6	—
9. Interpersonal competence	—	—	—
10. Confidence in handling change	5	—	—
11. Career preparation	—	—	—
12. Lifelong learning	2	4	—
13. Decision-making skills	6	1	2
14. Develop creativity and curiosity	7	2	—
15. Understand values	—	—	—

It would appear from this tabulation of goal choices that the faculty found it difficult to set career-oriented goals for students (i.e., low choices of goal #11), even though their college characteristics (Colleges Two and Three) stressed vocational concerns among the students. Likewise, choices of goals 5 and 6, which stressed personal growth, were low choices in Colleges One and Three, yet had been designated to be a focus of those institutions. This raises the basic educational question concerning whether the institution's program should reflect the needs and concerns of its students, or whether it should be organized and offered to those who may choose to accept it. It may be that faculty's personal goals do not coincide with those prescribed by college characteristics.

WORKSHOP MODIFICATIONS

In addition to the way the groups were divided and the method of administering the Delphi technique on goals, a new variable was built into the simulation design. Some feedback from Winona and Albion showed some participant frustration with the unrealities of designing a college for the year 2000. Therefore, the facilitators set the design for the year 1986. Facilitators were interested to see whether ten years into the future removed enough of the self-censoring barriers and facilitated development of the institution.

COLLEGES DESIGNED

Presentations of final college designs showed that College One (Western College) had many of the characteristics of a present college, although there was no Board of Trustees. The faculty was given significant responsibility, including the choice of Chancellor. The proposed calendar was a regular semester plan, and, in many respects, the academic organization of the college was like many present liberal arts colleges. Individually designed majors were encouraged and an integrative-comprehensive project was required. An interesting feature of College One was the requirement for a regular five-year reviewing of departmental programs. An additional feature involved students living in some fifty units of varying characteristics.

College Two took advantage of the highly favorable student-faculty ratio to institute a program of "reassignment." Faculty were "reassigned" with full salary every third year for further education, course development, research, internship, or administrative work. A division of experimental programs made up of faculty and students administered internships, interdisciplinary courses, and preprofessional interdivisional major programs. First-level administrators taught, and second-level administrators rotated every three years, coming out of the faculty and returning to it. Evaluation of administrators and departments occurred every four to five years by outside and inside evaluators, heavily involving advising skills and course evaluations. A full program of professional development was a predominant feature of College Two. Various student housing options were available, including houses scattered throughout the city. There were no intercollegiate athletics or Greek organizations.

College Three (Alluv U.) was a university committed to personal and communal development at all stages of life, for all people. The university maintained a policy of open admissions, with individual attention to designing a unique learning experience for each student.

Coming from a traditional liberal arts orientation, the curriculum was organized around six competency areas. The six competency areas were:

1. Communicating in verbal, quantitative, and social modes;
2. Dealing with the universe in physical and biological forms;
3. Being with oneself and others;
4. Creating in the expressive and aesthetic modes;
5. Relating to cultural, historical, and philosophical roots of humankind, and
6. Acquiring useful, salable, and productive skills and abilities (including preparation for graduate and professional skills).

Competency was to be determined by review committees of faculty from pertinent areas, including a student's mentor.

In addition, academic study typically carried out on campus during trimester terms was supplemented by one-term-in-three off-campus experiences in four categories: (1) social service; (2) adapting to environment and testing one's limits; (3) job experience, and (4) integrating projects, independent study, return to a previous experience. For the more mature students, alternatives to the formal experiential learning requirement were worked out. The total environment surrounding the university was viewed as a pool of resources both human and material.

College Three recognized no absolute distinction between faculty and administration. Individuals working for the University were expected to carry out many functions and to be open to frequent realignment of responsibilities. Salaries were published and bonuses were given only in recognition of special contributions to the University in a given year.

GROUP PROCESS OBSERVATION

The facilitators observed that the range of types of colleges created was quite extensive. Participants in College One sought to arrive at a summary of what now existed on their own campuses for the most part. Spouses generally sought to ensure that what was provided was adequate in preparing persons for responsible, solid positions. The groups were uniformly serious and purposeful and did not seem to have "fun," as was true for at least one of the colleges the first year. The harsh reality of the early date (1986) probably seemed partially responsible for this difference in tone.

PARTICIPANT EVALUATION

A different evaluation process was utilized, making it impossible to compare data from the two previous experiences with the simulation. Participants were asked to write comments about each of the events in the three-week workshop on the master schedule and to indicate, from a list of the major events, which they liked the most and the least. Retrospective evaluations were also sought, but the results of this last inquiry were not available as this report was written.

Outcomes from this evaluation exercise showed that the 1976 Winona group was not as positive in its evaluation as was the 1975 Winona group. In 1975 an outside evaluator had concluded that for many of the faculty the simulation was the highpoint of the workshop. Some of the comments generated by the new evaluation procedure at the 1976 workshop are as follows: Ten of the thirty-five comments could be clarified as negative ("frustrating, overorganized"). Eight or ten of the sixty participants rated this event as one of the least valuable parts of the workshop; a few said it was one of the most valuable. The scheduling of the simulation during the workshop, the nature of preceding events, the closeness of the projected date and some tensions within the total group (unrelated to the simulation) may have contributed to this difference.

V. *Summary and Recommendations*

These three experiences with the simulation "Designing a Liberal Arts College for the Future" showed it to be a moderately successful mechanism for a structured group discussion highlighting educational values in the future. The limited data and facilitator's comments showed that, generally, greater success existed with nonwork group participants than those from the same work group, although participants in both settings found value in the experience. In most groups the quality of the discussion was vigorous and substantial. Many participants highlighted their task force discussions as being both personally and professionally challenging. While the specific carry-over to current situations did not seem readily apparent, facilitators did observe most participants challenging their own and each others' philosophies and educational values.

In general, the designers recommend that care should be used to redesign process and content variables based upon the nature of the group participating in the exercise to maximize successful learning and interaction.

Other recommendations are: (1) The experience at Winona 1976 implied it would be best to structure the college to be designed some distance in the future (i.e., the year 2000) as a hypothetical institution; (2) while competitive groups can add to the sense of spirit, facilitators observed that groups should not be divided on any ideological basis without realizing the possibility of dangerous consequences in creating unproductive schisms in the faculty (particularly work groups); (3) ample time for discussions, perhaps in small groups, after the presentations could strengthen the simulation and point up possible transferral skills or insights; (4) a reaction by a guest expert to the goals selected in the Delphi process, their relation to the prescribed college background characteristics, and final presentations would serve as a useful summary; (5) even though tired, participants should include discussing their feelings and reactions to the format, emphasizing the decision-making process used in their task force and within their college grouping.

REFERENCES

Delbecq, Andre L., Van de Ven, Andrew H., and Gustafson, David. *Group techniques for program planning: A guide to nominal group and Delphi processes.* Glenview, Illinois: Scott, Foresman and Co., 1975.

Gardner, John W. *Self-renewal: The individual and the innovative society.* New York: Harper & Row, Publishers, 1963, 5-6.

Gustad, John W. Prolegomena to revision of the curriculum, *Liberal Education, LVII,* No. 3, October, 1971, 324-336.

Martin, Warren Bryan. The ethical crises in education. *Change, 6(5),* June, 1974, 28-33.

Part III

CHEMISTRY

The following paper by chemists Gilbert and Wismer briefly overviews some of the major ways simulation is used in chemistry. It includes a bibliography on computer simulations in chemistry.

3

COMPUTERS AND SIMULATION
IN CHEMICAL EDUCATION

Robert K. Wismer
George L. Gilbert

ABSTRACT

Computers and various simulation techniques have come recently to receive considerable attention in chemical education. This essay overviews sources of simulation and computer applications in chemistry, describes some of the work in chemical education carried out at Denison, and presents a bibliography of references for further research in the two areas.

I. *Introduction*

The concept of simulation as an activity in chemistry has an extremely long history if one views the laboratory experiences developed for instructional purposes in this way. Teachers of chemistry have long attempted to model or simulate activities in the laboratory that parallel the behavior of matter both qualitatively and quantitatively. This is true in the teaching of chemistry at all levels, high school, college, and university. In addition, biochemical research is an attempt to simulate the chemical reactions of living systems within the laboratory, and much industrial research simulates mass production processes on a small scale.

A recent focus on simulation, defined in a broader sense, points out that the range of activities available to chemists through simulation may encompass the use of some gaming and significant amounts of computer interaction to develop a beneficial program of instruction in chemistry. The number of activities that use this mode in chemistry is very small in comparison to the extent and success of computerized simulations. This is perhaps due to concern for presenting the subject matter in a serious manner, and a belief that "playing games" with chemistry, even in an instructional situation, would demean the character of the field of chemistry unnecessarily. In addition, those who have attempted to develop chemical games have found the procedure to be a difficult one and the results frequently not to be as attractive to students as to their developers. The latter result is probably attributable to the level of sophistication demanded of the user being too high.

The use of the computer in an interactive mode has been advantageous in a variety of simulation applications. Without stressing the obvious, the repetitive nature of interaction with the computer as a patient tutor for students in teaching the basis of new concepts, while including variations of parameters to enliven the subject matter, has received a great deal of attention. Other systems focus upon the ability of the computer to simulate chemical systems that are either too rapid in their activity or too slow for studens to deal with in the normal laboratory, or for which the equipment and chemicals are too costly. Thus, in simulation, the range of subject matter and materials with which the students can interact is extended. Furthermore, using simulations, students are able to deal with complex data and formulas as well as large amounts of data, using the capabilities of the computer and carefully developed programs to obtain correlations within such information. Finally, the computer allows the instructor the opportunity to keep records on student quiz and/or test performance. Students take such exams by interacting with the computer, and the results allow the professor to focus upon areas of difficulty, which can be further discussed or stressed in discussion groups or lectures.

II.   *Sources of Materials in Simulation in Chemistry*

Extensive work has been carried out at Denison, through the CONDUIT organization, and at the University of Iowa, to assemble bibliographies concerning materials used in simulation in chemistry. These materials have been collected, and many are included in the Appendix to this chapter.

Currently, there are very few materials available commercially, and thus a significant effort is being made to encourage a sharing of materials among the individuals at institutions that are actively using simulations in the teaching of chemistry. The *Journal of Chemical Education* serves as the principal medium of dissemination of this information.

III.   *Simulation Activities in Chemistry*

During the 1977 Denison Simulation Workshop, we attempted to focus upon the areas that have received the greatest attention and appear to be the most promising for the use of simulations in chemical education. Specific examples include materials that were developed at Denison, materials that have been made available from other computer centers, and materials that were brought together in a simulation workshop in chemistry during March, 1976, at Denison.

The use of simulations to extend experimental situations in such programs as PLANK and CHILDS, which model the photoelectric effect and kinetics reactions of the chemical reactions, respectively, are indicative of one of the better uses of simulation in the field of chemistry. PLANK allows the user-experimenter to examine the photoelectric effect by (1) selecting one of the five metals to be investigated; (2) choosing the relative intensity of the investigating X-radiation, and (3) searching for the retarding potential necessary to stop the photoelectric current flow. The program then presents the user with a plot of frequency *vs.* cutoff voltage, and the equation for the least squares line of the plot and asks the user a number of questions about the effect which has just been investigated. CHILDS allows the user to collect data of absorbance *vs.* time for the reaction:

$$BrCr^{III} + U^{III} = Cr^{II} + U^{IV} + Br^-$$

It allows control of the concentrations of $[H^+]$, $[Cr^{3+}]$ and $[U^{3+}]$. Finally, it permits the user to tabulate and graph the resultant data to determine the order of the reaction for each of the reactant species.

Work related to the laboratory in pre- and postlab instruction has been carried out locally to a very modest extent. These activities included presenting to the students a model of the experiment to be carried out on the computer. They may investigate the effects of varying the parameters so as to optimize the conditions under which they will carry out the experiments. In addition to learning about the optimum conditions, students also obtain a substantially better sense of what is happening in the chemical reaction and come to the lab better prepared to observe and understand what they are doing in the performance of the experiments.

Thus far, only one game activity has been developed for use on the computer. This game models the decay of a radioactive species. The user attempts to determine the number of radioactive "chips" remaining after preset periods of time. Because the decisions are backed by "bets," the object of the student is to "break the bank." It seems clear that more examples of this type could be developed in the field of chemistry, but they are receiving relatively little attention at the present time.

A recent development relating to simulations in chemistry has been the activity of Frank Marinaro, a Denison student, who has developed a BASIC interpreter for a subset of the DYNAMO language for dynamic modeling. This language is especially effective in investigating the kinetics of chemical reactions. During the 1976 and 1977 Summer Simulation workshops, this material was available to conferees, who found it to be of substantial benefit in developing simple-to-complex programs dealing with kinetics. In some cases, sample programs were developed for use at their home institutions. Because this development is quite recent, its application to chemistry programs at Denison is still in its initial stages and can be expected to include both the general chemistry course and, in a more sophisticated manner, the advanced laboratory course.

The computer also offers an opportunity to strengthen student background in concept areas, which are fundamental to science generally and would be specifically important in the field of chemistry. We have developed programs locally for teaching logarithms and the use of the metric system, as well as materials for teaching students about molecular structure and predictions of ionic character within materials. The relationship to simulation is more obvious in the latter material, where modeling of chemical systems is more direct and students can check their results against real substances with which they may deal.

A further area in which the computer assists the student is in the performance of long calculations. We have developed programs for the plotting of titration curves, for determining the percentage of various species present at different values of pH in monoprotic and triprotic acid systems, and for producing numerical maps of electron density within atoms. The principal benefit of these programs is that they allow the student to modify the parameters that determine the final results. Consequently, a student can more readily see the effect of various influences on these systems, but bypasses lengthy hand calculations that would otherwise be necessary.

Other uses of simulation in chemistry that have been developed locally include the collection and correlation of data from a laboratory class. This allows students an opportunity to handle moderately large amounts of data and find correlations within that data for a given laboratory experiment. In addition, we have found the computer useful in administering and constructing quizzes as a part of the chemistry program. The computer summations of the results of these quizzes provide a diagnosis of problem areas that can be clarified in subsequent lectures and discussions. These summations are not used to determine student grades. This latter activity is of recent origin, and the results of this work will be available during 1977-78.

We hope we have presented a comprehensive picture of current activity in simulation, especially materials that have been developed and/or used locally and that would find definite use at the college level.

IV.   *Research in Chemical Simulation for Education*

The question of research in simulation in chemical education relates more to the evaluation of chemical education techniques and to simulation as one of these techniques. To date, the amount of work in computerized simulation and its evaluation as an educational process is quite small. As more materials become available and are shared and checked by those involved in chemical education, it would be hoped that quantitative results concerning the impact of simulation might be available. As of the moment, however, this area is receiving relatively little attention.

APPENDIX

BIBLIOGRAPHY OF
CHEMISTRY COMPUTER SIMULATION REFERENCES

*(Compiled by George L. Gilbert
and James B. Summers, 1975)*

The following bibliography represents a brief scan of the literature for articles discussing computer systems and programs relating to chemical education. The sources covered include: The *Journal of Chemical Education, Chemistry, Science, The Journal of College Science Teaching,* and *Proceedings of the Conference on Computers in the Undergraduate Curricula.* The search is by no means intended to be exhaustive, but it should provide a starting point for those beginning in the field.

General Sources

Gibbs, G. I. *Handbook of games and simulation exercises.* Beverly Hills, California: Sage Publications, Inc., 1974.
Naylor, Thomas, H. (editor). *Design of computer simulations experiments.* Duke University Press, 1969.
Stolurow, Lawrence M. CAI, *Computer assisted instructions.*
Zuckerman, David W., and Horn, T. *Guide to simulations/games.* Information Resources, Inc., 1973.

Periodicals as General Sources

Simulation: Technical Journal of the Society for Computer Simulation. Simulation Councils, Inc., 1010 Pearl Street, La Jolla, California 92037.
Simulations and Games. An interdisciplinary journal of theory, design, and research. Beverly Hills, California: Sage Publications, Inc.
Simultation/Gaming News. Simulation Gaming News, Inc. Box 3039, University Station, Moscow, Idaho 83843.

Specific References

TUTORIALS/DRILLS IN GENERAL CHEMISTRY

Breneman, G. L. MCAI-Minicomputer aided instructions. *Journal of*

Chemical Education, 50, 469, 1973. A library of programs has been developed to instruct students in the trouble areas of general chemistry.

Breneman, G. L. A follow-up to the previous article, discussing recent developments. *Journal of Chemical Education, 52,* 627, 1975.

Castleberry, S. J., Culp, G. H., and Logowski, J. J. The impact of computer-based instructional methods in general chemistry. *Journal of Chemical Education, 50,* 469, 1973. A report on the theory, nature, and result of a full-scale program at the University of Texas.

Castleberry, S. J., and Lagowski, J. J. Individualized instruction using computer techniques. *Journal of Chemical Education, 47,* 91, 1969. University of Texas system to provide drills and remedial lessons to students of all levels.

Child, W. C., Jr., and Finholt, R. W. Ramette. Experiences with the PDP-8 system. *Chemistry Instructors Proceedings,* 1970.

Corrington, Joyce H., and Marshall, Sr. Patricia. *Proceedings of the Conference on Computers in the Undergraduate Curricula,* 1970.

Davis, L., and Macero, D. J. Computer assisted instruction in a chemical instrumentation course. *Journal of Chemical Education, 49,* 758, 1972. An excellent system for all courses of instruction in chemistry.

Empedocles, P. Fundamental theory of gases, liquids and solids by computer simulations, use in the introductory course. *Journal of Chemical Education, 51,* 593, 1974.

Eskinazi, J., and Macero, D. J. An interactive program for teaching pH and logarithms. *Journal of Chemical Education, 49,* 571, 1972.

Ewig, C. S. An interactive on-line computing system as an instructional aid. *Journal of Chemical Education, 47,* 97, 1969.

Grandey, R. C. The use of computers to aid instructors in beginning chemistry. *Journal of Chemical Education, 48,* 791, 1971. The PLATO system at the University of Illinois, system of practical problems, detailed help sessions and reviews designed to provide individual attention to the student at his own pace.

Grandey, R. C. *Journal of Chemical Education, 47,* 608, 1970; and *Science, 167,* 1582, 1970. More on the PLATO system.

Johnson, K. J. The use of Pittsburgh Timesharing System in computer-oriented curriculum, development in chemistry. *Proceedings of the Conference on Computers in the Undergraduate Curricula,* 1970.

Johnson, K. J. Computers and chemical education at Pittsburgh. *Proceedings of the Conference on Computers in the Undergraduate Curricula,* 1971.

Kapechi, J. A., and Switzer, W. BUF-A FORTRAN subset for the chemistry classroom. *Journal of Chemical Education, 47,* 111, 1969.

Lata, A. J. University of Massachusetts. An interactive timesharing basic tutorial program sequence in introductory electrochemistry. *Proceedings of the Conference on Computers in the Undergraduate Curricula, 1972.*

Lower, S. K. Audiotutorial and CAI aids for problem solving in introductory chemistry. *Journal of Chemical Education, 47,* 143, 1970.

Lower, S. K. Making the computer make a difference in college chemistry, *Proceedings of the Conference on Computers in the Undergraduate Curricula, 1973.*

Moss, D., Haglund E., and Flynn, J. General solutions of ionic equilibria problems. *Journal of Chemical Education, 43,* 582, 1966.

Neilson, W. B. Interactive computer programs for equilibrium and kinetics. *Journal of Chemical Education, 48,* 414, 1971.

Olson, M. V. Computer applications to chemical equilibrium problems. *Proceedings of the Conference on Computers in the Undergraduate Curricula, 1973.*

Reiter, R. C., and House, J. E., Jr. Teaching computer methods in undergraduate chemistry courses. *Journal of Chemical Education, 45,* 465, 1968.

Seitz, W. A. and Matsen, F. A. Computer augmented lectures. *Journal of Chemical Education, 51,* 192, 1974.

Smith, G. S., Chesquiere, J. R., and Auner, R. A. The uses of computers in teaching chemistry. *Journal of Chemical Education, 51,* 243, 1974. A brief evaluation of the effectiveness of the PLATO system of the University of Illinois.

Stevenson, P. E. DIATH 2: A program for demonstrating chemical bonding in hydrogen. *Journal of Chemical Education, 48,* 31, 1971.

Stevenson, P. E. Direct classroom use of a timesharing computer in chemical education. *Proceedings of the Conference on Computers in the Undergraduate Curricula, 1971.*

LABORATORY SIMULATIONS

Craig, N. C., Sheret, D. D., Carlton, T. S. and Ackermann, M. N. Computer experiments—some principles and examples. *Journal of Chemical Education, 48,* 310, 1971.

Francis, L. D. Computer-simulated qualitative inorganic chemistry. *Journal of Chemical Education, 50,* 556, 1973. A simulated experiment, reproducing the behavior of metal ions in solution under standard qualitative tests.

Garbarino, J. R., and Wartell, M. A. CAI in the laboratory—the photoelectric effect. *Journal of Chemical Education, 51,* 484, 1974.

Hogg, J. L. Computer programs in kinetics—an annotated bibliography. *Journal of Chemical Education, 51,* 109, 1974.

Jensen, R. E., Garvey, R. G., and Paulson, B. A. Determination of successive ionization constants—a computer-assisted laboratory experiment. *Journal of Chemical Education, 47,* 147, 1970.

Kozarek, W. J., and Fernando, Q. Location of the equivalence point in potentiometric titrations—a simulated laboratory exercise. *Journal of Chemical Education, 49,* 202, 1972.

Prager, S. Computer simulation of chromatographic columns. *Proceedings of the Conference on Computers in the Undergraduate Curricula,* 1971.

Schwendeman, R. H. Computer simulation of experimental data. *Journal of Chemical Education, 45,* 665, 1968.

COMPUTERIZED METHODS OF EVALUATION

Birkin, S. J. An analysis of the effectiveness of EXAMINER, a computerized question book and examination processing system. *Proceedings of the Conference on Computers in the Undergraduate Curricula,* 1972.

Collins, R. W., Purse, C. T., and Moore, J. W. The role of "Pseudo CAI" and computer-generated repeatable exams in a computer-oriented chemistry curriculum. *Proceedings of the Conference on Computers in the Undergraduate Curricula,* 1973.

Hammer, M., and Henderson, C. O. Improving large enrollment undergraduate instruction with computer generated repeatable test. *Proceedings of the Conference on Computers in the Undergraduate Curricula,* 1972.

Johnson, J. K. Pitts computer-generated repeatable chemistry exam. *Proceedings of the Conference on Computers in the Undergraduate Curricula,* 1973.

THE USE OF GRAPHICS IN COMPUTER INSTRUCTION

Allen, F. S., and Walters, E. A. Two computer problems dealing with graphics display in chemistry. *Journal of Chemical Education, 51,* 596, 1974.

Druding, L. F. A simple demonstration model of MO theory. *Journal of Chemical Education, 49,* 617, 1972.

Glasser, L. Contour maps and three-dimensional representations with a line printer. *Journal of Chemical Education, 50,* 421, 1973.

Kelley, T. G. A general graphics system for computer generation of visual arts. *Proceedings of the Conference on Computers in the Undergraduate Curricula,* 1971.

Legett, P. Computer-drawn diagrams. *Journal of Chemical Education, 51,* 502, 1974.

Mimocozzi, W. P., and Portugal, L. P. Computer-generated display and manipulation of a general molecule. *Journal of Chemical Education, 48,* 790, 1971.

Mortensen, E. M., and Penick, R. J. Computer animation of molecular vibrations. *Journal of Chemical Education, 47,* 102, 1970.

Solzberg, L. J. Teletype graphics for chemical education. *Journal of Chemical Education, 49,* 357, 1972.

Thomas, B. R. Computer animated films with a small computer and small budget. *Proceedings of the Conference on Computers in the Undergraduate Curricula,* 1971.

COMPUTER ASSISTANCE OUTSIDE OF GENERAL CHEMISTRY

Bader, M. A computerized physical chemistry experience. *Journal of Chemical Education, 46,* 206, 1969.

Child, W. C., Jr. A computer simulation of a kinetics experiment. *Journal of Chemical Education, 50,* 290, 1973. (Physical chemistry.)

Clark, H. A., Marshall, J. C., and Isenhour, T. L. An approach to computer-assisted drill in synthetic organic chemistry. *Journal of Chemical Education, 50,* 645, 1973.

Dannhauser, W. PVT behavior of real gases, computer-assisted exercises for physical chemistry. *Journal of Chemical Education, 47,* 126, 1970.

Gilman, Sister J. F. Interactive computer library programs in chemistry. *Journal of Chemical Education, 47,* 637, 1970. (Physical chemistry.)

Herman, H. B., and Leyden, D. E. Use of computers in analytical chemistry courses. *Journal of Chemical Education, 45,* 524, 1968.

Hornack, F. M. A qualitative organic identification game. *Proceedings of the Conference on Computers in the Undergraduate Curricula,* 1971.

Jones, D. O., Scamuffa, Portnoff, L. S., and Perone, S. P. On-line Digital computer applications to kinetics analysis—an undergraduate experiment. *Journal of Chemical Education, 49,* 717, 1972.

Perone, S. P. A laboratory course in Digital computers in chemical instrumentation. *Journal of Chemical Education, 47,* 105, 1970.

Peterson, D. L., and Fuller, M. E. Physical chemistry students discover the computer. *Journal of Chemical Education, 48,* 314, 1971.

Rodewald, L. B., Culp, G. H., and Lagowski, J. J. The use of computers in organic chemistry instruction. *Journal of Chemical Education, 47,* 134, 1970.

Smith, S. G. The use of computers in teaching organic chemistry. *Journal of Chemical Education, 47,* 608, 1970. A PLATO system.

Venier, C. G., Reineche, and Manfred, G. Armchair unknowns, a simple CAI qualitative organic simulation. *Journal of Chemical Education, 49,* 541, 1972.

Wise, G. Computer programs for undergraduate physical chemistry students. *Journal of Chemical Education, 49,* 559, 1972.

Part IV
LOGIC

The unusual application of simulation outlined in the following paper was designed by philosopher Straumanis as a tool to treat the problem of overcrowding in logic courses. Essentially, she created two computer programs, both of which "simulate" logical processes of sentential calculus. Straumanis describes these simulations, compares them to other similar approaches, and discusses possible theoretical and practical implications of their use.

4

LOGIC AND SIMULATION[1]

JOAN STRAUMANIS

ABSTRACT

A major problem in teaching symbolic logic is that of providing individualized and early feedback to students who are learning to do proofs. Ordinarily, the teacher first sees samples of such proofs only after notational and procedural errors are already ingrained, and must be unlearned. And some students have so much difficulty in getting started that they cannot produce completed proofs at all, and have nothing to submit for correction. In large classes the instructor is unable to offer the kind of concentrated and individualized help that may be needed.

To overcome this difficulty a computer program was developed that functions as a line-by-line proof checker in sentential calculus. The program, DEMON, first evaluates any statement supplied by the student to see whether it is well formed; second, it checks each line of the student's proof to determine whether it is a legitimate inference from the premises and earlier lines of the proof. This program, combined with a second that offers drill and feedback on translating English to and from logical symbols, is the key part of an integrated computer-assisted curriculum in informal and formal logic.

It is argued that these "simulations" of logical processes, together with the CAI approach in which they are embedded, produce a teaching system wherein college students acquire an understanding of symbolic logic more quickly and at a higher level than they do in courses using more conventional methods.

Further, it is argued that programs such as DEMON and BERTIE (a proof checker developed at Dartmouth College), which evaluates statements and arguments presented by students instead of being limited to a particular repertoire, are theoretically distinct from conventional models of computer-assisted instruction and constitute instances of "artificial intelligence."

I. *Simulation of Cognitive Processes*

In one sense "simulation" in logic is a misnomer. Logic, like mathematics, traditionally includes the construction and study of representations and models of its own structures within the discipline itself. So to the extent that a *simulation* of something must be a copy or imitation and not the thing itself, logic cannot be simulated; a model of logic *is* logic. But in a different sense, logic *itself* is a simulation of something else—it is a model so old we tend to forget that it is a representation at all. Of course, what logic simulates is the structure of thought itself; it is a model of cognitive processing.

In general, two different kinds of goals might be pursued by a simulator of a cognitive process such as logical inference (deduction). A psychophysiologist, for example, might want to model the *way* in which the process proceeds in a human subject. The details of such a model might be suggested by experimental findings regarding the actual steps and stages a human being goes through in performing an inference task, or the model might be strictly an heuristic device, a representation of an unconfirmed theory about what such a process might be like. The model might be based upon physiological events only, or else upon introspective reports—so-called "protocols" of thought (detailed answers to the question "What steps did you go through to get that answer?"), or both. But all of these, which I call "process" simulations, are essentially similar in that what is being simulated is the *way in which* the outcome is thought to be produced in the system being modeled. The criterion for classifying a model as a process simulation is not correctness of the model, but *intent* to model a process.

Logic is not a process simulation. Although Aristotle called his three axioms of logic "Laws of Thought," few psychologists or logicians have held that untaught reason goes through the very steps of a logical proof in making an "intuitive" inference. Instead, what logic does is provide a reliable route from "here" to "there." Building on the immediate plausibility of some inferences ("Rules of Inference"), longer and more complex problems can be solved than could be tackled by the unaided intuition alone. But even were we to assume that those same rules of inference are "wired" into the nervous system, there would be no reason to believe that complex human inferences proceed in the manner of a formal proof. And of course, formal logic does not show *why* the rules or axioms appear plausible to humans—it *depends* upon that plausibility. Therefore, logic no more simulates immediate inference than a telescope simulates sight. Both extend human capabilities. It may be fair to push the analogy a bit further and say that what both logic and the telescope "simulate" is a kind of superhuman capacity to reason or see, over and above the ordinary or lazy way of doing these things. We might say that telescopes (and eyeglasses) simulate "having better eyes" if the result of using these devices is like actually having better eyes, whether or not the optical system of the artificial device in any way models or resembles that of a pair of better eyes. For this reason, I call the telescope an example of an "input-output" simulation.

In an input-output simulation, "raw materials" similar to those processed by the system being modeled are transformed into a "finished product" resembling the output of the original system. But the mechanism by which the transformation takes place in such a dynamic simulation is irrelevant; it may be safely represented in the flow chart of the model by a black box. Examples of input-output simulations, in addition to the telescope, are artificial heart and lung machines, pacemakers and other functional but nonbiological body parts, the pitching and serving machines used in baseball and tennis, and so on. Such devices as vending machines, which "simulate" salespersons, are so familiar that it is easy to forget that they are indeed simulations.

Of course, calculators and computers are also simulations, and so are logic and mathematics. In fact, the former are input-output simulations of such cognitive processes as inferring and calculating. Hence a dynamic simulation such as a computer program, which "infers" or "calculates" by producing proofs or solving mathematical problems, deserves the designation "artificial intelligence." In my view, it is not necessary to have devised a process simulation in order to make such a claim.

II. *Simulating the Teaching of Logic by Computer (CAI)*

Two different modes of computer-assisted instruction (CAI) are utilized in our comprehensive program for the teaching of symbolic logic. One of them involves conventional CAI techniques, namely, the presentation of new material via alternating lessons and feedback exercises. The only sense in which this sort of computer program is a simulation is a trivial one; the computer "simulates" a part of the behavior of a classroom teacher conducting drill and review exercises. However, we also utilize a program that can be said to "constitute artificial intelligence" according to the criteria described in the previous section. This program falls into the broad class of computer-assisted instruction to be sure, but, because it independently arrives at logical conclusions through an "inferential" process, it provides feed-back of a sort that has been previously available only from a human instructor. Thus, it qualifies as an input-output simulation of cognitive processes. For example, first, our program checks logical sentences (formulas) provided by students to determine whether they are well formed and internally consistent. Second, it ascertains whether the formulas follow from the premises and/or previous steps of an argument.

In this, it is not limited to a stored repertoire of questions and answers as is the case with conventional CAI programs. Any problem furnished by the students (within very liberal limits) is capable of being analyzed by the computer. Third, the program has the capacity to diagnose a wide variety of logical and syntactical errors, and to provide hints and specimen solutions to problems.

III. *Objectives of CAI in Logic*

At a large university, the motive for computerizing instructional materials is often primarily economic. CAI appears to be a relatively efficient technique for administering mass education. At a small liberal arts college like Denison, our motives have been quite different. Because we offer only one all-purpose course in logic, the student clientele served by it tends to be heterogeneous, and the students' objectives in taking the course also vary considerably. CAI enables an instructor to individualize both the content of the course and the rate at which material can be presented. Because the students learn certain materials faster and more completely at the computer terminal than from lectures, the savings in class time can be utilized for curriculum expansion and enrichment. It is especially apparent that students can learn more material more quickly when certain kinds of topics such as translation into symbolic language and proof techniques are taught outside of class. This is because the rate of mastery of these topics is particularly a function of student ability. The computer enables practically all students to reach a minimum threshold of understanding, although they may require different amounts of time in which to do it. CAI contributes to a more efficient use of the time of instructors and assistants as well. Formerly, teachers were required to repeat material many times before feeling confident that a majority of class members had reached a satisfactory level of understanding. Now an instructor can concentrate upon the conceptual elements in a course such as Logic, leaving much of the teaching of skills and techniques to the computer. Student morale appears to be enhanced by this combination of teaching methods.

By contrast, the conventional method for teaching students to do proofs involves demonstrating a few specimen proofs in a lecture setting and having students attempt some exercises at home. Under this system, the student receives no feedback until examination time, when errors are likely to be ingrained. Also, by then the evaluation process has begun, creating an environment in which new learning and error correction are eclipsed in importance. Indeed, under the traditional approach, some students never reach the first threshold of competence in doing proofs, and thus receive no helpful feedback at all. In contrast, the computer provides early, instantaneous, and detailed feedback in an environment that is nonjudgmental and maintains the student's privacy. Virtually all students manage to begin to produce proofs in this setting. This dramatic fact alone justifies the use of CAI in the teaching of logic.

IV. *The Denison FRAME Programs*

The conventional CAI component of our integrated computer package in logic consists of a series of exercises we call FRAME programs. This is because they are keyed to *frames* of the programmed textbook[2] we use for the teaching of translation to and from symbolic language. The FRAME programs provide explanations, corrections, additions, extra practice exercises and feedback, each one related to a particular lesson in the textbook. Like other conventional CAI programs, the FRAME programs are limited to the specific repertoire of exercises stored in the computer's memory and offer the student feedback to only those of his or her responses that the designers of the programs were able to anticipate. Experience with these programs will enable us to make them more versatile, but not to overcome this inherent handicap of conventional CAI programs.

V. *Proof-Checking Simulations: DEMON and BERTIE*

The most innovative feature of our computer package in logic is, of course, our proof-checking program, which we call DEMON ("Demonstration"). The major credit for the programming of DEMON belongs to Robert Manfredi, a Denison senior Chemistry major, who had been a teaching assistant in Logic. When DEMON was designed, we believed that it was the only simulation of its kind, but later we learned of the existence of BERTIE, a computer program with identical objectives that was developed at Dartmouth College by two faculty members, James Moor and Jack Nelson. BERTIE and DEMON have the following features in common: Both allow the student to choose whether to solve practice problems stored in the computer's memory or to furnish his or her own. The repertoire of problems that the programs can assist students in solving is thus unlimited. Both programs are capable of providing a series of exercises carefully graduated in difficulty and designed to provide practice in the use of all applicable rules of inference. Both check each line of student input for coherence as well as correctness (DEMON specifies which logical or syntactical error is being made), and both have the capability of evaluating the student's claimed justification for each line of proof. Both are able to evaluate any proffered solution, and to certify any correct proof, no matter how circuitous. BERTIE goes further than DEMON in providing instruction in doing proofs in two different symbolic languages, Sentential (Propositional) Calculus and Predicate Calculus, while DEMON handles only proofs written in the former language.

VI. *Evaluation of the Denison CAI Package in Logic*

This is the first semester in which the complete Denison CAI package is available for classroom use. Data have been collected establishing norms for student achievement in Logic during previous semesters when conventional teaching methods were employed exclusively. As many factors as possible are being held constant to facilitate the evaluation of the CAI Logic Project. These include syllabus, class size, contact hours, instructor, and textbooks used. Student achievement is evaluated by means of objective written tests compiled by the instructor from a pool of problems of similar difficulty. The evaluation process does not utilize the computer in any way; a basic premise of the project has been that the computer serves exclusively as an instructional device. Although variations in the capabilities of the students who elect to study logic could distort our evaluation data, admissions statistics for the period of the study suggest that no such effect is likely.

A report on this comparative evaluation of our project will be available by early Summer, 1977. Inquiries about the project are welcome, and we are willing to share our programs with others who are engaged in the teaching of symbolic logic. In the same spirit, we would like to acknowledge the generosity of the designers of BERTIE and their distributing agents, CONDUIT of Iowa, who have unhesitatingly shared their work with us.

VII. *Technical Information*

Language of FRAME and DEMON: Basic Plus, Ver 06A.

Language of BERTIE: "Dartmouth" Basic (The distributing agent for BERTIE is CONDUIT, P.O. Box 388, Iowa City, Iowa 52240.)

Denison Computer: Digital Equipment Corporation, Model PDP 11/45; Operating System RSTS/E. Nine-track magnetic tapes, 800 bpi (8 bit ASCII) and PDPii type DEC tapes are available at cost for transfer of FRAME and DEMON.

NOTES

1. This paper was presented at the Annual Meeting of the American Educational Research Association; New York, April 4-8, 1977.
2. Schagrin, Morton L. *The language of logic* (New York: Random House, 1968).

Part V
URBAN STUDIES

The first of the following two essays by anthropologist David Potter outlines briefly a rationale for using gaming forms of simulation in sociology and anthropology courses. The essay does not thoroughly review current materials, because several reviews are already available; however, it does mention in passing a number of main approaches.

The second essay in this section provides an introduction to the use of the Community Land Use Game (CLUG) in an urban studies course taught with a cross-disciplinary focus. It also outlines some considerations relevant to evaluating the success of the use of CLUG in that course.

Together these two foci demonstrate the typical course of development of faculty skills in simulation, at least as we have experienced it at Denison. The first step for most faculty has been to decide what was wanted from the use of simulation. Next, careful and extensive investigation of simulation materials already available is usually made. Third, there was generally selection of, rewriting of, or individual development of simulations so as to fit particularly the heuristic need. Finally, there is usually an attempt to evaluate both the cognitive and affective results of using the simulation material. Potter's work, as can be seen, followed this pattern, yielding some insights into what is needed for effective use of simulation in urban studies areas.

5

A REVIEW OF SOME URBAN SIMULATIONS AND GAMES AND AN ASSESSMENT OF THEIR UTILITY

DAVID L. POTTER

ABSTRACT

After considering briefly the functions and historical development of urban simulations, this essay outlines several typologies of urban games. Three major kinds of urban simulations are reviewed in detail: role-playing, gaming-simulations, and urban simulation models. For each type, representative games are listed.

Gaming-simulations are presented as the most effective form for classroom use. An extensive delineation of this type's core features and major assets is offered. Particular stress is given to the distinction between formal and systemic games.

Difficulties involved in urban simulation models are then discussed as these affect the possible pedagogical uses of such simulations. Proliferating goals for the utilization of these models, problems of fit between the model and the real urban system, and the potential for integrating the gaming experience with other aspects of an urban studies course are some of the issues addressed. An alternative use of urban simulation models—for professional, cross-disciplinary interaction and communication—is offered in conclusion.

In his comprehensive *Scientific Methods of Urban Analysis,* Catanese (1972) effectively distinguishes among some often confused terms. First, discussing modeling and simulation, he notes that the former "*represents* the urban system" while the latter "*imitates* an urban system." However, he continues, "these fine distinctions are hardly needed for simulation and modeling because, in general, simulation is a way of using models"

(Catanese, 1972, 219; *cf.* Inbar and Stoll, 1972, 28-31). Operationally, simulations are imitations that are utilized to "perform vicarious experimentation" or for "testing alternative solutions to urban problems" (Catanese, 1972, 219).

Gaming is then defined as one of four major functions of simulation in urban analysis:

> It often occurs that the urban problem is too difficult, complex and unwieldy to model. When these conditions occur, usually involving numerous outcomes of decisions and intervening human behavioral values, it is necessary to formulate alternative simulations of the problem. This function is called gaming. . . . (Catanese, 1972, 220)

Special qualities of gaming include its contribution to *learning* about and *understanding* urban problems and processes, generally through roleplaying, in order to make decisions for hypothetical problems. Sometimes "actual data from real urban systems are used as well" (Catanese, 1972, 251). This essentially educational function of gaming permits investigation of its pedagogical potential for students of urban studies.

To begin, one can follow Philip Patterson's (1974, 352) caveat that:

> The potential user [of urban games] should find out the portion of the urban system that is modeled, the portion that can be gamed, and the portion that is missing in any urban gaming model he contemplates using.

Patterson's differentiation between *modeled* and *gamed* elements reflects the Catanese contrast between simulations (or models) and gaming (as decision-making). Urban gaming-simulations incorporate a model (the way "the resources, events and outcomes . . . interact") and a gamed portion (the way "the players interact, set objectives, make decisions, and evaluate outcomes") (Patterson, 1974, 352).

This essay will discuss several urban simulations and games. The focus will shift from a description of various types of games useful for classroom play to a comment on the modeled portions *per se*. Relationships between the two foci will be placed in the context of alternative uses of simulations and games.

An Historical Note

The genesis of modern gaming is found in military applications of war games (see Catanese, 1972, 252; Taylor, 1971). Business schools, education programs, and eventually social scientists (especially political scientists and economists) followed by adapting the technique to their uses. Parallel simulation developments in the general field of education (role playing, T-groups, psychodrama, etc.) and in decision, organization, and systems theories infused the design process. The systems approach in particular was used beneficially by urban planners, enabling them to shift from a mechanistic, deterministic to a dynamic, interactive paradigm (Taylor, 1971).

Gaming functions were added to early research models to reflect this paradigmatic interaction between social and economic dynamics and physical artifacts. Elements of the urban system involving humans were not so easily quantified in mathematical models. Consequently, gaming-simulation arose to express qualitative institutional, administrative, and political decision-making processes. The resulting mix of modeled and gamed components permitted flexible strategies and approaches.

The generic evolution of gaming owes an additional theoretical debt to von Neuman's and Morganstern's (1944) work on gaming theory. Catanese (1972) outlines the underlying theoretical strategies on which urban games are based, and notes that many urbanologists have found this theoretical base less useful than others for comprehending urban systems (see, e.g., Taylor, 1971, 16). Nevertheless, assumptions of risk and uncertainty undergird the purposes of gaming in urban analysis, including:

(1) learning about complex urban problems and understanding risks and uncertainties inherent in many of them;
(2) testing alternative solutions to complex urban problems and examining the risks and uncertainties attached to alternative solutions; and
(3) approximating models of decision-making processes for complex urban problems which are subject to conditions of risk and uncertainty. (Catanese, 1972, 253)

The second and third purposes emphasize the modeling aspects of simulations and will be discussed later. The educative purpose of "learning . . . and understanding" is the concern of our next remarks.

Types of Urban Games

Feldt, Eckroad, and Moses (1972) have identified common elements for all gaming applications as composed of: people playing roles, a scenario, and an accounting system. These commonalities yield three varieties of games—role playing, gaming simulations, and computer simulations. This typology parallels another frequently used one: man, man-machine, and machine games (Inbar and Stoll, 1972). Historically, man simulations have been used for teaching purposes. These games incorporate few, if any, modeled relationships, instead constructing situations suitable for extensive role-playing. Many of these games were developed for secondary education.

In both man and man-machine games, players participate as decision-makers. In the latter, however, the computer or some other external object (a board, a grid) symbolizes a second element of the environment responsive to players' actions. When the other object is an actual machine (e.g., computer), a script for its role must be provided, giving the computer the capability to respond to all possible player responses. Likewise, players (or game directors) must be given a language with which to communicate with the computer. Early man-machine games used the computer primarily for bookkeeping. Later, complex and sophisticated models of the urban system were incorporated to elicit player response. Alternative objects to computers often are employed to represent the model of the urban system. This form accounts for the broader category of gaming-simulation, within which one can place man-machine games. These games have been used for numerous purposes, including research, training, planning, and education.

Likewise, machine (or computer) simulations are multifunctional. In this form, the computer is used to generate gaming processes, or sequences of behavior. Programming is essential and is analogous to procedural rules that govern roles in the other forms. Directions for performing operations must, of course, be made more precise and sequenced rigorously in this case (see Inbar and Stoll, 1972, Chapter 1, for this history). Thus, the modeled portion of the game is the center of attention.

Inbar and Stoll find unity among these three types of simulations. For them the decision to use one or another is a practical matter. They do suggest, however, that for teaching purposes the man or man-machine (gaming-simulation) types are advantageous for players who wish to learn about the process in question. More generally, the computer mode is preferable for processes about which we know a great deal, while the other forms can be used for phenomena about which we know only the general outlines. To anticipate a later argument, one might add that problems of desirability, feasibility, and utility vary with the purpose one has in using the games, and that these goals are not always congruent. As a result, gaming-simulations or elaborate machine models may be disadvantageous for classroom use.

Taylor (1971), however, subsumes all purposes for using games under the educational heading. He also offers a broader typology than the tripartite ones described above, though one that can be condensed for a discussion of urban games. This typology is based on the criterion of increasing abstraction. The continuum begins with "realistic" forms that have been used for several areas of study (including case studies, in-basket or in-tray methods, and incident processes). The remaining three increasingly abstract forms correspond to our three-part typology above (for a similar scheme see Schran, 1972, 309-311). His extensive observations about their qualities merit repeating as a way of introducing examples of urban games.

Role-playing (or man) games involve

> a process requiring spontaneous mock performances from a group of participants in which an attempt is made to create realistic and life-like situations. . . . It is a technique used to gain empathy with pre-scribed roles . . . [and] insight into human interplay in the context of a safe learning environment and relies on spontaneous enactments to illustrate and dramatize human problems or actions. (Taylor, 1971, 12)

The following table lists urban-related games that are known to, or seem to, have major emphasis on role-playing aspects of the simulation. Games with asterisks have been taken from Taylor's (1971, 149-158) annotated "Appendix 2: A directory of selected urban development simulations." All others are found in the Denison University Simulation Center library. The games are organized according to this author's best judgment of the problems or processes for which empathy and insight are the desired products.

Taylor describes his second category, gaming simulations, as "cus-tomarily consist[ing] of human decisions-makers interacting with a simu-lated environment; this environment is represented by other humans in combination with various models of the real world" (Taylor, 1971, 13). While players perform roles in these games, the genesis of their activities is not determined by the role definition or arbitrarily assigned situation, but by a structured environment to which the actors respond:

TABLE 1
A PARTIAL LIST OF URBAN
ROLE-PLAYING GAMES BY TOPIC

Economics
BUDGET
BUDGETARY POLITICS AND
  PRESIDENTIAL DECISION-
  MAKING
BUDGET AND TAXES

Education
EDPLAN
*EDUCATION SYSTEM PLANNING
  GAME
THE METRO HIGH SCHOOL CRISIS
NEW SCHOOL

Environmental/Population Problems
BALANCE
BLIGHT
EXPLOSION

*POLLUTION
SACRIFICE
SMOG

Land Use
INNER-CITY HOUSING GAME
*LOW BIDDER
OPEN SPACE
*OPERATION SUBURBIA
*POGE (Planning Operation Gaming
  Experiment)
TRACTS
WHIPP (Why Housing Is a Problem
  and a Priority)

Politics and/or Intergroup Conflict
THE CITIES GAME
*DEKALB
ESCALATION

THE LAFAYETTE LAND DISPUTE
METROPOLITICS
*PLANS
POLICE PATROL
PRESSURE
THE RAINBOW PARK LAND DIS-
    PUTE
*SECTION
STARPOWER
YES, BUT NOT HERE

Planning
COMMUNITY
COMPACTS
IMPACT
IMPASSE (Rapid Transit)
INNER CITY PLANNING
*NEIGHBORHOOD

*ROUTE LOCATION GAME
TRANSIT
*URBAN PLANNING SIMULATION

Poverty
GHETTO
RURAL POVERTY AND
    COMMUNITY DEVELOPMENT
WHAT'S BEST FOR THOSE IN
    NEED

Race
HANG-UP
THE HILLTOP HOUSING DISPUTE
*INSIGHT
SUNSHINE
WHITE TO WHITE
WIN-LOSE SIMULATIONS MODEL
    (PACT)

> In other words, the game resources, constraints and goals have been
> largely determined in relation to prescribed real-world or hypothetical
> systems. . . . Decisions generally have a bearing on the state of the
> simulated environment. . . . (Taylor, 1971, 15)

In this author's opinion, gaming-simulations are intrinsically more
rewarding than their role-playing counterparts. A more complex model
of the real world (or its hypothetical surrogate) has been added, re-
placing the often static definitions of the situation found in role-playing
exercises. Learning can now focus not only on player interactions and
performances but also on the simulator's model of the environment. The
latter can be utilized to raise questions about its accuracy, and to ascertain characteristics of the modeled environment that influence player performances and are in turn altered by player decisions. Additionally, when
the model constitutes a "complex system," students can experience its
"counterintuitive behaviors" that "cause many of the failures and frustrations experienced in trying to improve [its] behavior" (Forrester, 1969,
107. *Note:* Forrester has an extensive discussion, pages 107-129, of the
qualities of complex models and their virtues for representing urban
dynamics). This function may be limited, however, depending upon the
type of model constructed. This problem will be discussed later in the
essay.

Gaming-simulations, then, are well suited for the urban studies
teacher, offering a blend of environmental complexity and human interaction that can be effectively applied to pedagogical purposes. In addition,
unlike many of the final category of machine games, many of these simulations are more readily available and in a format feasible for educational
use.

Several generations of gaming-simulations in urban studies have passed since their beginnings in the early 1960s. (For a generational breakdown see Taylor, 1971, Chapter 1; and Catanese, 1972, 263-277.) Catanese refers to such gaming-simulations as *operational games,* stating:

> When games are concerned with urban problems, whether hypothetical or real, and when game theory is used to derive decision rules for urban analysis, the procedure is generally referred to as *operational gaming.* Operational gaming usually takes data from real urban systems and simulates problems, alternate solutions, and effects of moves. (1972, 263)

For a genealogy of these games, see Appendix 1 to this article.

Core features of these games most often used by urban planners are:

(1) models which are "simple abstractions of relatively complex aspects of hypothetical or real world situations";

(2) simplicity achieved through "reducing complex operations into a series of simply expressed actions controlled by explicit rules";

(3) exposing participants "to certain preselected features under relatively controlled and risk-free circumstances";

(4) allowing "concerted use of physical models, mathematical representations and human operations";

(5) requiring participants "to assume roles involving various degrees of cooperation, competition and conflict . . . and making decisions which reflect their understanding of key features of the model";

(6) producing "certain decision 'pay-offs'—rewards or deprivations— . . .";

(7) providing "varied experience in controlling the course of events over a series of 'time' spans where the state of the simulated environment is continuously altered in response to the quality of accumulated decision-making";

(8) "compressing 'time' and as a result . . . provid[ing] rapid feedback on the results and consequences of decisions," and

(9) progressing in "predetermined decision stages or periods," each generally representing a 'time' span (Taylor, 1971, 18).

Genealogical histories of urban gaming vary according to the author's purpose. A few are worth discussing to show the range of gaming-simulations and their salient characteristics. Catanese (1972, 263-277) offers an evaluation of a small number of operational games acclaimed for classroom use. First-generation representatives are New Town, METROPOLIS, and CLUG (Community Land Use Game). Second-generation games, which are "extensions of first-generation games to modeling, simulation, and decision-making for real urban systems," include Region I and City I (especially its TELECITY version). Third-generation games "push the generality of the game to the full limit of scientific and technological capabilities in order to represent any urban system" and were created to overcome a problem perceived in second-generation games—i.e., that, while good for teaching, these games "had little policy implications for decision-making in real urban systems." Further, the "current thrust of third-generation games is directed toward the development and implementation of modular games." The strategy of modular games is to construct subsystem models that interact to form a total system (e.g., national, regional, metropolitan, central city, and neighborhood modules). For Catanese, this structure "is much more reflective of real urban systems in an open-system context, and the hierarchy of decision-making is realistic." Representative games for this generation are Region II, City II, and SIMSOC.

This schema reflects changing goals and methodologies among simulators. In later generations attention is focused on building a sophisticated and realistic model rather than on the gaming component. This is especially true when the simulations are viewed as research or experimental devices rather than teaching tools. As these simulations move in this direction, their utility for teaching may decline, revealing tradeoffs between modeled and gamed elements of the simulation.

Appendix 1 to this essay represents a more conventional summary of gaming-simulations. Taylor speaks of a first and second "wave," the latter with conceptual debts to the "pioneering planning games" of the first wave—CLUG, METROPOLIS, and POGE (Planning Operation Gaming Experience). Second-wave games discussed by Taylor include: Northeast Corridor Transportation Games, Land Use Transportation Simulation (LUTS), GSPIA, CITY I, REGION, New Town, Land Use Gaming Simulation (LUGS), COMEXOPOLIS, APEX, METRO, and BUILD. (All games listed here and/or found in the genealogy offered by Taylor are annotated in his Appendix II [Taylor, 1971, 149-158].)

Patterson (1976, 3-8) brings the emphasis on the modeled portion of the game to explicit focus in his categorization, by differentiating two major types of urban gaming models represented in his chronology of games. Somewhat confusingly, Patterson uses the term "gaming model" to refer to both the gamed and modeled portion of the simulation. A formal gaming model is one in which players are given resources and generally assigned well-defined roles and objectives. Their task is to compete in a designated situation to achieve goals defined as appropriate for their respective roles (Patterson, 1976, 3-4). In contrast, in a *systemic gaming model* players are given resources but not necessarily objectives. Rather, players are expected to evaluate the status of the system and their own resources and set goals that they try to achieve (Patterson, 1976, 4-5).

In formal gaming models, the modeled portion is little more than a series of events within which roles make decisions on resource allocation. In systemic gaming models, however, the designer must "build" a systems model relating inputs and outputs in the modeled portion.

Players are encouraged to base decisions on their understanding of the nature of the systems model rather than on a role definition assigned for the game.

Patterson's characterization crosscuts our previous distinctions among man, man-machine, and machine games. His formal gaming models include man games as well as some gaming-simulations that have relatively simplistic models. Systemic gaming models are found in more complex gaming-simulations and in large-scale machine models.

The intellectual tasks involved in these two types of gaming experience are different. In formal games qualities of empathy, imagination, and performance predominate. In systemic games, analysis, calculation, and prediction are more significant. Likewise, one can see again an increasing concern for the modeled portion of the simulation as we move along the continuum toward the more abstract end.

Representatives of the two types of games listed and described by Patterson (1976, 5) are:

Formal Games	*Systemic Games*
Our Town	CLUG
LOC	Urban Dynamics
METROPOLIS	WALRUS
SITTE	SURVIVE
Fair City	New Town
	BUILD
	River Basin
	SIMSOC
	METRO
	GSPIA
	CITY I
	APEX
	TRANSPORTATION
	ACRES

For systemic games, Patterson also identifies the type of model on which the system is based.

For other sources containing extensive information on urban gaming-simulations see Duke (1964), Lee (1974), Nagelburg (1970a and 1970b), Steinitz and Rogers (1971), Taylor and Carter (1969), and Taylor (1971). The Steinitz and Rogers source has a valuable breakdown of the subjects addressed, functions displayed, theories embodied, and methodologies employed to build twenty urban planning models.

Urban Simulation Models

We have tried to suggest that the development of urban games is increasingly diversified as a product of methodological and function concerns. For example, River Basin, a recent large-scale model, has been described as intended "for purposes of training, policy formulation, citizen participation, and elementary indicative planning" (Patterson, 1974, 349). This proliferation of purposes and models requires a note of caution for the educator interested in pedagogical uses of simulation. Incompatibilities among purposes emerge that limit classroom potential of some simulations. The nature of these incompatibilities is not merely economic (i.e., their costliness) but is inherent in the design process:

> One measure of the quality of the simulation is the "quality" of the abstraction or how well the simulation represents the section of life which is to be conveyed. The difference, however, lies in the "level" of abstraction. For research purposes, the level should be as near as possible to reality; while a "high" level of abstraction or simplification is desirable for a more generalized model representing basic social and political concepts. In designing simulation games, it has been pointed out that simplification is not necessarily synonymous with less effort in the design and development process of a game. (Kennedy, 1974, 366)

Patterson (1974, 352) characterizes this dilemma as one between "playability" and "reality."

Given this situation it is important to identify the purpose for which the simulation was intended to determine its likely utility for one's purposes. As Catanese has specified, the functions of simulation include gaming as well as others (1972, 219-220). The same author cautions that mixing the functions, as when games are used for predicting and estimating behavior and decision-making patterns in the real world, is a dubious strategy (Catanese, 1972, 251).

Others (Hendricks, 1974; Lee, 1974) have identified further problems with large-scale machine (computer) simulations. Thus, while such simulations present a number of practical problems for the teacher having pedagogical aims (e.g., cost, availability, time required, etc.), these models also may have limited utility for understanding or representing real urban systems. In fact, Lee argues that the large-scale computer models suffer from endemic problems. Despite his rather overdrawn condemnation of computer simulations, Lee does concede that such models do help one learn about modeling (though not about urban systems).

One need not accept Lee's bald assertion that large-scale models tell us nothing about the urban system. But his assessment does suggest a significant potential educational use of such urban simulations. One benefit of classroom use of gaming-simulations is the necessity for student participants to become conscious of the suppositions about urban life embodied in the modeled component. Evaluation of that model can be an effective means of integrating the gaming experience with other parts of the course. One can require students to articulate the model and analyze validity in the context of course readings that presumably identify other elements of urban life not found in the game.

One can extend this learning experience to include model-building or modification of existing gaming models. Such an exercise need not be limited to student assignments; but may be a genuine opportunity for faculty to refine their understanding of the urban system. The game (or model) design process demands that the creator articulate his conceptions (or preconceptions) of key variables and their interaction in the urban process. As Kaplan (1964, 269) has commented:

> The model saves us from a certain self-deception. Forced into the open, our ideas may flutter helplessly; but at least we can see what bloodless creatures they are. As inquiry proceeds, theories must be brought out into the open sooner or later; the model simply makes it sooner. . . . [And] the model allows the scientist to make clear to others just what he has in mind.

This enhanced precision of thought may have professional consequences for faculty, but it may also redound to the benefit of the classroom. Definitions of key variables may be translated into course objectives—by commitments to expose students to literature stressing these factors, in selection of a gaming-simulation that illustrates these variables, or in modification of games already used. Finally, possibilities for interdisciplinary (see Inbar and Stoll, 1972) or interinstitutional cooperation in this process of game design or modification are exciting though largely unexplored.

For those interested in initiating this process, literature on the designs of urban models will be instructive. The Lee article (1974, 324-325) has a good bibliography of urban models. The issue of *Ekistics* for May, 1974, has several articles that describe specific models (see especially, Doxiadis Associates 1974, 326-329; Rech and Koebel, 1974, 349-354). Extensive descriptions of specific large-scale models also are found in Rogers and Steinitz (1970) (which describes a very ambitious interdisciplinary and inter-course project), Forrester (1969) (the Urban Dynamics model), Duke (1975) (which outlines the METROPOLIS model), House (1973) (which translates components of the urban system into sectors, and which formed the basis for the CITY series of games from Environmetrics), Birch, Reilly, Sardstrom, and Stach (1974) (the New Haven model), and Steiss, Dickey, Phelps and Harvey (1975) (a model of social change). With these efforts as background, and cognizant of the limitations of model-building (cf. Kaplan, 1964, 274-284), we can proceed with this process as an educational means of communicating with colleagues and students.

APPENDIX

A GENEALOGY OF SELECTED URBAN SIMULATIONS

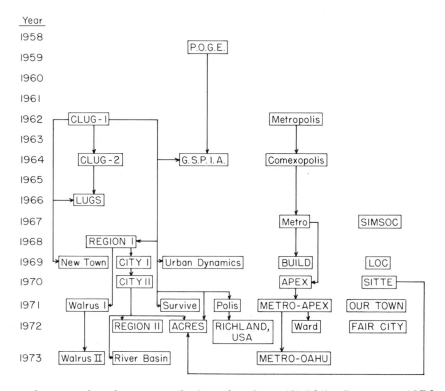

A composite of two genealogies taken from (1) Philip Patterson, 1976, 4; and (2) Richard Duke, 1975, 7.

REFERENCES

Birch, David, Reilly, Atkinson, Sardstrom, Sven, and Stack, Linda. *Patterns of urban change.* Lexington, Massachusetts: Lexington Books, D. C. Heath and Co., 1974.

Catanese, Anthony. *Scientific methods of urban analysis.* Urbana, Illinois: University of Illinois Press, 1972.

Doxiadis Associates. A concept plan for future development—The

Northern Ohio Urban System Research Project. *Ekistics, 37,* No. 222, May, 1974, 326-339.

Duke, Richard. *Gaming simulations in urban research.* East Lansing: Michigan State University (Institute for Community Development), 1964.

――――. *Metropolis: The urban systems games.* Volume II—Participant's Manual. New York: Gamed Simulations, Inc., 1975, 7-18.

Feldt, Alan, with Moses, David, and Echroad, James. *Introduction to gaming simulation techniques,* In *WALRUS I.* Water and Land Resource Utilization Simulation. Technical Report No. 28. Environmental Simulations Laboratory, School of Natural Resources. The University of Michigan, May, 1972, 4-14.

Forrester, Jay. *Urban dynamics.* Cambridge: The M.I.T. Press, 1969.

Hendricks, Francis. Problems of large-scale simulations. *Ekistics 37,* No. 222, May, 1974, 312-315.

House, Peter. *The urban environmental system. Modeling for research, policy-making and education.* Beverly Hills, California: Sage Publications, 1973, 64-80.

Inbar, Michael, and Stoll, Clarice. *Simulation and gaming in social science.* New York: Free Press, 1972.

Kaplan, Abraham. *The conduct of inquiry. Methodology for behavioral science.* San Francisco: Chandler Publishing Co., 1964.

Kennedy, Magrit. Perspectives on urban simulation games for education and planning. *Ekistics, 37,* No. 222, May, 1974, 365-367.

Lee, Douglas, Jr. Requiem for large-scale computer models. *Ekistics, 37,* No. 222, May, 1974, 316-325.

Nagelburg, M. *Selected urban simulations and games.* Working Paper No. 4. Institute for the Future. Middletown, Connecticut: 1970a.

――――. *Simulations of urban systems—A selected bibliography.* Working Paper No. 3. Institute for the Future. Middletown, Connecticut: 1970b.

Patterson, Philip. Games as an urban laboratory. *Ekistics, 37,* No. 222, May, 1974, 349-354.

――――. Recent developments in urban gaming. *Simulations Council Proceedings* Series 2, No. 2, La Jolla, California: The Society for Computer Simulations, 1976.

Rech, Charles, Jr. and Koebel, Charles. The neighborhood model: A structured urban decision process. *Ekistics, 37,* No. 222, May, 1974, 340-344.

Schran, Henning. Urban systems gaming. Developments in Germany. *Simulation and Games 3,* 1972, 309-328.

Steinitz, Carl, and Rogers, Peter. *A systems analysis model of urbanization and change.* Cambridge: The M.I.T. Press, 1970.

Steiss, Alan, Dickey, John, Phelps, Bruce, and Harvey, Michael. *Dynamic change and the urban ghetto.* Lexington, Massachusetts: Lexington Books, D. C. Heath and Co., 1975.

Taylor, John. *Instructional planning systems. A gaming-simulation approach to urban problems.* Cambridge, England: University Press, 1971.

Taylor, John, and Carter, K. A decade of instructional simulation research in urban and regional studies. In Armstrong, R., and J. Taylor (Eds.), *Instructional Simulation Systems in Higher Education.* Cambridge Institute of Education: Cambridge Monographs on Education, No. 2, 1969.

von Neumann, John, and Morganstern, Oskar. *Games and economic behavior.* Princeton: Princeton University Press, 1944.

6

USING GAMING-SIMULATIONS IN URBAN STUDIES

DAVID L. POTTER

ABSTRACT

This essay describes the process of selecting and integrating an urban simulation into an interdisciplinary course on the study of urbanization. Included in the paper are: (1) a rationale for gaming-simulation in urban studies courses; (2) criteria for selecting a game; and (3) strategies used for evaluating the effectiveness of the gaming-simulation.

The course is described in detail to illustrate characteristics that made gaming-simulation an attractive teaching device. The interdisciplinary nature of the course, heterogeneity of student backgrounds, and the desire to dramatize urbanization in process are some salient arguments relevant to this issue.

An outline of the simulation used in the course—Community Land Use Game (CLUG)—is offered to illustrate its qualifications for use as well as the ways in which the game could be fitted with other course materials. The problem of integration of simulations and other learning experiences is highlighted to demonstrate the effectiveness of gaming-simulations when care is taken to define clear objectives for their use.

Finally, several instruments were developed to measure the impact of the gaming-simulation on students' learning. These tests are described and some tentative conclusions offered as to the utility of the simulation experience.

The Course

Several characteristics of the course on urbanization made use of a simulation potentially worthwhile. First, the course introduces students to the concept of urbanization, a term with a broad range of meanings and a process of great complexity, historical diversity, and bewildering scope. Simplification and organization are necessary to reduce the phe-

77

nomenon to manageable proportions for students. Gaming-simulation is especially capable of providing clear models of the urbanization process because of its roots in organization and systems theories, and its flexibility in expressing simultaneously both qualitative and quantitative aspects of the system. (See Taylor, 1971, for an extensive discussion of theoretical antecedents of urban gaming-simulations.)

A model of urban development can also provide a graphic means for students to experience and examine an urban system in action. Referring to gaming's capacity to help students learn and understand about urban phenomena, Antony Catanese (1972) quotes James Coleman, who said:

> Students have too long been taught things that are *known* and have too seldom been allowed to discover for themselves the principles governing a situation. . . . The fascination with . . . games [is] the opportunity to learn about social organization by forming a *caricature* of such organization and then observing the caricature. . . . The student is learning how to incorporate this experience into his own life, learning to recognize the dominant aspects of the social environment so that he can respond appropriately to them when he meets such an environment in his own life. (Catanese, 1972, 251-252)

This potential opportunity to discover the principles of urbanization through gaming augments simulation's model-building capacities as a contribution to the course.

A second salient characteristic of the course in question is its interdisciplinary nature. College faculty members are well aware of the difficulties in achieving meaningful unification and integration among disciplines. Gaming-simulation shows promise of being a vehicle to overcome these problems:

> By emphasizing the interconnectedness of knowledge, gaming-simulation may help to reduce the artificial barriers erected between disciplines and demonstrate gaps and overlaps between different disciplinary approaches. . . . [This is of special significance] in fields such as urban and regional studies which are essentially multi- or interdisciplinary. . . . Games offer particular advantages in the way that they can present an integrated or synoptic view as well as providing a generally freer means of communication. (Taylor, 1971, 68)

The "Study of Urbanization" has been taught several years by teams of faculty from the urban studies coordinating committee. Most often the format could be described as a set of modules introducing various disciplinary perspectives on urbanization, usually including economics, political science, sociology, and/or history. Integration was left to the students or attempted in the interstices between disciplinary frameworks. Frustration dominated the enterprise for students and faculty. The former felt unable to synthesize the segments without transcending principles to guide them; the latter could find no common universe of discourse or analytic framework.

An initial attempt at reform resulted in a formal mode of integration being applied to course material. Urbanization was conceived as an independent, intervening, and dependent variable related to other socioeconomic and political phenomena. Literature was presented illustrating how one could demonstrate the variable properties of urbanization. However, a substantive focus was still missing; and the search for a sophisticated simulation model of the urban system was begun with hope it might provide a substantial, if selective, base.

A final relevant characteristic of the urbanization course is the heterogeneous mix of students it serves. While ideally being the introductory course for urban studies majors, the course actually includes students with background in the several disciplinary urban studies courses at Denison, as well as others who elect the course for other intellectual or personal reasons. For the former group, redundancy with the other courses must be avoided while the latter students are given an introduction to the field. The gaming-simulation was designed to provide a common experience that the whole group could use for discussion and analysis. Both the gaming experience and the model underlying the game became the background for student dialogue.

In summary, we utilized a gaming-simulaton as an integrative device —to give a coherent image of urbanization that could be validated or challenged by other course materials, and to contribute a common experience that would be available for classroom use.

The Gaming-Simulation

The Community Land Use Game (CLUG) has a relatively long and distinguished history as an urban simulation. Taylor (1971) considers CLUG one of three prototype games among the "pioneering planning games" developed in the early 1960s. Genealogical relationships among urban simulations reveal CLUG's status as a progenitor of several major models of varying complexity, availability, and feasibility for classroom use. (For two genealogies see Patterson, 1976, 4; and Duke, 1975, 7.)

CLUG was selected over its competitors for several reasons. First, urban simulations often require large time and preparation commitments, as Taylor observes:

> One point [is] . . . clear: the extraordinary demands placed upon accommodation, timetables and equipment by gaming sessions in comparison with other teaching methods more commonly used in planning education are exceptional. . . . Very few games, relevant to urban and regional development, are available in a form which can be run ade-

quately in the standard classroom and in the conventional lecture or "studio" period. (Taylor, 1971, 63)

However, "If costs are related to use, then possibly only the CLUG model has so far demonstrated its widespread applicability and potential high cost effectiveness" (Taylor, 1971, 3). In this case, CLUG was adaptable to a two-hour session per week throughout the course, with two other hours reserved for lectures.

A second advantage of CLUG is the systemic nature of its underlying model. Patterson (1976, 3-6) distinguishes between *formal* and *systemic* gaming models. In the former design, players are given resources and placed in a situation in which they compete to maximize those resources. The game design assigns the reward system, the distribution of resources, and the limits of player freedom. Thus the formal model has defined objectives and players represent different types of decision-makers related through formalized relationships.

Systemic models portray a system that relates outputs to inputs. Players are given resources but not necessarily objectives. Instead, players are encouraged to look at the status of the system represented and their own resources, and then to evolve roles and objectives they wish to achieve. Unlike the formal model, the systemic model requires the designer to "build" a model to interrelate resources and events.

CLUG is a good example of the systemic approach (in contrast to its major American competing prototype METROPOLIS). CLUG is a game "in which the players' strategies and roles are determined only in response to the rules of the game (the system relations) and the behavior of the other players" (Feldt, in Patterson, 1976, 5).

Another way of stating this classification of games is to distinguish between player-controlled and role-defined games, i.e., systemic and role-playing games (Inbar and Stoll, 1972). In the latter, situations are generated for which players must try to achieve goals peculiar to the roles assigned them. Typically, dissimilar (or conflicting) objectives are given for the roles, as are dissimilar (or unequal) resources with which to achieve the goals. In these games, then, the *roles* constrain the players and dominate the dynamics of play.

Systemic games, as noted, enable players to choose similar or dissimilar objectives and often allocate resources equally among players. "In terms of structure CLUG is a sophisticated hybrid of 'Chess and Monopoly.' This is because the strategies are determined only by the rules of the game; therefore, role-playing is only a response to the rules of the game" (Catanese, 1971, 267). For the course, the relative artificiality of role-playing was believed to be a potential distraction from concentrating on the model of urbanization. Consequently, a game in

The Integration Process

which the *rules* (rather than the roles) were the constraints was preferred.

To avoid having the gaming-simulation process become an isolated element in the course, the game must be related to other aspects of the course. This concern influences both the choice of game and subsequent determinations of course content. The CLUG model is an economic one that "presumes that basic industry is the primary mover for city growth. Nonbasic industry (services, suppliers, and government) grow to accommodate basic industry. Population and residences grow to provide labor for all of the basic and nonbasic employers" (Patterson, 1976, 5).

More specifically,

> the rules of the game for CLUG include a set of predetermined factors: (1) the location and efficiency of the highway network; (2) the location of major points of access to other urban systems; (3) a structure of real property taxation to pay for the building and maintenance of needed community services; and (4) a range of land use categories. Each player is given a fixed amount of capital with which he can buy land and construct buildings in order to get a return on his investment as well as to make profits from the operation of his investments. (Catanese, 1971, 267)

Alternative goals to economic maximization also are possible, as noted.

Experiments with the rules of Basic CLUG have added complexity to this model and permitted alternatives to be introduced into the course. Such experiments include, for example, different ecological and transportation arrangements, zoning, public finance, rural-urban interdependence, environmental, and political issues. (For a complete description of basic rules and experiments, see Alan Feldt, *Community Land Use Game. Player's Manual* [1972].) This flexibility allowed correlation of different versions of the game with various course topics and readings.

The literature counterpart to CLUG as a central focus was Warner's (1972) *The Urban Wilderness.* This history of American urbanization emphasizes factors easily exemplified by the game. Warner's major thesis is that value preferences supportive of a capitalistic ethos combined with advances in transportation-technology to shape our urban growth. He delineates three historical types of American cities, each having a characteristic ecology and reflecting the dynamics of economic values with available technology. Urban problems are identified for the three eras, arising from issues such as planning (or its lack), zoning, transportation, housing, centralization/decentralization, public versus private interest, and segregation/integration.

CLUG was well suited for dramatizing elements of Warner's thesis. The basic model demonstrates how ecological and transportation variables influence urban decision-making and growth. Experiments mirroring transportation advances for Warner's three eras can be offered. Various other experiments highlight the issues of concern to Warner.

Interactions among players illuminate the role of values in decision-making. Given the systematic nature of the game, players can operate as capitalist entrepreneurs by striving to maximize profit in competition with other teams. Consequences of this style of play for urban growth reflect in simplified form some of Warner's conclusions for American history.

Alternative modes of relating to each other may arise as students become aware of different values they would like to incorporate into the game. Experiments permit this formally, but students may devise their own interaction modes or rules.

Limits to the gaming model also become evident in comparison to the richness of Warner's historical material. These weaknesses can generate concern for changing the model that can be a basis for class discussion.

Sjoberg's (1960) *The Pre-Industrial City* proposes an ideal typology for the preindustrial city that can be compared both with Warner's tripartite typology of industrializing America and the CLUG model. Such comparisons emphasize that the gaming model is appropriate for a particular historical, technological, and ecological context, and dramatize that urbanization is not a unilinear process. Differences between preindustrial and industrial forms can be discussed in terms of how the gaming model might be altered to reflect the former.

Owen's (1972) *Accessible City* proposes changes in urban ecology and networks that would transform currently "accidental cities" into more accessible ones—through effectively integrating transportation with other systems of urban activity. The book's focus on transportation's contribution to urban form and function obviously is relevant to the gaming experience. Systemic effects of transportation can be observed in the game. Further, Owen's contrast between presently unplanned, "accidental" cities and possible planned "accessible" cities reiterates a major theme in Warner. Planning experiments in CLUG, used as sequels to the basic free market version, permit observations of ecological consequences for public developmental strategies.

Rodwin's (1961) *The Future Metropolis* includes a number of selections describing past and future urban forms. CLUG yields a visual image of a growing city as the board grid takes shape during several rounds of play. Determinants of form are represented as rules of the games. Evaluations of these models are possible when the articles in Rodwin analyze factors creating past and future urban forms.

Finally, Feagin's (1973) *The Urban Scene* examines a number of urban problems. While a few of these issues are available within the game or its experiments, this book functions best as a challenge to the

CLUG model. The economic base of CLUG's system restricts its capacity to represent sociological processes or products of urbanization. Social and political issues are not well represented in the game. This raises questions about the model and about the proper relationships among economic, political, and social urban subsystems. Students can be urged to consider revisions of the model that might more accurately reflect actual urbanization. In the course, this was done formally by requiring a term paper asking students to: (1) identify the variables influencing urbanization in the CLUG model; (2) describe how those variables worked together to produce the varied results of the game versions played; and (3) criticize the gaming model by citing evidence (from course readings and lectures) that critical variables are missing or misrepresented in the model.

(*Note:* This last assignment was a culminating attempt to link the experiential and cognitive components of the course. In retrospect, another step might well be taken by asking students to design their own experiment based on the CLUG model. In fact, some observers believe the modeling process should be an intrinsic element of using games in educational settings. These advocates see the design process as a "fundamental instructive activity which requires detailed data collection, systemic analysis and an ability to recognize and synthesize essential and important relationships. Even when a satisfactory model is not achieved, investigators believe that they have obtained considerable insight into the nature of the phenomenon under study" [Taylor, 1971, 66].

(While modification of an existing model is less ambitious than the entire process described here, this more modest assignment may prove valuable. William Gamson (in Inbar and Stoll, 1972, 67) notes that once students have played, analyzed the play, and thought about what happened, they often are eager to construct their own picture of the simulation and to understand the process:

> The use of games for teaching seems to me most successful when the students are asked to make the jump from player to simulator. As players they accept constraints . . . and use resources to achieve certain objectives specified or suggested by the rules. When the students become simulators, the *rules themselves* become the resources and they can manipulate these resources—hypothetically or actually—to see whether the resulting process will take the form they believe it will. Developing simulations is too enjoyable and valuable a learning experience to be hoarded by professors.

(Gamson's enthusiasm for model-building or modification should be tempered by recognition that a systemic model is scaled and linked in ways that require care in making alterations. A seemingly small change may have wide ramifications that are unintended and unanticipated.)

The Evaluation

Experimental conditions for evaluating the effectiveness of the gaming experiences were not met, given the absence of a control group. Nonetheless, several steps were taken to ascertain what was learned during the semester. The results, which will not be extensively described here, but are available upon request, must be interpreted as a measure of the total course experience rather than of the gaming component *per se*. They are, however, suggestive of how the various pedagogical techniques employed worked together.

Our evaluation strategy was based on the presumption that not all students would benefit fully from the gaming experience. Gamson has observed that not all students like games, which require an active, instrumental, and controlling posture toward the environment. He predicts that those who are shy or passive, or who simply like to let things happen, will not enjoy simulations. Whether or not this typology is empirically sound, Gamson does identify a type of student response that is all too common—the passive. Our concern was whether this or other types of students would meet Gamson's further assertion that it is not necessary to like a game in order to learn from it (in Inbar and Stoll, 1972, 67).

To accomplish this goal, a cognitive style test was devised to characterize learners' styles in the course. Each student was asked to assess his preferences for kinds of learning experience. Differences among students were then correlated with measurements of learning change obtained from our other instruments.

Two other instruments were used to measure changes during the course. A set of adjective pairs were presented to the students in a standard continuum format (e.g., good__ __ __ __ __bad). Students were asked to locate their positions on each continuum in response to the statement "Cities are . . . ." Both a pretest and posttest were given at the appropriate times to discover if student attitudes toward the city had changed during the semester.

A second instrument listed a number of possible factors influencing urbanization. Students were asked to estimate the importance of each factor listed according to their own best knowledge. Again a pretest and a posttest were given at appropriate times to determine if ratings for each factor changed during the course.

Significant changes in attitudes toward cities, though mixed, tended to show enhanced appreciation of the complexity of cities. Changes in the ratings for variables influencing urbanization generally reflected increased recognition of the factors dramatized by the game and the readings.

Finally, each student was asked to evaluate the gaming experience through a series of questions. When positive and negative evaluations were correlated with cognitive style measurements, interesting and significant differences appeared. This suggests that special consideration should be given to questions about how different kinds of students learn best. It also suggests that continued and refined evaluation of pedagogical innovations should be an important component of course development.

Conclusion

Adopting gaming-simulation as a learning experience involves a number of decisions. First, one needs to specify course objectives in order to evaluate whether or not a game will satisfy course goals. In the case discussed, special emphasis was given to contributions that gaming-simulation models can make to an understanding of urban processes. Second, criteria for choosing a particular game need to be clear. Practical considerations as well as structural characteristics of the game are limiting factors. Third, the gaming-simulation must be an integral part of the entire course. In this way a symbiosis is effected between experiential and cognitive learning. Fourth, knowledge of the actual impact of the gaming-simulation is needed to judge whether or not the innovation was successful.

REFERENCES

Catanese, Antony. *Scientific methods of urban analysis.* Urbana, Illinois: University of Illinois Press, 1972.

Duke, Richard. *Metropolis: the urban systems games.* Volume II—Participant's Manual. New York: Gamed Simulations, Inc., 7-18. 1975.

Feagin, Joe (Ed.). *The urban scene. Myths & realities.* New York: Random House, 1973.

Feldt, Alan. *CLUG Community land-use game. Player's Manual.* New York: The Free Press, 1972.

Inbar, Michael, and Stoll, Clarence. *Simulation and gaming in social science.* New York: The Free Press, 1972.

Owen, Wilfred. *The accessible city.* Washington, D.C.: The Brookings Institute, 1972.

Patterson, Philip. Recent developments in urban gaming. *Simulations Council Proceedings Series, 2,* No. 2. La Jolla, California: The Society for Computer Simulations, 1976.

Rodwin, Lloyd (Ed.). *The future metropolis.* New York: George Braziller, 1961.

Sjoberg, Gideon. *The pre-industrial city.* New York: The Free Press, 1960.

Taylor, John. *Instructional planning systems. A gaming-simulation approach to urban problems.* Cambridge, England: University Press, 1971.

Warner, Sam Bass, Jr. *The urban wilderness. A history of the American city.* New York: Harper & Row, Publishers, 1972.

Part VI

ECONOMICS

The two papers on simulation in economics take very different approaches to analyzing how simulation can be best used as a teaching device. In the paper by economist Fletcher and mathematician Karian, computer simulation of a regulatory commission that the authors developed is described, as are some of its classroom uses. The authors then go on to attempt to evaluate the simulation, at least in terms of its teaching effectiveness.

The second economics paper was written by individuals who object to both the format and the heuristic use of computer simulations like that of Fletcher and Karian. Bartlett and Amsler criticize the computer simulation approach on the basis of an argument that the simulations used rarely if ever achieve a satisfactory level of "real world" validity, that, instead, one is left with an abstract mathematical model that may have apparently little predictive or even postdictive accuracy. To remedy this argued shortcoming, Bartlett and Amsler suggest combining data, role-playing activities, and theoretical models into what they call a "synergistic" simulation, that is one in which "two discrete [simulation] techniques [are combined] such that the total result is greater than the sum of their individual results." The authors, after critiquing current simulation approaches to teaching economics, and after suggesting synergistic simulations, then go on to outline Bartlett's simulation of the Federal Open Market Committee, which they consider to fulfill the requirements for "synergism," and to encourage their own brand of simulation for the teaching of economics.

7

USING INTERACTIVE SIMULATION IN TEACHING REGULATION OF BUSINESS[1]

DANIEL O. FLETCHER
ZAVEN A. KARIAN

ABSTRACT

COMMISSION is a simulation developed at Denison University to facilitate the teaching of regulation of public utilities. It enables the student to take the role of regulator and try to satisfy his various constituencies. The simulation is explained in some detail and classroom experience is outlined. Most satisfactory experience was gained where the simulation was used as homework, closely tied to classroom discussion.

"A realistic way of confrontation as if I was really in control." "The computer is an excellent diversion from the book-lecture system and definitely created interest." These are two comments from a class that used a computer simulation of a regulatory commission, called COMMISSION, at Denison University. The model is one we developed at Denison in the BASIC-PLUS language for use on a PDP 11/45 computer with 104K words of memory and 16 terminals dedicated to a student body of 2,100. The primary purpose of the model is to enable students to appreciate the inherent difficulties in sustaining a healthy industry while keeping the public satisfied through regulation. The object is to give the student the feel of being a regulator and present him with some of the problems and constraints felt by the conscientious regulator. The student should be able to recognize problems and results that have been discussed in class as he receives responses to his decisions at his terminal. The student is able to run the simulation as often as he wishes at terminals scattered around campus, which are available twenty-four hours a day. Many students tried thirty or more examples using a variety of approaches and strategies.

I. *The Student Role*

In the simulation, the student is in the position of the commissioner (with no other members to bring up the problem of votes and disagreements), with four possible courses of action. He may change the price that the regulated firm charges any time he wishes. He may subsidize the firm, although the possibility is opened only when the firm has already gotten into some financial trouble. He may issue a "quality order" when the service provided by the firm fails. The implication of this order is that the firm is required to improve service to cut customer complaints, although additional costs are involved. Last, the "commissioner" may change the allowable rate of return on capital—the famous "fair return on a fair value" of *Smyth vs. Ames*. This last course of action is available only when the firm makes a request for a change in rate of return and, in most cases, results in a "Court Decision" that is rather favorable to the firm.

The last two of the above courses of action are contained in an options program. That is, the simulation may be run without the quality order and the changing rate of return possibilities. The intention is to have each student run the simulation without these options once. Then, by executing the options program, the instructor is able to insert these new possibilities into the program and the students are asked to run the simulation again. In addition, the options program enables the instructor to change the magnitude of the initial capital investment in the utility and to change the general magnitude of the demand. Demand is randomly selected for each play of the simulation, but changes make the simulation more difficult for the student and make it different when he plays it several times.

The student is to keep in mind the dual responsibility of the commissioner: to provide good quality service to the public and to provide a reasonable level of profits to the company involved. The type of company is not specified, but all of its characteristics, such as inelastic demand and high fixed costs, are consistent with a transit company or an electric power company.

His progress is reported each "year" and is based on his keeping the company's rate of return in line with the allowable rate of return and complaints down. He is also annually urged to keep his eye on the capital/labor ratio (the Averch-Johnson effect). Sample Output 1 illustrates the initial instructions.

```
                    SAMPLE OUTPUT 1

DO YOU WISH TO START AT THE BEGINNING?  YES
WOULD YOU LIKE INFORMATION CONCERNING THE SIMULATION?  YES

YOU ARE THE HEAD OF A COMMISSION REGULATING A PUBLIC UTILITY.
THERE WILL BE CERTAIN DECISIONS THAT YOU WILL HAVE TO MAKE
CONCERNING PER CENT RETURN ON CAPITAL--QUALITY OF SERVICE--PRICE/
UNIT--AND OTHER RULES AND REGULATIONS.
YOU ARE TO MINIMIZE THE COST TO THE PUBLIC BUT AT THE SAME TIME
YOU MUST SEE THAT THE QUALITY OF SERVICE IS KEPT UP AND THAT
THE COMPANY REMAINS SOLVENT AND IN SOUND OPERATING CONDITION.
REMEMBER THAT THE COMPANY IS ENTITLED TO A 'FAIR RETURN' ON ITS
OPERATING CAPITAL.  THIS IS CALLED 'ALLOWABLE RETURN ON CAPITAL'
IN THE SIMULATION.  AT THE BEGINNING AND THE END OF EACH QUARTER
YOU WILL BE GIVEN FEEDBACK CONCERNING THE DECISIONS THAT YOU
MADE IN THE PREVIOUS PERIOD.  ---IMPORTANT---  THERE IS DEPRE-
CIATION OF CAPITAL AND A BUSINESS CYCLE FACTOR INCORPORATED AND
BOTH WILL AFFECT DEMAND SO TAKE THIS INTO ACCOUNT.  ...GOOD
LUCK

THE SERVICE QUALITY IS DEFINED BY USING A QUALITY INDEX RANGING
BETWEEN -100 AND 100, 100 BEING ASSOCIATED WITH GOOD QUALITY,
-100 BEING ASSOCIATED WITH MISERABLE SERVICE.  QUALITY ORDERS
WILL HELP RAISE THE QUALITY, BUT WILL CAUSE ADDITIONAL CAPITAL
INVESTMENT AND WILL RESULT IN A DECREASE IN ACTUAL RETURN.

HOW MANY QUARTERS WOULD YOU LIKE TO RUN?  12
```

II. *The Lower End Routine*

If the student allows the profits earned by the firm to fall too far below the legally allowed levels, he gets into the "lower end" routine. The firm complains and begins a bargaining routine. At the same time, consumer complaints rise and this is accompanied by an irritating ringing of the bell on the terminal. (Lower profits presumably mean poor maintenance and poor service.) Political pressure on the commissioner follows and he is approached about providing a subsidy. If he is unable to lift the utility back to profitability through the subsidy or a price increase, he is eventually removed from office.

"LOWER END" ROUTINE - OUTPUT 2

PERIOD 7

DEPRECIATION	$29,655
REPLACEMENT INVESTMENT	$26,475
NEW INVESTMENT	$ 0

TOTAL CAPITAL INVESTMENT	$1,183,001
CAPITAL/LABOR RATIO	3.549/1
ELASTICITY OF DEMAND	0.102162

ALLOWABLE RETURN ON CAPITAL/YR.	6%
ALLOWABLE RETURN ON CAPITAL/QRTR.	1.5% $17,745
ACTUAL YEARLY RETURN ON CAPITAL	2.30% $24,593
PAST QUARTER'S RETURN ON CAPITAL	0.44% $ 5,196

LAST QUARTER'S PRICE/UNIT	$1.90
LAST QUARTER'S DEMAND IN UNITS	204,605
BUSINESS CYCLE FOR NEXT PERIOD	0.00

TOTAL COST/UNIT	$1.80
VARIABLE COST/UNIT	$0.47
MARGINAL COST	$0.74

FIRM UNHAPPY--NOT ENOUGH PROFIT TO SUSTAIN QUALITY.
A PRICE INCREASE TO $2.15 IS REQUESTED. WHAT PRICE
DO YOU PROPOSE? 1.90

OUR COST FOR THIS SERVICE/QRTR. IS	$91,992
OUR RETURN/QUARTER	$97,187
OUR PROFIT/QUARTER	$ 7,886

CALL FROM GOVERNOR WARNING YOU NOT TO BLOW IT!!
VISIT FROM UTILITY'S UNION LEADERS
NOT VERY HAPPY *?%$&'♪!!!

DO YOU WANT TO SUBSIDIZE THE FIRM? NO
HOW ABOUT RAISING THE PRICE TO $2.15?
YOUR PROPOSAL? $1.90
UTILITY REJECTS YOUR PROPOSAL!!

PERIOD 8
{SUBSTANTIALLY REPEATS PERIOD 7}

OUTPUT 2 (CONT'D.)

PERIOD 9

DEPRECIATION	$29,549
REPLACEMENT INVESTMENT	$26.014
NEW INVESTMENT	$ 0

TOTAL CAPITAL INVESTMENT	$1,178,423
CAPITAL/LABOR RATIO	3.535/1
ELASTICITY OF DEMAND	0.102162

ALLOWABLE RETURN ON CAPITAL/YR.	6%
ALLOWABLE RETURN ON CAPITAL/QRTR.	1.5% $17,676
PAST QUARTER'S RETURN ON CAPITAL	0.03% $ 394

LAST QUARTER'S PRICE/UNIT	$1.90
LAST QUARTER'S DEMAND IN UNITS	188,102
BUSINESS CYCLE FOR NEXT PERIOD	0.00

TOTAL COST/UNIT	$1.89
VARIABLE COST/UNIT	$0.45
MARGINAL COST	$0.74

FIRM UNHAPPY--NOT ENOUGH PROFIT TO SUSTAIN QUALITY.
A PRICE INCREASE TO $2.27 IS RQUESTED.

WHAT PRICE DO YOU PROPOSE? $1.90
YOU REALLY BLEW IT!!!!
LEGISLATION HAS REMOVED YOU FROM OFFICE
BYE---

READY

III. *The Upper End Routine*

On the other hand, if the student lets the returns to the company rise too high above the legally allowable limits, he finds himself in the "upper end" routine. He finds that the "Consumer Welfare Organization" is complaining and more political pressures appear. This pressure is made tangible by the slowing of the program. While "tied up in litigation" is printed, the program stops printing output. Each period the return is still too high, this delay increases. Within a few periods, this delay becomes intolerable and the student finds that he must come up with an answer through reducing price or the subsidy if there is one being given.

"UPPER END" ROUTINE - OUTPUT 3

CONSUMER WELFARE ORGANIZATION FINDS FIRM'S
RETURN TOO HIGH, OPERATIONS WILL BE SLOWED.

                            PERIOD 18
TIED UP IN LITIGATION
SUBSIDY $50,000
DEPRECIATION $49,887
REPLACEMENT INVESTMENT $40,721
NEW INVESTMENT $ 0

TOTAL CAPITAL INVESTMENT $1,986,309
CAPITAL/LABOR RATIO   5.959/1
ELASTICITY OF DEMAND   0.159937

ALLOWABLE RETURN ON CAPITAL/YR.   6%
ALLOWABLE RETURN ON CAPITAL/GRTR.   1.5% $29,795
PAST QUARTER'S RETURN ON CAPITAL   2.53% $50.196

LAST QUARTER'S PRICE/UNIT $2.00
LAST QUARTER'S DEMAND IN UNITS   81,763
BUSINESS CYCLE FOR NEXT PERIOD   0.04

TOTAL COST/UNIT $1.99
VARIABLE COST/UNIT $0.53
MARGINAL COST $0.82

DO YOU WISH TO CHANGE SUBSIDY? YES
INPUT TOTAL AMOUNT/QUARTER? 90000

DO YOU WANT TO CHAGE PRICE/UNIT? YES
INPUT NEW PRICE/UNIT? 0.90

CONSUMER WELFARE ORGANIZATION FINDS FIRM'S RETURN
TOO HIGH, OPERATIONS WILL BE SLOWED.

IV. *The Use of Options*

If the "quality order" option has been activated, the student receives
a quality index in his output tables instead of general comments about
consumer complaints. This index is from -100 to $+100$ and falls as
the company is unable to earn sufficient revenues to keep the service up.
If the index falls below 70, the student is asked if he desires to issue a
"quality order." If he does, the quality index the next period will go up
but costs will shift upward and new investment will be made by the
company, presumably in order to make the necessary quality improvements. This, in turn, will upset the profit and rate of return figures,
causing the student to rethink this decision. This routine is illustrated in
Output 4.

PERIOD 2

DEPRECIATION	$24,957
REPLACEMENT INVESTMENT	$14,216
NEW INVESTMENT	$ 0

TOTAL CAPITAL INVESTMENT	$997,550
CAPITAL/LABOR RATIO	2.993/1
ELASTICITY OF DEMAND	0.102586

ALLOWABLE RETURN ON CAPITAL/YR.	6%
ALLOWABLE RETURN ON CAPITAL/QRTR.	1.5% $14,963
PAST QUARTER'S RETURN ON CAPITAL	0.66% $ 6,559

LAST QUARTER'S PRICE/UNIT	$2.00
LAST QUARTER'S DEMAND IN UNITS	124,435
BUSINESS CYCLE FOR NEXT PERIOD	0.022

TOTAL COST/UNIT	$1.79
VARIABLE COST/UNIT	$0.58
MARGINAL COST	$0.82

QUALITY INDEX	44

WANT TO SEND A QUALITY ORDER?   YES

A PRICE INCREASE TO $2.27 IS REQUESTED
WHAT PRICE DO YOU PROPOSE? $2.00

SERVICE QUALITY WILL DETERIORATE

PERIOD 3

DEPRECIATION	$24,939
REPLACEMENT INVESTMENT	$21,137
NEW INVESTMENT	$101,085

TOTAL CAPITAL INVESTMENT	$1,094,834
CAPITAL/LABOR RATIO	3.284/1
ELASTICITY OF DEMAND	0.102586

```
                    OUTPUT 4 (CONT'D.)


PERIOD 3 (CONT'D.)


ALLOWABLE RETURN ON CAPITAL/YR.           6%
ALLOWABLE RETURN ON CAPITAL/QRTR.         1.5%    $16,423
ACTUAL YEARLY RETURN ON CAPITAL           3.07%   $31,065
PAST QUARTER'S RETURN ON CAPITAL          0.40%   $ 4,375
----
LAST QUARTER'S PRICE/UNIT                 $2.00
LAST QUARTER'S DEMAND IN UNITS            127,369
BUSINESS CYCLE FOR NEXT PERIOD            0.00
----
TOTAL COST/UNIT                           $1.86
VARIABLE COST/UNIT                        $0.56
MARGINAL COST                             $0.82
----

QUALITY INDEX                             81
```

If the option is activated that enables the allowable rate of return to be changed, the company will request a new higher rate of return on capital at times specified in the program. Up to this point, the student has worked entirely with a 6% rate of return as the goal. The firm will present certain "evidence" as illustrated. The student is asked to accept or reject this suggestion. If he accepts, we go back to simulation. If he rejects it, he finds himself in "court" and the court decision is made. This is a compromise between the present rate and the proposal. Hence, it usually, but not always, results in a higher legal rate of return being set. After this point, the new rate is used as the standard for all decisions in the simulation.

```
                    RATE OF RETURN CHANGE - OUTPUT 5

                             PERIOD 1

DEPRECIATION                                $25,000
REPLACEMENT INVESTMENT                      $21,000
NEW INVESTMENT                              $      0
----
TOTAL CAPITAL INVESTMENT                    $996,500
CAPITAL/LABOR RATIO                          2.999/1
ELASTICITY OF DEMAND                        0.179248
----
ALLOWABLE RETURN ON CAPITAL/YR.                6%
ALLOWABLE RETURN ON CAPITAL/QRTR.            1.5%      $14,948
PAST QUARTER'S RETURN ON CAPITAL            0.20%     $ 2,036
----
LAST QUARTER'S PRICE/UNIT                    $2.00
LAST QUARTER'S DEMAND IN UNITS              939,292
BUSINESS CYCLE FOR NEXT PERIOD               0.00
----
TOTAL COST/UNIT                             $1.99
VARIABLE COST/UNIT                          $0.49
MARGINAL COST                               $0.79
----

FIRM UNHAPPY--NOT ENOUGH PROFIT TO SUSTAIN QUALITY.
----

UTILITY REQUESTS INCREASE IN PERCENTAGE OF ALLOWABLE
RETURN.  EVIDENCE FOR THIS REQUEST:

        PRIME RATE IS                       8.6%
        ALTERNATE PROFIT OPPORTUNITIES      19.4%
        OUR COST OF CAPITAL                 17.1%
THE UTILITY SUGGESTS A RETURN OF            18.0%
DO YOU ACCEPT OR REJECT?  REJECT

UTILITY HAS TAKEN YOU TO COURT
COURT RAISES ALLOWABLE RATE TO              16.4%
SORRY, BUT IT IS OUT OF YOUR HANDS
```

The other two options cause the capital and the demand figures to be of a much higher magnitude. The result is that the student finds it much more difficult to keep the profit levels and prices within acceptable limits. The degree of difficulty can be varied by the instructor in this way to give a great deal of flexibility.

There are, of course, many possible strategies for the student to pursue. He may elect to try to keep the company's profits within the legal limits by adjusting price to its requirements (Sample Output 6). Another possible strategy is to force the firm to charge marginal costs and make up the difference through the subsidy (Sample Output 7). An even more radical approach is to set the price at zero and provide the company's entire needs from the public treasury (Sample Output 8). This example refers to free urban transit or free medical service.

OUTPUT 6

PERIOD 1

DEPRECIATION	$25,000	
REPLACEMENT INVESTMENT	$22,939	
NEW INVESTMENT	$ 0	

TOTAL CAPITAL INVESTMENT	$997,939	
CAPITAL/LABOR RATIO	2.994/1	
ELASTICITY OF DEMAND	0.134804	

ALLOWABLE RETURN ON CAPITAL/YR.	6%	
ALLOWABLE RETURN ON CAPITAL/QRTR.	1.5%	$14,969
PAST QUARTER'S RETURN ON CAPITAL	1.54%	$15,387

LAST QUARTER'S PRICE/UNIT	$2.15	
LAST QUARTER'S DEMAND IN UNITS	139,658	
BUSINESS CYCLE FOR NEXT QUARTER	0.00	

TOTAL COST/UNIT	$1.71	
VARIABLE COST/UNIT	$0.47	
MARGINAL COST	$0.72	

DO YOU WANT TO CHANGE PRICE/UNIT?   NO

PERIOD 2

DEPRECIATION	$24,948
REPLACEMENT INVESTMENT	$20,110
NEW INVESTMENT	$ 0

TOTAL CAPITAL INVESTMENT	$993,100
CAPITAL/LABOR RATIO	2.973/1
ELASTICITY OF DEMAND	0.134804

ALLOWABLE RETURN ON CAPITAL/YR.	6%
ALLOWABLE RETURN ON CAPITAL/QRTR.	1.25% $14,897
PAST QUARTER'S RETURN ON CAPITAL	1.55% $15,387

LAST QUARTER'S PRICE/UNIT	$2.15
LAST QUARTER'S DEMAND IN UNITS	139,658
BUSINESS CYCLE FOR NEXT PERIOD	0.04

TOTAL COST/UNIT	$1.71
VARIABLE COST/UNIT	$0.47
MARGINAL COST	$0.72

DO YOU WANT TO CHANGE PRICE/UNIT? NO

PERIOD 5

SUBSIDY	$58,000
DEPRECIATION	$14,803
REPLACEMENT INVESTMENT	$21,173
NEW INVESTMENT	$ 0

TOTAL CAPITAL INVESTMENT	$988,505
CAPITAL/LABOR RATIO	2/965/1
ELASTICITY OF DEMAND	0.175020

ALLOWABLE RETURN ON CAPITAL/YR.	6%
ALLOWABLE RETURN ON CAPITAL/QRTR.	1.5% $14,828
PAST QUARTER'S RETURN ON CAPITAL	1.52% $14,982

LAST QUARTER'S PRICE/UNIT	$0.64
LAST QUARTER'S DEMAND IN UNITS	218,259
BUSINESS CYCLE FOR NEXT PERIOD	0.00

TOTAL COST/UNIT	$1.43
VARIABLE COST/UNIT	$0.44
MARGINAL COST	$0.64

DO YOU WISH TO CHANGE SUBSIDY? NO

DO YOU WANT TO CHANGE PRICE/UNIT? NO

PERIOD 9

SUBSIDY	$103,000
DEPRECIATION	$ 29,587
REPLACEMENT INVESTMENT	$ 27,108
NEW INVESTMENT	$ 0

TOTAL CAPITAL INVESTMENT	$1,181,002
CAPITAL/LABOR RATIO	3.543/1
ELASTICITY OF DEMAND	0.175020

ALLOWABLE RETURN ON CAPITAL/YR.	6%
ALLOWABLE RETURN ON CAPITAL/QRTR.	1.5% $17,715
PAST QUARTER'S RETURN ON CAPITAL	1.62% $19,152

LAST QUARTER'S PRICE/UNIT	$0.00
LAST QUARTER'S DEMAND IN UNITS	255,358
BUSINESS CYCLE FOR NEXT PERIOD	$0.00

TOTAL COST/UNIT	$1.31
VARIABLE COST/UNIT	$0.47
MARGINAL COST	$0.64

DO YOU WISH TO CHANGE SUBSIDY?   YES

INPUT TOTAL AMOUNT/QRTR.?   101500

DO YOU WANT TO CHANGE PRICE/UNIT?   NO

V. *Classroom Experience with Commission*

The simulation was used three times in classroom situations during the first year. Each of these situations was substantially different, and the success of the simulation seemed to differ in the three experiences. The simulation was first used in an upper division course, Industrial Organization and Public Policy, populated mostly by junior and senior economics majors. This course deals in public policy issues, including antitrust laws and regulation of business, as well as some theoretical and empirical material. The two sections of the course in the fall semester used simulation in different ways. Both sections had completed the material on concentration, empirical evidence, and antitrust laws. Both were ready to begin discussion of public regulation.

Section I was put directly to work on the simulation without any formal classroom discussion of the problems of public regulation. They were given a week to work on the terminals without other assignments or classes. At midweek, the options program was used to change the simulation, introducing new complexities, and each student had to hand in his results from before and after the changes. After this week, we returned to regular classes and discussed the material on regulation. Before this discussion started, the students took a short factual test and an attitudinal test on their views of regulation that had also been administered before work on the simulation began. It was clear that their views on regulation had not changed enough to change their performance on the attitudinal test. On the factual test, the students appeared to understand the simulation mechanics, but drew a blank on the underlying theory and the underlying real forces in the situation. For instance, a question on why the capital/labor ratio changed brought a mechanical answer but no discussion of the possible reasons for this.

Section II spent a week discussing regulatory theory and the history of regulation. We talked about everything from *"Smyth vs. Ames"* to the so-called "Averch-Johnson Effect." Then the section was given a week to work on the simulation in the same format as the other section. The program was changed at midweek and two printouts were to be handed in. Again, tests were administered to try to discover attitudinal and factual changes. This time a very slight increase in the student's sympathy toward the regulator—the role he had been playing—was seen. This was, however, a very small change. On the factual test, greater differences were evident. A question on why the capital/labor ratio had changed now was answered by reference to the "Averch-Johnson Effect." Many of the students reacted well by saying, "Yeah, that's what we talked about in class," and explaining. Some, of course, simply recognized a remembered phrase from class. The simulation did seem to be more meaningful to these students.

By far the most satisfying use of the simulation, however, was in a section of basic economics. These students were primarily freshmen and sophomores and none had taken a previous course in economics. This was the second semester and they had had about eight weeks of general economics, but no specific discussion of regulation or other government policy. Here, for nine classes, the simulation was used as text and homework. After introducing the computer terminal, the simulation, and the subject, the work on the simulation was tied directly to the classroom work. We would spend a day in which, as an example, the strategy of marginal-cost pricing for utilities was discussed. The homework assignment was then to work out such an example on the simulation and turn it in the next class day. We would review that strategy and go on to the possibility of zero pricing and heavy subsidy. The assignment for that night would be to work out such an example in the simulation. This use of the simulation seemed to work very well. Interest was high. The simulation seemed to make sense because we had discussed the background in class. The class was interesting because it related to the homework assignment coming up. Altogether, it was a most satisfying experience from the instructor's viewpoint. (The only problem was that we had a bit too many days for this particular simulation.)

In all three cases, it was clear that the students enjoyed using the terminals and the simulation. It was a welcome change from the usual classroom format. Only a few students had had much computer experience, although most had been on the terminals at least a few times before. Technical expertise on the part of the students appears to be somewhat undesirable, though, because these students want to get into the program and see how it works, rather than paying attention to the problem. The reaction of the students, in general, indicated that interactive use of the computer terminals is an exciting and different way of getting their attention on a legal-economic subject.

NOTE

1. The authors wish to thank Richard Castor for his programming assistance. Copies of the program are available from Professor Zaven Karian, Department of Mathematical Sciences, Denison University, Granville, Ohio 43023.

   If you send a DEC tape or magtape (9 track 800 BPI), we will supply you with the programs.

8
SIMULATIONS AND ECONOMICS

Robin L. Bartlett
Christine E. Amsler

ABSTRACT

Typically, economists who use simulations as a teaching technique
employ a computer-oriented type of simulation. The psychological, sociological, and political aspects of the economic decision-making process
are rarely incorporated into these simulations. Consequently, simulations
intended to represent some economic decision-making process fail to do
so and instead represent one aspect of the total process.

The synergistic approach to simulations in economics attempts to
correct for this failure. A simulation is synergistic if it combines the
three basic techniques of case study, role-playing, and model-building
in such a way as to produce a result greater than the sum of the individual
techniques.

A rationale for this approach is developed by reviewing the use of
simulations by other social and physical scientists. The purposes served,
the various types employed, and the criteria used for validation by these
scientists are compared with those of economists. The comparison suggests that the synergistic approach may indeed have a greater impact on
students than the specialized technique of economists, because it is more
representative of the observed decision making process.

Finally, *A Synergistic Simulation of the Federal Open Market Committee* is presented in detail. This simulation is an example of the synergistic approach to simulations in economics. Although the simulation
focuses on one particular economic decision-making process, it is easily
adapted to others.

Simulations are not new to economists. Economists have built models
for research and simulated results for centuries. Traditionally, their simulation efforts have been more pedagogical or positive than normative.
More recently, however, economists have employed simulations to fore-

cast and to prescribe policy alternatives. The new emphasis evolved as a result of refinements in econometrics, advances in computer technology, and demands of modern policymakers. Despite methodological and technical advances, economists have found it difficult to quantify, and therefore to incorporate, psychological, sociological, and political facets of the market framework into their models. But policymakers, operating within the larger "market plus" framework (Samuels, 1966, 7), have to consider these facets when making decisions. Consequently, a simulation of an economic decision-making process needs at least to recognize the influence of these institutional variables.

This paper introduces just such a simulation, *A Simulation of the Federal Open Market Committee.* This simulation is unique in the sense that it not only attempts to achieve a variety of purposes, but it also employs three basic simulation techniques, in order to achieve these purposes. Properly to ascertain the validity, effectiveness, and appropriateness of this simulation as a teaching technique, a review of simulation techniques used by social and physical scientists is undertaken. Section I of this paper briefly develops a perspective on simulations in general. Section II focuses on the simulations of economists. Section III presents a rationale for a new approach to simulations, a synergistic approach, as demonstrated by *A Simulation of the Federal Open Market Committee.* A description of this simulation is in Section IV. Finally, Section V concludes with an additional comment on the synergistic approach.

I. *Simulations in General*

In academia many physical and social scientists adopt simulations as one teaching technique in their repertoire. To find one definition of simulation that is encompassing is a formidable task. An adequate, yet simple, definition is provided by lexicographers. According to Webster's Dictionary, simulation means:

1.   The act of simulating; pretense, feigning, or
2.   False resemblance as through imitation.
                    (Webster, 1964, 1360)

Thus to simulate is to pretend, to imagine, or to play. As a teaching technique, simulation is a modeling process employed to bridge the gap between classroom experiences and the real world. Additionally, some simulations are designed and executed to motivate students, sensitize and even change their attitudes, enhance their retention and analytical abilities, and develop their social skills. (Slesnick, 1965, 2).

In bridging the gap between the classroom and reality, simulations are used for at least one of the following five specific purposes: First, simulations are used as a means of *instruction;* that is, aspects of the real world are presented in a form that provides knowledge of and insight into the situations or problems being studied. Second, simulations are used as a tool for *theorizing*. Some notions about the real world are best understood and articulated in an abstract form. Many models are developed in this case that specify hypothetical behavioral relationships and assumptions. If hypotheses already exist, moreover, simulations can also be used to *test* them. Third, once a testable hypothesis is accepted, simulations aid in *predicting* or *forecasting* future events. Fourth, simulations are used to *demonstrate* the outcome of suggested strategies or policy alternatives in a laboratory-like setting. Examples are numerous. Engineers test the effects of changing atmospheric pressures on mock models of aircraft or submarines on computers without risking human life. Economists predict the impact of changes in government spending on employment and prices with their macro-models. Students test and use their knowledge of decision-making without having to suffer the consequences of a bad decision. Finally, some simulations attempt to achieve some *combination* of these purposes (Hermann, 1967).

The type of simulation technique used generally depends on the purposes to be achieved. Several authors describe the various types of simulations that have been developed by referring to a continuum. Figure 1 is a copy of a continuum developed by Taylor (1971, 11).

REALITY   *ABSTRACTION*
                                                            INCREASING

Case - - - Study	In-Basket - - - or In-Tray Method	Incident - - - Process	Role - - - Playing	Gaming - - - Simulation or Game— Simulation	Computer - - - Machine or Simulation
Observations on the Real World	Non- Interacting One-to-One Representation	Interacting One-to-One Representation	Informally Structured Group Portrayal	Structured Group Representation	

FIGURE 1
TAYLOR'S CONTINUUM

At the two extremes of the continuum are case studies and machine or computer simulations. Case studies tend to be very realistic or representative of actual situations.

Graham and Gray (1969), who deal specifically with business simulations, disaggregate case studies into four additional categories. On the other extreme, machine simulations tend to be very abstract and self-contained. These types of simulations often are employed by economists and physical scientists. The techniques in between, such as role-playing, are typically used by social scientists in history, psychology, and sociology. A more inclusive continuum of simulation techniques is presented

by Shannon (1975, 8). His continuum, as illustrated in Figure 2, ranges
from what he calls "exactness" to "abstractness." Many of the simulation

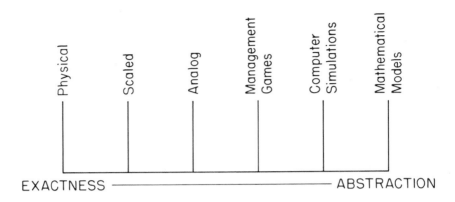

FIGURE 2
SHANNON'S CONTINUUM

techniques used by the physical scientists such as scaled or mock models
are represented. Taylor, Shannon, Graham and Gray give excellent
descriptions of these simulation techniques.

In order to determine whether or not a particular simulation fulfills
its purposes, an evaluation is made at several levels (Thorson, 1975).
On the initial level, the validity of the simulation is established; that is,
does the simulation accurately represent that which it is supposed to
represent? Depending upon the purposes to be served, Hermann (1967)
suggests that several aspects of validity be examined. First, a simulation
must exhibit "internal validity." Here the observed results of the simulation are attributed to the simulation itself and not to extraneous influences.
Second, a simulation must possess "face validity" or give an initial impression of representativeness. Third, a simulation must have "variable-
parameter validity." Here the concern is over whether the simulation
uses variables and parameters found in the observed world. Fourth, a
simulation needs "event validity." In this respect, the results of the simulation are compared to observed results. Finally, "hypothesis validity"
means that the variables in the simulation bear the same relationships
among themselves as they do in the observed world. The exhaustive
criteria of Hermann is found simplified in Shannon (1975, 29). In brief,
the validity of a simulation depends on the representativeness of the
underlying assumptions and on whether the outcomes of the simulation

are expected, given the inputs. If these two conditions hold, the simulation is valid.

The criteria necessary for validation expressed by Hermann and Shannon are modified and expanded in the literature. Three criteria, however, are repeatedly mentioned. First, a simulation needs face validity as defined by Hermann. In conjunction with face validity, simulations need to be structurally sound. This means that, in order for a simulation to be valid in this sense, it must be internally logically consistent with observed behavior. Finally, the simulation should demonstrate the capacity of generating outcomes that are comparable to those in the real world. In a general sense, if these three criteria are met, a simulation is valid.

At another level of evaluation, the concern is for effectiveness or whether the simulation achieves the original teaching objectives. Thorson reviews the literature on the pros and cons of pre- and posttesting the simulation experience. She cautions against drawing conclusions without absolute control over external events. In light of this caution, it is difficult to give credence to those who have attempted to quantify the effectiveness of particular simulations. This issue is no doubt the most debated and least researched area in simulations.

Finally, when evaluating a simulation as a teaching technique, there is always the issue of appropriateness. Here the question is whether the best teaching technique was used to achieve the objective. In some instances, simulation techniques may be indeed the best or only way of instructing, theorizing, forecasting, or generating alternative outcomes from different strategies or policy decisions. In other instances, other teaching techniques are appropriate. Here the literature is sparse and inconclusive. The measurement problems are even more difficult than those concerning effectiveness. Some judgment from experience, however, can be made on a personal level in terms of the cost and benefits associated with a variety of techniques.

II. *Simulations in Economics*

In other disciplines, simulation is perceived as an additional teaching technique that is relatively new. Most economists, however, are unaware of the fact that they frequently use simulations in their teaching because the theory they teach is itself a simulation in the broadly defined sense of the lexicographers. Rather, a typical economist today perceives simulation as a specific type of or use for an econometric model. Although perceptions of the role of simulation in economics vary, economists simulate the real world with their models.

Economists use simulations for the very same purposes as the physical or social scientists; that is, economic models are used for instruction, theorization, prediction, and demonstration. Defining simulation first in its broadest sense, this section traces the role of simulation in economics to its present narrow definition and use.

An economic theory consists of a set of basic definitions and assumptions about the real world. From these definitions and assumptions, economists draw conclusions in a deductive manner (Dutta, 1972, 2). Their models may try to explain the economic behavior of individual units in the economy, such as households or business firms, or they may try to explain the economic behavior of economic aggregates, such as the gross national product, total employment, and the general price level. The former models are the subject of microeconomics, while the latter are the subject of macroeconomics. One of the earliest economic models is the *Tableau Economique,* an input-output model of the French economy developed by Thomas Quesnay in 1758 (Gherity, 1969, 115). Even by today's sophisticated standards, Quesnay's model is a good representation of the eighteenth-century French economy.

More recent uses of simulations in economics are well documented by Thomas Naylor (1966, 1971), who has written at length on this topic. In one of his earlier works (Naylor, 1966), where he describes the use of simulation in economics up to 1966, he presents the models of Cournot and Edgeworth as documentation of simulative efforts in early economic writings. These models were developed to explain how much each entrepreneur would produce in a duopoly situation. Another model Naylor presents is the Cobweb Theorem, which provides for students studying economics an opportunity to simulate the equilibrating forces of the hog cycle. Other examples of numerous microeconomic models are found in Ferguson (1972), Henderson and Quandt (1971), or Hirshleifer (1976). The tradition of macroeconomic model-building is equally voluminous, as illustrated by any standard macroeconomics text such as Shapiro (1974), Crouch (1972), or Allen (1968). Such micro and macro models as these, whether developed long ago or more recently, are used by economists as pedagogical tools in the classroom to *instruct* and to *theorize.*

But these are only some of the models created by economists. With the developments and refinements in econometrics and computer technology, new demands were placed upon economic models. First, economists wanted to test empirically specific hypotheses, and the application of econometric techniques enabled them to do so. In any field within economics, there exist numerous empirical studies that try to accept or reject various hypotheses. Second, besides accepting or rejecting hypotheses, economists wanted to determine the actual values of particular variables. By applying econometric techniques, economists determine the magnitude as well as the direction of changes in model variables.

Obviously, such information is of critical importance to policymakers

(Maisel, 1973). For example, a legislative group, if properly informed in an idealistic sense, should be able to determine *ex ante* whether consumers would spend more, and how much more, as a result of a tax cut. Given the desired increase in consumer spending, legislators could then determine the appropriate size of a tax cut. Unfortunately, econometrics is not yet that exact a science. But this exactness has not deterred economists from expanding their models into whole systems consisting of several hundred equations. There are at least six working models of the U.S. economy (Anderson and Carlson, 1970; deLeeuw and Gramlich, 1968; Duesenberry, Fromm, Klein, and Kuh, 1969; Dugal, Klein, and McCarthy, 1974; Evans and Klein, 1968; Hymans and Shapiro, 1974), and even more industry and market models (Cyert and DeGroot, 1970; Griffin, 1974; MacAvoy and Pindyck, 1973; Naylor, Blintfy, Burdick, and Chu, 1966; Vinon, Rives, and Naylor, 1969). These models are important to firms within industries because they need to know the impact of government regulation, inflation, and money supply growth upon their industries. The use of these models will undoubtedly continue as the role of forecasting in the decision-making process increases.

There are, however, some historical distinctions to be made between econometric models and simulation models. Naylor cites Cohen as the first economist to differentiate between the types of models. According to Cohen, the econometric model is a one-period change model that is usually static, while the simulation model is a self-contained multiperiod dynamic model. Specifically, Naylor quotes Cohen as saying:

> Computer simulation models of economic systems or "process models" differ from traditional econometric models primarily in the treatment of lagged endogenous variables. The equations of the model, together with the observed time paths of the exogenous variables, are treated as a closed dynamic system; each period, the values of the predetermined endogenous variables are the values generated by the model, not the known or actually observed values. (Naylor *et al.*, 1966, 190)

Naylor gives many examples of macroeconomic econometric models, a few of which were developed by Klein, Christ, and Tinbergen. The simulations models of Dusenberry, Eckstein, Fromm, Adelman, and Adelman, and the Brookings Institute are also reviewed by Naylor.

Pindyck and Rubinfeld, however, in their recent book, blur this distinction by referring to econometric simulation models. According to these authors, "simulation is a set of simultaneous equations" (Pindyck and Rubinfeld, 1976). Note that there is no reference to the lagged structure of different variables. Pindyck and Rubinfeld review many of the updated versions of the models Naylor presented, without categorizing them as econometric or simulation models. The reason they do not separately identify the two types of models is that Pindyck and Rubinfeld focus upon the objective of demonstrating policy alternatives. In their presentation of econometric simulation models, Pindyck and Rubinfeld use econometric models to trace the time paths of variables within the model. This is completed first without structural or exogenous changes. Once the solution to the model is traced, they then trace alternative solutions resulting from changes in various elements of the model.

This ability to demonstrate policy alternatives is again very important to policymakers such as legislative bodies, the executive branches of government, and the Federal Reserve. Each of these institutions has particular policy instruments at its disposal that can affect the time paths of economic aggregates or disaggregates. A policy decision to change one of these instruments can have an unanticipated adverse effect on the economy. This can sometimes be mitigated using econometric simulation models, and that is their most frequent use. To most economists, therefore, simulation is using an econometric model to *forecast* and to *demonstrate* alternative outcomes either internally or externally generated. But the classroom simulations of entire economies or industries also can serve the purposes of *instruction* and *theorization*.

A few economists use simulations in the classroom as other disciplines. Their usage, however, tends to focus more on issues of business administration rather than economics. As Naylor points out, business simulations or management games should not be considered part of the discipline of economics proper (Naylor *et al.,* 1966, 186).

Just as the definition of simulation in economics is more specific for an economist, so too are the types of simulations used. Both economic models and economic simulation models are very abstract and, when placed on Taylor's or Shannon's continuum, they fall into the mathematical or computer simulation category. Moreover, econometric simulations are on the more abstract end of all economic models because they are usually self-contained and often dynamic.

In regard to the evaluation of simulations, economists are concerned mainly with the validity of the simulation in a mathematical or statistical sense. Some economists believe a simulation is valid if it is internally logically consistent, while others believe a model is valid if its equations display a "good fit." Measures such as the coefficient of determination and Student's t-test are just a few of the statistics used (Pindyck and Rubinfeld, 1976, 309). Still other economists are concerned only with the reliability of the predictions generated by the models, and again statistical measures are used (Pindyck and Rubinfeld, 1976, 319).

Economists are rarely concerned with the effectiveness and appropriateness of their models. In terms of the previous definition of effectiveness, most economic models pass the test. But in other terms, they do not. Economics by definition is a science of choice; that is, allocating scarce resources, such as time and money, among competing ends. The variables taken into consideration are readily quantifiable. That is not to say other variables are not important and/or lack influence, but that they do not lend themselves well to the economic modeling process. The question is whether this is an accurate presentation of reality or economic reality in a vacuum. If the latter is the case, then a strong case for a synergistic approach to economic simulation can be made.

III. *A Rationale for the Synergistic Approach to Simulations in Economics*

Synergism is the act of combining two discrete techniques such that the total result is greater than the sum of their individual results. A synergistic approach to simulation, when used in the teaching of economics, is the incorporation of the three basic simulation techniques into one simulation. The rationale for posing such a combination is to provide students with a more meaningful representation of the real world. Casual empiricism dictates this approach. A brief examination of the many economic policymaking bodies in the United States reveals that economic models are used as input into their decision-making processes.

The Council of Economic Advisors, the Federal Reserve Board of Governors, and the Federal Communications Commission all use economic models, particularly econometric simulation models, to give their deliberations direction and insight. The weight given to these models by particular groups is a function of the personalities, the social and political backgrounds and aspirations, and the unintentional ignorance of their members (Maisel, 1973). Because decisions are made in the real world, often in an economic sense, with many currently unquantified variables as parameters, economic simulations used for teaching should include these factors.

The various simulation techniques described by Naylor can be simplified into the three basic techniques shown in Figure 3. It is evident that

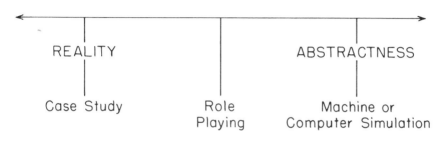

FIGURE 3
THREE BASIC TYPES OF SIMULATION TECHNIQUES

the more a simulation specializes in a particular technique, the less representative of observed behavior it becomes. The more abstract a simulation technique is, the less it deals with facts and interpersonal relationships. And the more a simulation focuses on case studies and facts, the less it includes abstract notions. Specialization in a simulation technique, therefore, tends to invalidate the simulation in terms of the real world.

This point is elaborated in Figure 4. Each participant in the decision-making process uses combinations of the attributes described by the various simulation techniques. A decision-maker, given his institutional, personal, and social position, assumes a particular role. Generally, he has some perception of the facts which he analyzes within his own theoretical framework acquired from formal training or from personal experience. Although his perception of the facts and his theoretical framework may be inaccurate and incomplete, he continues to make decisions either by active choice or by default. Hence a specialized type of simulation provides an unrealistic view of the total decision-making process, even though it may accurately represent one facet of that process.

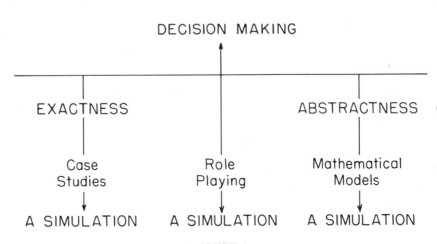

FIGURE 4
THE SYNERGISTIC APPROACH
TO SIMULATION IN ECONOMICS

A simulation that combines several techniques gives a more representative impression of the real world. For this reason, the synergistic approach to simulation establishes an additional criterion for validation. This is easily accomplished by ensuring that a simulation includes facts, requires role-playing, and contains an abstract theoretical model. Such a criterion for validation implies that a valid economic simulation puts the use of economic models into a proper perspective within the entire decision-making process.

There are three major advantages to the synergistic approach for simulations in economics. First, the synergistic approach shows students the environment in which the economic models are employed. Second, the approach amplifies the limitations of the economic models by demonstrating that more is involved in decision-making than studying the output of a model. Third, the synergistic approach reduces the possibility of misrepresenting the decision-making process by either oversimplifying the complexities involved or by overemphasizing one particular aspect of the process.

In sum, by providing a rationale and establishing additional evaluation criteria, the synergistic approach promotes the development of economic simulations that illustrate the overall decision-making process. The next section explains one example of such a simulation.

IV.   *A Synergistic Simulation of the Federal Open Market Committee*

One example of the synergistic approach in economics is a simulation of the Federal Open Market Committee (FOMC) of the Federal Reserve System. This section reviews the structure and objectives of the Federal Reserve System and provides a detailed explanation of the context, objectives, stages, and evaluation of the FOMC simulation.

The Federal Reserve System is the country's central bank. Its major objective "is to regulate the flow of money and credit in order to promote economic stability and growth" (*The Federal Reserve at Work,* 1969, 5). In formulating and executing monetary policy the Federal Reserve tries to maintain a high level of employment, stable prices, a reasonable rate of growth, and a reasonable balance of payments position for the United States. Often the interdependency of these goals inhibits the effectiveness of monetary policy. The Federal Reserve System consists of five groups: the Board of Governors, the Federal Open Market Committee, the Federal Advisory Council, the twelve Federal Reserve Banks, and the member banks. Although several comprehensive publications by the Federal Reserve explain its purposes and functions in more detail, a brief comment about each group follows (*The Federal Reserve System,* 1974; *The Federal Reserve at Work,* 1969).

The Board of Governors is the most influential group in the Federal Reserve System because its primary task is to formulate monetary policy. At its disposal, the Board has two general tools with which to execute policy: (1) it approves changes in the discount rate charged by the twelve District Banks to their member banks, and (2) it possesses the authority to change member bank reserve requirements within the statutory limits. The Board of Governors consists of seven members appointed to staggered fourteen-year terms by the President of the United States, with the advice and consent of the Senate. The President designates one member as chairman and one as vice-chairman for renewable four year terms.

The most important group in the Federal Reserve System, however, is the *Federal Open Market Committee* (FOMC). This group is responsible for monetary policy on a day-to-day basis because its main task is to conduct Open Market Operations. That is, it has the power to buy and sell government securities, acceptances, and foreign exchange in the Open Market, which directly affects the size of the money stock and the structure of interest rates, directly or indirectly. Because the directives issued by the FOMC are executed by the Trading Desk at the New York Federal Reserve, the President of the New York Federal Reserve Bank is always one of the twelve members of the FOMC. The eleven other members are the Board itself and an annually rotating panel made up of four of the other eleven Federal Reserve Bank Presidents.

Two of the remaining groups, the Federal Advisory Council and the twelve District Banks, ensure that regional interests are represented at the deliberations of the FOMC and the Board. The final group, consisting of the six thousand member banks, is required to cooperate in policy matters to promote a sound banking system.

These five groups within the Federal Reserve System act together to formulate monetary policy that attempts to promote full employment, stable prices, reasonable growth, and a reasonable balance of trade. They achieve these goals by altering the flow of money and credit in our economy. For example, when the economy is recovering from a recession and economic activity is increasing, households and businesses increase their expenditures. As more transactions occur, the growth in the supply of money or the rate at which money changes hands must increase at a rate equivalent to the increase in expenditures. If the money supply is not sufficient to accommodate all desired transactions, the recovery is thwarted. On the other hand, if the Federal Reserve overreacts and creates too much money, inflation ensues. The decision-making process used by the FOMC to determine the "right" amount of money to be created obviously is complex. Economic considerations are but one facet of the total collage. The FOMC members are also subject to domestic and international political pressures, the criticisms of the press, the constraints of their own institutional roles, and their own personal beliefs. In short, the making of monetary policy encompasses not only economic considerations but many other considerations as well.

Context: The FOMC simulation is used to acquaint college-level Money and Banking students with the operations of the Federal Reserve System.

It can be conducted in an introductory or intermediate-level class on a one-time basis or as a continuing part of the course. It is suggested that FOMC meetings be held every two or three weeks during the semester, because students become more adept at analyzing, forecasting, and debating monetary issues as they become more comfortable with the format of the simulation.

Objectives: The objectives of the FOMC simulation are the same objectives sought by simulations in general. That is, the FOMC simulation is designed to *instruct,* to *theorize,* to *predict,* and to *demonstrate* policy alternatives. These general objectives pertain to the FOMC simulation in the following way. The first objective is to instruct Money and Banking students in the operations of the Federal Reserve System. The second objective is to enable students to theorize about the monetary sector and, in a simplistic yet comprehensive way, to construct models that explain the economic behavior they observe.

The third objective is to ask students to predict intuitively the consequences of changes in their theoretical models. For instance, the students might have to decide whether an increase in the money supply will increase output and employment because investors desired to increase expenditures, or will decrease output and employment because investors feared galloping inflation. The fourth objective of the FOMC simulation is to encourage students to debate the merits of competing monetary policies. For example, although all students may agree that the level of unemployment needs to be decreased, some student may favor an increase in government spending for public works programs, while others may favor the imposition of an investment tax credit.

As previously mentioned, the fifth objective of simulations in general is the combination of some or all of these objectives. It is apparent that this simulation combines at least the first four objectives. But the FOMC simulation causes a synergistic effect to take place when these four objectives are combined. In addition to instructing, theorizing, predicting, and demonstrating, the FOMC simulation forces students to become adept at communicating their ideas and to become aware of the impact of political events, the limitations of statistics and models, the variety of theories that are put forth to explain interrelationships among variables, and the role of individual beliefs in the decision-making process.

Stages: The simulation of the FOMC is patterned after the actual composition, functions, and activities of the FOMC (Maisel, 1973) and is composed of four stages: preparation, briefing, debate, and decision. A detailed description of each of these four stages follows.

Preparation. The synergistic approach requires that the three basic types of simulation techniques be included in the simulation. This means that students must perform a case study or collect data, participate in role-playing, and construct theoretical models or frameworks. All of these begin in the preparation stage of the FOMC simulation.

Throughout the semester the students and the teacher should keep abreast of economic events by constructing a "green book." It is called "green book" because it is similar to the "green books" or statistical reports that the Washington staff economists actually prepare for the FOMC members before each monthly meeting. In these "green books" the students and the instructor should organize and record the data they have gathered about all the sectors of the economy. The teacher may wish to employ a student assistant to compile his "green book."

A current source of data and information to which all students have ready access is the only expense required when the FOMC simulation is used in a Money and Banking course. The *Wall Street Journal* is a particularly good source, which is easily adapted to meet this need. As students clip out pertinent articles each day they can construct their own "green books." It is essential for the professor to point out that only articles that contain facts or economic measures and not speculation about future facts should be clipped. The time spent at this activity can be minimized to approximately five minutes a day with the use of the authors' *Wall Street Journal Journal.*

At the beginning of the semester, a class of at least twenty-four students is divided into two groups. The first group consists of eleven students who are willing to assume the roles of FOMC members or are chosen to do so. These students have two primary responsibilities. First, they are responsible for researching the background of their respective member, distributing a brief written biography of their member to other students, observing the actions and comments of their member in the daily press, and presenting the views of their member in the FOMC simulations.

Second, they are responsible for directing the activities of student staff economists assigned to them. This aspect of the FOMC simulation deviates slightly from the actual functioning of the FOMC in Washington. There, Associate Advisors to the Board of Governors manage the research efforts of the staff economists. But, given the limitations of class size and the need to ensure that each student is well prepared for classroom simulations, students designated to be FOMC Committee members manage the staff economists. The result is that each student in the class not only collects and organizes data about the entire economy but also becomes an expert on a particular sector of the economy. Depending upon the size of the class, a student Committee member may have one or more student staff economists assigned to him.

The students in the second group serve as staff economists under the direction of the Committee member. Each sector of the economy should either be chosen by or assigned to a single or group of staff economists. How many sectors of the economy for which each staff economist is responsible depends upon the number of students in the class. Typical sector subdivisions might be auto production, key interest rates, housing construction, and durable goods orders.

The teacher acts as the Chairman of the Board. His responsibilities include (1) keeping abreast of the latest economic developments in order to serve as a check on student reports, (2) conducting the FOMC meetings while portraying the views of the present chairman, and (3) distributing a background biography of the Chairman, similar to those prepared by the student Committee members. Also, the teacher should make certain that students understand their roles and are prepared for FOMC simulation meetings.

It is assumed that the students are exposed to the simple Keynesian cross model and the fundamentals of the banking system in a previous principles class. If the FOMC simulation is being conducted every few weeks, the instructor can incorporate more sophisticated models, such as the Bailey model, as the semester progresses.

Briefing: The simulation actually begins with the briefing. The classroom should be arranged in a conference format, with a conference table that seats twelve people. If a conference table is unavailable, the seats in the classroom should be arranged into two circles. The inner circle should have twelve seats, and the remaining seats should be in the outer circle. Name cards should be placed in front of Committee members, and a makeshift podium should be placed in one corner of the room.

When all arrangements are complete, the Chairman calls the meeting to order. As the first order of business, the Chairman asks the President of the New York Federal Reserve Bank to refresh the Committee's memory about its last directive and to outline the steps that were taken to achieve that directive. Then the Chairman calls upon particular staff economists to review the current and past economic situations, to present their own analysis of why events have taken place in their areas of expertise, and to predict future trends. Reports should never continue for more than five minutes. Moreover, if the class is large, one student should summarize the findings and conclusions of several staff economists. During the briefing, the Chairman makes sure that all new and relevant information has been presented properly. The Chairman may allow Committee members to ask questions intermittently if time permits.

Debate. In the third stage of the simulation, Committee members take active roles. Having heard the staff reports, they must now integrate the facts into a cohesive description of the economy. The Committee members must determine how much credence should be given to the available information and must judge for themselves the direction in which the economy is heading. They must bear in mind the goals of the Committee. Also, they must consider the tools at their disposal for effecting changes in the monetary sector and the limitations of these tools.

Decision.   Based upon their judgments about the economic situation, the Committee members must decide what target rates they want the New York Federal Reserve Bank to achieve by buying and selling U.S. Government securities, acceptances, and foreign exchange in the Open Market. When the Chairman senses that a consensus is being reached, he asks the Committee members to suggest policy alternatives, then integrates and summarizes the suggestions, and makes his own suggestions to the Committee. If any member strenuously objects to these suggestions, the Chairman may permit further argument. If the argument is persuasive, the Chairman may change his suggestion. Finally, the Chairman's original or revised suggestion is placed before the Committee for a vote. When affirmed, as is commonly done (Levine, 1976, 1), the suggestion is written in the form of a directive and is given to the President of the New York Federal Reserve Bank, who is responsible for its execution. Then the Chairman adjourns the meeting.

Evaluation.   The FOMC simulation, like other simulations, is evaluated in terms of validity, effectiveness, and appropriateness. Moreover, because the FOMC simulation is synergistic, it must meet the additional criteria of incorporating the three basic types of simulations.

A simulation has validity if it appears to be realistic, is internally logically consistent, and meshes well with the outside world. The FOMC simulation is valid in each respect. First, the simulation appears to be realistic. The amount of preparation, the variety of props, and the atmosphere in which it is conducted tend to achieve this objective. Second, the briefing, debate, and decision stages of the simulation parallel those of the real FOMC. Finally, within this artificial framework, the input of facts, roles, and theories generates outcomes or policy recommendations similar again to those generated in Washington.

A simulation is effective if it fulfills its stated objectives. This is measured through a culminating experience. Students can be required to write brief position papers that include a review of the current economic situation, a standard theoretical model for analysis, and a set of policy recommendations that the Board is encouraged to adopt. The quality of these papers indicates the effectiveness of this simulation.

A simulation is appropriate if it is the best way to achieve the instructor's objectives. Given the cost and benefits of sending students off to Washington to observe the decision-making for themselves, this simulation is the next best thing to being there.

A simulation is synergistic if it employs all three basic simulation types. This simulation employs all three: facts, role-playing, and theoretical constructs. In doing so, the FOMC simulation gives each type equal weight. Theory is not more meaningful than facts, and facts alone cannot negate theory and roles. In summary, the FOMC simulation fulfills each criterion.

V. Conclusions

Simulation in economics can mean a variety of different things to different people. Observers from other disciplines view most economic models as simulations, while economists view simulations as a particular use of an economic model. A few economists use simulations as a teaching technique, and most of these simulations are computer-oriented. Despite these perspectives, any use of simulations in economics as a teaching technique is invalid if it specializes in one simulation technique. The objection is the fact that a simulation of this sort fails to portray properly the use of economic models and econometric simulation models in the real world of decision-making. The remedy is straightforward. A valid simulation needs to follow the criteria of being synergistic; that is, it must employ the three basic simulation techniques.

A Synergistic Simulation of the Federal Open Market Committee is just one example of how the gap between classroom experiences and the real world can be effectively bridged. This simulation has as its goals not only instruction, theorization, prediction, and the demonstration of possible effects of different policy alternatives, but also synergism. The combining of simulation goals or objectives is not enough unless they are integrated in such a way as to ensure a total impact greater than the sum of the individual impacts. This objective is met with the use of the three basic simulation techniques found in the FOMC simulation.

REFERENCES

Allen, R. G. D. *Macro-economic theory: A mathematical treatment.* London: MacMillan, 1968.

Anderson, L. C., and Carlson, K. M. A monetarist model for economic stabilization. *Federal Reserve Bulletin of St. Louis, Monthly Review,* April, 1970, 7-25.

Brown, T. M. *Specification and uses of econometric models.* London: MacMillan, 1970.

Chandler, L. V. *The economics of money and banking,* 6th ed. New York: Harper & Row, Publishers, 1973.

Crouch, R. L. *Macroeconomics.* New York: Harcourt Brace Jovanovich, Inc., 1972.

Cyert, R. M., and DeGroot, M. H. Bayesian analysis and duopoly theory. *Journal of Political Economy,* September/October, 1970, 1168-84.

deLeeuw, F., and Gramlich, E. The Federal Reserve-MIT econometric model. *Federal Reserve Bulletin,* January, 1968, 11-40.

Duesenberry, J. S., Fromm, G., Klein, L. R., and Kuh, E. (Eds.). *The Brookings model: some further results.* Chicago: Rand McNally, 1969.

Duggal, V. G., Klein, L. R., and McCarthy, M. D. The Wharton model Mark III: A modern IS-LM construct. *International Economic Review,* October, 1974, 572-94.

Dutta, M. *Econometric methods.* Cincinnati: Southwestern Publishing Co., 1975, 346-53.

Evans, M. K., and Klein, L. R. *The Wharton econometric forecasting model,* 2nd ed. Philadelphia: Wharton School of Finance and Commerce, University of Pennsylvania, 1968.

The Federal Reserve System: Purposes and functions. Washington: Board of Governors, September, 1974.

The Federal Reserve at work. Richmond: Federal Reserve Bank of Richmond, 1969.

Ferguson, C. E. *Microeconomic Theory,* 3rd ed. Homewood: Irwin, Inc., 1972.

Gherity, J. A. *Economic Thought: A historical anthology.* New York: Random House, 1969, 114-58.

Graham, R. G., and Gray, C. F. *Business games handbook.* New York: American Management Association, Inc., 1969.

Griffin, J. M. The effects of higher prices on electricity consumption. *Bell Journal of Economics and Management Science,* 1974, *5,* 515-39.

Henderson, J. M., and Quandt, R. E. *Microeconomic theory: A mathematical approach,* 2nd ed. New York: McGraw-Hill, 1971.

Hermann, C. F. Validation problems in games and simulations with special reference to models of international politics. *Behavioral Science,* 1967, *12,* 216-231.

Hirschleifer, J. *Price theory and applications.* Englewood Cliffs, New Jersey: Prentice-Hall, Inc., 1976.

Hymans, S. H., and Shapiro, H. T. The structure and properties of the Michigan Quarterly econometric model of the U.S. economy. *International Economic Review,* 1974, *15,* 632-53.

Levine, R. J. Fed's high turnover diminishes expertise, seems to bolster Burns. *Wall Street Journal,* July 30, 1976, *56,* No. 203, 1.

MacAvoy, P. W., and Pindyck, P. S. Alternative regulatory policies for dealing with the natural gas shortage. *Bell Journal of Economics and Management Science,* 1973, *4,* 454-98.

Maisel, S. J. *Managing the dollar.* New York: Norton, Inc., 1973.

Naylor, T. H., *Computer simulation experiments with economic systems.* New York: Wiley, 1971.

Naylor, T. H., Blintfy, J. L., Burdick, D. S., and Chu, K. *Computer simulation techniques.* New York: Wiley, 1966.

Pindyck, R. S., and Rubinfeld, D. L. *Econometric models and economic forecasts.* New York: McGraw-Hill, 1976, 308-416.

Samuels, W. J. *The classical theory of economic policy.* New York: The World Publishing Company, 1966, 237-88.

Shannon, R. E. *Systems simulation: The art and science.* Englewood Cliffs, New Jersey: Prentice-Hall, Inc., 1975.

Shapiro, E. *Macroeconomic analysis.* 3rd ed. New York: Harcourt Brace Jovanovich, Inc., 1974.

Slesnick, F. Simulations in managerial finance curriculum. Unpublished manuscript, June 1975. Available at Denison Simulation Center, Denison University, Granville, Ohio.

Taylor, J. L. *Instructional planning systems: A gaming-simulation approach to urban problems.* New York: Cambridge University Press, 1971.

Thorson, E. *Simulation in the liberal arts college: Evaluation at three levels.* Paper presented at the meeting of the National Simulation and Gaming Conference, Los Angeles, October 1975.

Vernon, J. M., Rives, N. W., Jr., and Naylor, T. H. An econometric model of the tobacco industry. *Review of Economics and Statistics,* May, 1969, 149-58.

Webster's new world dictionary of the American language, College ed. New York: The World Publishing Company, 1964.

Part VII

VALUES CLARIFICATION

The three papers on values clarification, ethics, and simulation take very different approaches to the relationships. One paper discusses how existing values games can be modified to increase their philosophical sophistication and their teaching effectiveness. A second goes to philosophical foundations of value systems and discusses how these foundations relate to values clarification as often practiced by educators. A third talks about what possible effects "playing games" might have on the value systems of college students. The range of these papers reflects the wealth of possibilities that simulation techniques might provide for those experimenting with ways to treat ethical and moral questions in the classroom.

9

THE MODIFICATION OF VALUES GAMES: BEYOND VALUES CLARIFICATION

ERIC STRAUMANIS
ROBERT J. AUGE

ABSTRACT

The explicit aim of values clarification is limited, that is, to make persons aware of their values and of the processes by which they acquired them. Many of the games used in values clarification fail to distinguish between unjustified preferences and justifiable values, and it can be argued that this omission makes these games inadequate for sophisticated audiences. Because it is often easier to modify an existing game than to construct a new one, a reasonable approach is to modify values games (VG) so that they go beyond values clarification by providing the players structured opportunities for formulating justification arguments. This paper presents for discussion the criteria that sophisticated VG might meet and offers some specific routines or strategies that can be used in games worth modifying.

The explicit aim of values clarification is to make persons aware of their values and the ways such values influence decision-making. However, values clarification activities often fail to distinguish between unjustified preferences and justifiable values. The purpose of this paper is to examine selected values games and develop strategies for modifying values games and gamelike simulations so that teachers might use them to attain goals that go beyond the limited aims of values clarification. In selecting the games for discussion we considered restricting activities to resource allocation (RA) games. We subsequently decided that such a narrowing of focus would make it difficult for us to illustrate levels of evaluative reasoning. Consequently, we considered both RA and non-RA values games as well as some nongaming values simulations.

Values Education

The word "value" is ambiguous. We can speak of the value of things or the value(s) that a person holds. The value of things (or states of affairs) is an evaluative property (the capacity to satisfy certain normative criteria) whose magnitude can be determined by appraisal. The values of persons, on the other hand, are dispositions to behave in certain ways. These dispositions can be ascertained by observing either the nonverbal actions or the discourse of persons (Rescher, 1969).

If we assume that the broad aim of values education is to foster sound values and correct valuing, then values education includes at least the following two kinds of procedures: (1) Educational processes that enable individuals to come to know the value of things; for example, consumer education aims at imparting knowledge of the prices and priorities of various things. (Notice, however, that it is usually *not* part of consumer education to foster specifically the *disposition to use* such knowledge.) (2) Educational processes that tend to establish in persons dispositions to behave in desirable ways; for example, in moral education and aesthetic education, the aim is not only to impart knowledge about correct value assessments but also to foster the dispositions to act in a manner that meets moral and aesthetic norms, respectively.

Moral Education

The main interest in values education has been, of course, in the area of moral education. Moral choices have far greater social significance than, say, aesthetic choices. The very concept of a moral norm has the implication that moral norms take precedence over all other types of norms.

In order to come to an understanding of the aims of moral education it is necessary to be clear on the following concepts and distinctions:

(1) A *moral* action is action according to *duty* or *obligation:* it is to be distinguished from a merely prudential or self-interested action.

(2) *Actions* are either *right* (in accordance with norms) or *wrong* (in violations of norms)—never good or bad. (Actions can also be morally indifferent—neither required nor proscribed by norms.) It is *things,* or *states of affairs,* that are either (nonmorally) *good* or (nonmorally) *bad,* depending upon whether or not they tend to confer a benefit upon someone.

(3) In order for a set of moral norms (a normative theory of moral obligation) to become linked with the real world, what is *morally right* must in some way depend upon what is *nonmorally good* (Rescher, 1969). That is, when we judge that a person has acted rightly, we are assuming that the dispositions and actions of that person lead to the realization of states of affairs that will confer a nonmoral good or benefit on someone.

Given the preceding distinctions we can state what moral education encompasses. Moral education consists of (1) the teaching of what we shall loosely call *moral theory,* and (2) *moral training.* Some further explanation of these two dimensions of moral education is in order.

To be a competent moral thinker or "theorizer" is to have the ability and skills for formulating and understanding some framework of moral norms (*rules,* e.g., one ought to keep one's promises; and *principles,* e.g., respect for persons) and to be able to use such a framework in arriving at and justifying what one ought to do in particular cases. Moreover, successful moral thinking will often require skill in making nonmoral value assessments or appraisals because, to repeat, what is morally right in some way ultimately depends upon what is nonmorally good.

But competence in moral thinking is not all there is to being a full-fledged autonomous moral agent. As is well known, the knowledge of what one *ought* to do is very often insufficient for *moving* one to do it and for *sustaining* such action. Various terms have been used in the literature of moral philosophy to describe this condition: for example, weakness of will and "backsliding." Some kind of moral training (of the will) seems to be required in addition to the teaching of moral theory in order to establish in persons the attitudes, dispositions, inclinations, traits, or habits that initiate and sustain the actions that a person believes it is right or obligatory to perform. For example, *A*'s correct moral judgment that *A* ought to protest *X* may remain sterile either because *A* lacks the skills for effective public speaking (assuming that this is what is necessary in this case) or because *A* lacks courage or the capacity to withstand public ridicule. Because such cases abound in ordinary life, nearly all who advocate moral education believe that it should include a moral training dimension. But what kind of "training of the will" is effective and morally permissible is still an unresolved issue. Still, there is virtually universal agreement that the informal education (or values socialization) to which everyone is exposed, virtually since birth, too often falls short of providing us with the knowledge, skills, and dispositions for full-fledged autonomous moral action. This fact provides the warrant for deliberate efforts at moral education.

Theories of Moral Development

The socialization of moral beliefs and behaviors is one of the main tasks of all viable cultures. Given this concern, one might ask: How does moral development occur? How can we describe it? What are the factors responsible for various levels of moral sophistication? In essence, we are asking, what are the *causes* of moral beliefs and behaviors? In our discussion of values simulations we focus on three general theories of moral development (Hoffman, 1970).

A first major theory is psychoanalysis. This theory of moral development tends to concentrate upon affective components of morality, e.g., guilt and remorse. Unfortunately, psychoanalytic theory, although of substantial historical importance in the evolution of contemporary psychological theory, has not generated substantial systematic research that can withstand critical analysis. It has received decreasing attention from researchers over the years.

In contrast, the cognitive developmental theories of Jean Piaget and Lawrence Kohlberg concern major contemporary positions regarding moral development (Piaget, 1932; Kohlberg, 1969). Within the context of these theories moral development is viewed as progressing through invariant sequences of stages reflecting the increasing cognitive complexity of the child, which in turn is a function of the child's biological maturation and social interaction. Both of these theorists, and particularly Kohlberg, have had substantial impact on current discussions of moral education and moral philosophy. Accounting for changes and differences in the form and content of moral judgments as the human matures is the primary task of the cognitive developmentalists. Whereas Piaget has emphasized the role of peers, Kohlberg has pointed out the importance of role-taking and interactions with those at relatively advanced stages in the development of mature moral judgments. A considerable amount of research has gained empirical support for cognitive moral development theory (e.g., Hoffman, 1970).

Based on the cognitive view of moral development, the objective of moral education is to accelerate the progress of those who are slow in moving from a lower to a higher stage, and to dislodge those who seem to be arrested at a stage lower than the highest. If this theory of moral development is valid, then moral educators should fashion their teaching techniques in accordance with the research findings. If they fail to do so, then two errors are likely to be committed. First, one's moral education techniques might fail to stimulate the student because they are aimed at a stage of moral thinking that he has already passed through. Second, one's techniques could fail to engage the student because they are appropriate for a level of moral development several stages beyond the student's present capabilities.

Unlike the previous two general theories of moral development a third theoretical stance has emphasized the profound importanec of social learning as regards the development of moral behavior (Bandura and Walters, 1959; Bandura, 1969). This position argues that much of human behavior is the result of social interactions involving the observation and modeling of one individual's behavior by another. Especially within the last fifteen years, social learning theorists have undertaken a systematic analysis of modeling and observational learning as a means for acquiring both prosocial and antisocial behaviors. In the case of moral behavior, children and adolescents often reproduce behaviors they have observed in, for example, parents, teachers, peers, and other significant individuals with whom they have interacted. In general, social learning theorists argue that moral affect, judgment, and behavior are strongly influenced by situational factors, i.e., the stimulus setting conditions, the observable behavior, and the various kinds of consequences that follow the behavior. Only in a very general sense, however, have social learning theorists identified the processes involved in observational learning or modeling; a detailed, refined understanding of moral behavior awaits the results of additional research. Social learning theory suggests that the educational value of games and role-playing is a complex function of the interactional dynamics of the activities, the participants, the possible behaviors, and the possible consequences of those behaviors in simulation experiences.

The Role of Simulation and Gaming in Moral Education

In what respects are simulation and gaming activities superior to conventional teaching procedures in moral education? We shall answer this question after a brief explanation of conventional techniques of moral education.

The conventional approach depends heavily on the case study method —a method that involves a great deal of open-ended discussion. In the case study approach the teacher can use either the so-called rational strategy or the so-called conflict strategy (Hall and Davis, 1975). In the first, the student is presented with an open-ended moral situation where she/he is required to formulate alternatives, calculate consequences, evaluate reasons, and justify the decision. The rational strategy aims at the development of systematic moral thinking or "theorizing." In the second, the conflict strategy, the student is presented with a moral dilemma which focuses the issue on questions of the form "Should *A* do *X* or *Y?*" or "Should *A* do *X*, yes or no?" Although the dilemma approach is compatible with moral reasoning and justification, it usually fails to make use of the *full* range of moral deliberation relevant to the case because the dilemma tends to polarize the discussants (see Appendix 1 for an example of a moral dilemma).

The rational strategy does well with respect to the first aim of moral education—the development of moral thinking, reasoning or "theorizing," but it fails with respect to the second goal—the development of the capacities and inclinations required for initiating and sustaining moral action. In particular, the rational strategy fails to perform the diagnostic task that values clarification approaches reputedly perform well. That is, when the rational strategy is used students tend to solve cases on the basis of values they believe they *ought* to hold, not on the basis of values they *actually* hold. It is doubtful whether the conflict strategy does any better than the rational strategy in the area of values diagnosis, although it can be argued that discussion of moral issues that have been cast in the form of a dilemma provides *some* of the realism required for giving participants an idea of how they are likely to make moral judgments in real-life situations.

Values simulation games, gamelike values simulations, and non-gaming values simulations might be viewed as superior to either variant of the case study method in regard to values diagnosis or values clarification. Simulation activities can, for instance, incorporate a variety of social roles. That is, the rules of the activity may require players to make moves according to the norms that guide statesmen, military leaders, police and judicial officials, abortion counselors, etc. The rules in effect formalize the role relationships that are often vague or indeterminate in social reality. It is these role relationships that are being simulated by the activity. When participants attain high identification with their role they are perhaps more likely to employ their *actual* values, rather than their *professed* values, in the decision-making required by the simulation activity.

Finally, we do not believe that values simulations and games are superior to nonsimulation, nongaming values activities or exercises (such as the variants of the case study approach) in respect to their potential for encouraging students to attain the goals of moral *training* that we described earlier as the second component of moral education. It has been widely held that the capacities, inclinations, or habits that are the mainsprings of sustained moral action can be developed or acquired only in real-life situations. For example, if we wish to develop the kind of moral courage that can prevail against ridicule and social disapproval, we must place the person in the actual situation and hope that she/he will have enough success to strengthen this characteristic. So-called "action-learning" programs that require participants to, say, investigate certain social injustices and then to present the evidence to officials, write letters, demonstrate, etc., are one kind of device that has been employed by some moral educators. But, obviously, these are nonsimulation activities! Still, it might be possible to modify existing simulations so that much of the convenience of simulation remains but certain desirable features of action-learning are incorporated. For instance, some of the key roles in a values simulation game might be occupied by "guest-participants," persons who have these roles in real life.

Classification of Simulation and Gaming
Materials in Values Education

We estimate that there are between seventy-five and one hundred values simulations/games[1] presently available from a variety of commercial and academic sources. In many instances it is difficult to determine whether a simulation/game belongs in the *values* category. Quite a few simulations/games in history, sociology, and anthropology, for example, require evaluative judgments in which the player's moral values are involved. Even if the game designers fail to list values clarification or values education as one of the objectives of their game, it still might be used as a values education activity. Furthermore, simulation and gaming catalogs do not usually list values education as one of their major categories. Those looking for values simulation/games are advised to search through all of the humanities and social science categories if they are not to miss relevant materials.

With a very few exceptions all of the values simulations/games are noncomputerized. Four out of five, in our opinion, would fail the strict criteria for games. (A game must have (1) explicit rules, (2) at least two players, and (3) a determinate outcome or "payoff.") The bulk of values activities should be classified either as gamelike simulations or nongaming simulations. Some of the values activities listed in simulation/gaming catalogs fail to qualify as simulations, i.e., the activities do not include *dynamic* models of reality. These would have to be classified as nongaming, nonsimulation values activities or exercises.

The classification schemes in simulation/gaming catalogs and handbooks include an age level or grade level rating. Although such a rating tells the prospective user something about the complexity and interest level of the activity, it is inadequate as an indicator of the level of moral development for which the values activity is appropriate. The fact is that most values simulations/games require very little sophistication in moral reasoning.

In this brief discussion of the classification of values simulations/games we have omitted all mention of *particular* games, classification systems, and handbooks or guides. The handbooks and guides are readily available (e.g., Stadsklev, 1975) and most contain annotated bibliographies, which, despite their classification shortcomings, are a good source of information about the content and function of values simulations/games. In the next section we will discuss particular simulations/games that serve as good examples for the modification strategies we proposed, and that were used in a four-day workshop on "Simulation and Values Clarification" (Denison University, June 18-22, 1976).

Play, Analysis, and Modification of Selected
Values Simulations/Games

By way of introduction to the general area of values simulation and gaming the authors provided a brief overview of values education to workshop participants. Furthermore, because this area is intimately related to the psychology of moral development, that topic too was briefly discussed with the aid of handouts (see Appendices 1, 2, 3, and 4) and a *Psychology Today* film on moral development. Following the first day of the workshop the participants engaged in the actual play and analysis of various values games interspersed with discussions of strategies for modification (see Appencies 2, 3, and 4). Of course, it was necessary to be selective in choosing games (sometimes in shortened form) to be played. The games played on days 2 through 5 of the workshop were as follows.

DAY 2:

Timao and *My Cup Runneth Over* (MCRO) (both published by Pennant Educational Materials, 1971) are typical values clarification games. The two are very similar: *Timao* attempts to develop the ability to recognize when and how a variety of events brings about either the realization or the deprivation of particular values; *MCRO* employs the same list of values but concentrates on the communication and expression of values realization and values deprivation. Both games attempt to generate (and hence, to simulate) the cognitive processes of value assessment.

We selected these two games for play in the workshop because they illustrate the following:

(*a*) *Timao* is merely a "prudentialist" game, i.e., it requires no more than judgments about what affects one's self-interest. This makes *Timao* relevant to the stage 1 or stage 2 (preconventional) level of the Kohlberg moral development scale (see Appendix 1 for a description of Kohlberg's stages).

(*b*) Both games relegate issues requiring *moral* reasoning to the postplay *informal* discussion period. Any moral reasoning that is learned by the discussants is at best a remote or indirect result of game play. That is, there is good reason to believe that a "rap session" *alone,* say, on the topics that arise in the game, would produce the same results as playing the game plus the postgame informal discussion.

(*c*) *Timao* and *MCRO* are good cases for the application of the modification strategies we recommend. For example, the list of values in the two games can be improved both from the standpoint of clarity and classification.

DAY 3:

Sacrifice (Education Ventures, Inc., 1971) is a nonzero-sum role-play simulation of evaluative deliberations among various community interest groups. The objective of the game is to achieve consensus on the allocation of limited resources. This game was selected for play in the workshop for the following reasons:

(*a*) Sacrifice allows for the whole range of evaluative reasoning; unlike *Timao* and *MCRO,* the moral reasoning in *Sacrifice* is part of the game proper and has not been relegated to an informal postgame discussion.

(*b*) The level of sophistication of the moral reasoning in *Sacrifice* is, however, wholly dependent upon the sophistication of the participants; no formal mechanisms in the game *force* players to engage in complex values deliberations. The modification strategies we recommend could be used to formalize the moral deliberations in *Sacrifice.*

(*c*) As a *role-play* simulation *Sacrifice* has some potential for developing those characteristics of agents that initiate and sustain moral action. The game tends to encourage sophisticated social interaction in the form of deliberation, rational exchange, and community discussion of complicated environmental problems.

DAY 4:

Planning Future U.S. Worlds (Denison University Simulation Center, 1975) is a nonzero-sum resource allocation game of considerable complexity. Because it requires at least two days for play, we did a systematic three-hour "walk-thru," asking participants to perform only some of the key steps in the game. Over the past two years *Planning Future U.S. Worlds* has been conducted by Denison faculty and staff at several conferences and workshops. The game has gone through two versions and is still under development. We selected it for consideration in the workshop because: (*a*) it is one of the more sophisticated and complex values games, and (*b*) it represents a challenge for anyone attempting to modify its presently inadequate moral deliberation and justification stages. There seem to be two levels of justification required in the game—the justification of particular resource allocation moves and the justification of the human actions that are likely to be brought about by the various possible resource allocation patterns. Again, we feel that the modification strategies that appear in Appendices 2-4 can help facilitate the development of sophisticated justification stages in *Planning Future U.S. Worlds.*

DAY 5:

Future Decisions: The I.Q. Game (SAGA, 1974) is a *gamelike* values simulation because there is no determinate "payoff" or outcome specified. The objective of the activity is to allocate a benefit (chemically produced high I.Q.) and to support the allocated choices with moral reasoning. *The I.Q. Game* is designed to simulate the moral deliberations of the members of a hospital board. We chose *The I.Q. Game* for play in the workshop module primarily because it is a good, engaging example of a gamelike simulation (it does not fulfill formal criteria for a *game*). With this simulation/game, as well as the others, we discussed modification strategies and procedures but did very little actual modification due to time limitations.

Our experiences in the module suggest the following general conclusions and recommendations. First, the content of most values simulations/games is not particularly intellectually stimulating even though the activity might be socially significant. Many designers seem to try to remedy this shortcoming by adding, almost as an afterthought, challenging questions to the postgame discussion period. Although we agree that the debriefing is an important phase of a simulation game, much of the *subject matter* of such questions should be structured into the game proper. On the other hand, some values simulations/games appear more sophisticated and refined than they actually are as a consequence of being "tested" on academicians familiar with evaluative reasoning. Second, to our knowledge there are no simulations/games designed to take into account research findings on moral development. We want to emphasize that an important distinction needs to be drawn between being able to *play* and being able to *benefit,* in terms of moral development, from a simulation/game. Although very few persons are so unsophisticated as to be unable to play the available values simulations/games, most people, we feel, derive little benefit from these activities in terms of an increase in the sophistication of their moral thinking. Third, we believe that many values simulations/games could be improved by computerization. This would be the case particularly with games requiring complex evaluative and moral reasoning; the rapid display of relevant facts as well as lists of values and rules encompassed by principles would be a great aid to structuring moral deliberations. Of course, before such expensive development is undertaken, a great deal more empirical research needs to be done on the connection between values simulation/gaming and moral development.

NOTE

1. We shall employ the term "simulations/games" whenever we wish to refer *generally* to the various different activities in this area— nonsimulation games, simulation games, gamelike simulations, and nongaming simulations.

APPENDIX 1

AN OVERVIEW OF KOHLBERG'S WORK
WITH THE SIX STAGES OF MORAL
DEVELOPMENT

A moral dilemma:

> In Europe, a woman was near death from cancer. One drug might save her, a form of radium that a druggist in the same town had recently discovered. The druggist was charging $2,000, ten times what the drug cost him to make. The sick woman's husband, Heinz, went to everyone he knew to borrow the money, but he could only get together about half of what it cost. He told the druggist that his wife was dying and asked him to sell it cheaper or let him pay later. But the druggist said, "No." The husband got desperate and broke into the man's store to steal the drug for his wife. Should the husband have done that? Why? (Kohlberg, 1969, p. 379)

Kohlberg's Six Stages of Moral Development

PRECONVENTIONAL LEVEL

Stage 1:

Punishment and obedience orientation. The physical consequences of an action determine whether it is good or bad. Avoiding punishment and bowing to superior power are valued positively.

Stage 2:

Instrumental relativist orientation. Right action consists of behavior that satisfies one's own needs. Human relations are viewed in marketplace terms. Reciprocity occurs, but is seen in a pragmatic way, i.e., "You scratch my back and I'll scratch yours."

CONVENTIONAL LEVEL

Stage 3:

Interpersonal concordance (good boy-nice girl) orientation. Good behaviors are those that please or are approved by others. There is much emphasis on conformity and being "nice."

Stage 4:

   Orientation toward authority ("law and order"). Focus is on authority or rules. It is right to do one's duty, show respect for authority, and maintain the social order.

POSTCONVENTIONAL LEVEL

Stage 5:

   Social-contract orientation. This stage has a utilitarian, legalistic tone. Correct behavior is defined in terms of standards agreed upon by society. Awareness of the relativism of personal values and the need for consensus is important.

Stage 6:

   Universal ethical principle orientation. Morality is defined as a decision of conscience. Ethical principles are self-chosen, based on abstract concepts (e.g., the Golden Rule) rather than concrete rules (e.g., the Ten Commandments).

THE TYPE OF MORAL REASONING EMPLOYED AT VARIOUS STAGES IN RESPONSE TO THE PROBLEM OF HEINZ

Stage 1:

   Action is motivated by avoidance of punishment, and "conscience" is irrational fear of punishment.

Pro—If you let your wife die, you will get in trouble. You'll be blamed for not spending the money to save her and there'll be an investigation of you and the druggist for your wife's death.

Con—You shouldn't steal the drug because you'll be caught and sent to jail if you do. If you do get away, your conscience would bother you thinking how the police would catch up with you at any minute.

Stage 2:

   Action motivated by desire for reward or benefit. Possible guilt reactions are ignored and punishment viewed in a pragmatic manner. (Differentiates own fear, pleasure, or pain from punishment-consequences.)

Pro—If you do happen to get caught you could give the drug back and you wouldn't get much of a sentence. It wouldn't bother you much to serve a little jail term, if you have your wife when you get out.

Con—He may not get much of a jail term if he steals the drug, but his wife will probably die before he gets out so it won't do him much good. If his wife dies, he shouldn't blame himself, it wasn't his fault she has cancer.

Stage 3:

Action motivated by anticipation of disapproval of others, actual or imagined-hypothetical (e.g., guilt). (Differentiation of disapproval from punishment, fear, and pain.)

Pro—No one will think you're bad if you steal the drug, but your family will think you're an inhuman husband if you don't. If you let your wife die, you'll never be able to look anybody in the face again.

Con—It isn't just the druggist who will think you're a criminal, everyone else will too. After you steal it, you'll feel bad thinking how you've brought dishonor on your family and yourself; you won't be able to face anyone again.

Stage 4:

Action motivated by anticipation of dishonor, i.e., institutionalized blame for failure of duty, and by guilt over concrete harm done to others. (Differentiates formal dishonor from informal disapproval. Differentiates guilt for bad consequences from disapproval.)

Pro—If you have any sense of honor, you won't let your wife die because you're afraid to do the only thing that will save her. You'll always feel guilty that you caused her death if you don't do your duty to her.

Con—You're desperate and you may not know you're doing wrong when you steal the drug. But you'll know you did wrong after you're punished and sent to jail. You'll always feel guilt for your dishonesty and lawbreaking.

Stage 5:

Concern about maintaining respect of equals and of the community (assuming their respect is based on reason rather than emotions). Concern about own self-respect, i.e., to avoid judging self as irrational, inconsistent, nonpurposive. (Discriminates between institutionalized blame and community disrespect or self-disrespect.)

Pro—You'd lose other people's respect, not gain it, if you don't steal. If you let your wife die, it would be out of fear, not out of reasoning it out. So you'd just lose self-respect and probably the respect of others too.

Con—You would lose your standing and respect in the community and violate the law. You'd lose respect for yourself if you're carried away by emotion and forget the long-range point of view.

Stage 6:

Concern about self-condemnation for violating one's own principles. (Differentiates between community respect and self-respect. Differentiates between self-respect for general achieving rationality and self-respect for maintaining moral principles.)

Pro—If you don't steal the drug and let your wife die, you'd always condemn yourself for it afterward. You wouldn't be blamed and you would have lived up to the outside rule of the law but you wouldn't have lived up to your own standards of conscience.

Con—If you stole the drug, you wouldn't be blamed by other people but you'd condemn yourself because you wouldn't have lived up to your own conscience and standards of honesty.

Source: Rest, 1968.

APPENDIX 2

MODIFYING SIMULATIONS

The following list of questions was designed to get one started in the analysis and modification of simulation games and activities.

1. How can the instructions for a game be modified to improve the clarity of the game?
2. What are the advantages and disadvantages of "keeping score" or having a payoff in a game?
3. How can the simulation be made more realistic? Can chance factors be reduced if they subtract from realism? If they add to realism . . . ?

4. How does one adjust the intellectual caliber of a game?
5. Might certain audiovisual aids, etc., improve the quality and realism of the simulation?
6. How does one ensure that all participants are *actively engaged* in the game? What mechanisms can be built into the game for this purpose?
7. How might instruments be designed to allow the players of a game to evaluate critically and improve the game and their performance in playing the game?
8. Was enough information provided for decision-making at various stages? How might such a deficiency be remedied without interfering with the game?
9. Are the "task load" and the time available for the game optimal? Might the game be improved by breaking it into parts separated by breaks, etc.?
10. Can vague or ambiguous aspects of the game be improved, clarified, or eliminated?
11. Is there additional background information for a particular game that would improve its worth as a simulation game, activity, etc.?
12. Are the rules, means, and goals specified clearly and unambiguously?
13. How can one assess the impact (e.g., learning, behavioral change, etc.) of a particular simulation?

You might also wish to consult: Adair, C. H., and Foster, J. T. *A guide for simulation design: theoretical and practical procedures for the development of instructional simulations.* Tallahassee, Florida: Instructional Simulation Design, Inc., 1972.

APPENDIX 3

MOVING BEYOND VALUES CLARIFICATION: ADDITIONAL GAME* ANALYSIS QUESTIONS

(1) In games that contain lists of "values" (which players usually are asked to arrange in a hierarchy), are the values statements of the same type or generality? If not, does this introduce confusion into the

---

*The word "game" has been used here as a term of convenience to cover both values gaming activities and nongaming values simulations.

game? Can such a list be modified so that players are not required to arrange hierarchically a "mixed bag" of values statements?

(2) Does the game distinguish between moral and nonmoral values?

(3) What kinds of evaluative reasoning does the game require?

(*a*)   Mere approval or disapproval of actions that are described in the game (i.e., players are not required to formulate any action plans because the actions are already spelled out for them)?

(*b*)   The formulation of specific action alternatives *without* any requirement for giving reasons?

(*c*)   The making of explicit inferences to the value(s) subscribed to by players (such inferences are usually made on the basis of players' approval or disapproval of some action alternative)?

(*d*)   The making of specific moral decisions regarding particular actions *and* the rationalization of the decision by the citing of the underlying value? (This move is not enough to justify the action because the value remains unjustified.)

(*e*)   The making of specific decisions regarding particular actions *and* supporting such decisions with the giving of reasons that refer not only to underlying values but also purport to justify the values by locating them in a framework of moral rules and principles that the agent accepts?

For further explanation of (*d*) and (*e*) see Cochrane, 1975, p. 40.

(4) Does the game provide an adequate amount of relevant factual information for value decisions? If not, does it require players to seek or generate such factual information before proceeding with evaluative judgments?

(5) Is the game competitive? If so, how does this affect the evaluative thinking that is required of players?

(6) Does the playing of the game require that participants have developed the so-called "moral emotions"—e.g., sympathy, empathy? Is the playing of the game likely to foster or enhance in participants the development of such moral emotions?

(7) Does the playing of the game require skills or abilities (of a predominantly nonrational kind) that *enable* an agent to act in accordance with his or her rational decision? Does playing the game foster or enhance

the learning or development of such skills or abilities—e.g., learning to listen, to console, to speak out in public, to lobby, picket or protest, etc.?

(8) Does the playing of the game require that participants have certain psychological capacities that initiate and sustain moral action? Some of these are traditionally known as "the will"—courage, perseverance, capacity to delay self-gratification, etc. Does playing the game foster or enhance the development of these capacities?

For further explanation of (6), (7), and (8) see Cochrane, 1975, part IV.

APPENDIX 4

SUGGESTIONS FOR MODIFYING THE EVALUATIVE REASONING COMPONENTS OF GAMES AND SIMULATIONS

I. If the values game contains an incoherent list of values statements, try to substitute an improved list. For example, one type of error contained in values games (especially values clarification games) is permitting players to rank value X (say, FRUGALITY) above value Y (say, WEALTH) when X is instrumental for (or the means to) the attainment of Y. Another example is a list of terms, all of which *purport* to refer to values, but some of which turn out to name *value objects* rather than values.

II. If a values game attempts to simulate the process of value justification by asking participants merely to *discuss* their value differences, try to replace this instruction with rules requiring structured discussion or play. For example, suppose player A endorses the evaluative judgment "The making of welfare payments is morally wrong" and suppose that player B disagrees. In the ensuing discussion A and B should be required to identify both the *facts* and the norms on which they have either tacitly or explicitly based the specific judgment. One device that could be built into a game to structure deliberations is the Evidence Card (see pp. 50-51 of Jerrold R. Coombs and Milton Mieux, "Teaching Strategies for Value Analysis," in *Values Education,* ed. Lawrence E. Metcalf [Washington, D.C.: National Council for the Social Studies, 1971], pp. 29-74).

The evidence card lists the specific value judgment, the relevant fact(s) and the governing norm.

> *Value judgment:* The making of welfare payments is morally wrong.
> *Fact:* Welfare payments are made to people who haven't earned the money on the job.
> *Norm:* Practices which give money to people who haven't earned it are morally wrong.

The requirement either to supply or select relevant facts and norms exposes them to the kind of examination that is often missing from unstructured discussions.

III. Once the norm that is presupposed by a particular value judgment has been explicitly identified, further systematic moral deliberation is possible. Coombs and Mieux (1971, pp. 54-61) describe four tests for the acceptability of norms or principles. These tests (new cases test, subsumption test, role exchange test, universal consequences test) are intended by them to be used in nongaming contexts. The challenging design problem for those working in the area of values simulation and gaming is the adaptation of the four tests to gaming situations.

REFERENCES

Bandura, A. *Principles of behavior modification.* New York: Holt, Rinehart and Winston, Inc., 1969.

Bandura, A., and Walters, R. H. *Adolescent aggression.* New York: Ronald, 1959.

Cochrane, Don. Moral education—A prolegomenon. *Theory into practice,* October, 1975, *14,* 236-246.

Future decisions. The I.Q. game. Lebanon, Ohio: Simulation and Gaming Association, 1974.

Gibbs, G. E., ed. *Handbook of games and simulation exercises.* Beverly Hills, California: Case Publications, Inc., 1974.

Hall, Robert T., and Davis, John Y. *Moral education in theory and practice.* Buffalo, New York: Prometheus Books, 1975.

Hoffman, M. L. Moral development. In P. H. Mussen (Ed.) *Carmichael's manual of child psychology.* Vol. 2. New York: Wiley, 1970, 261-330.

Kohlberg, L. *Stages in the development of moral thought and action.* New York: Holt, 1969.

Metcalf, Lawrence E., ed. *Values education.* Washington, D.C.: National Council for the Social Studies, 1971.

My cup runneth over. San Diego, California: Pennant Educational Materials, 1971.

Piaget, J. *The moral judgment of the child.* New York: Harcourt, Brace, 1932.

Planning future U.S. worlds: technological change in human values. Denison University Simulation Center, 1975. This is an adaptation of *Simulating the Values of the Future* by Olaf Helmer in K. Baier and N. Rescher (eds.) *Values and the Future.* New York, 1968, 193-202.

Rescher, Nicholas. *Introduction to value theory.* Englewood Cliffs, New Jersey: Prentice-Hall, Inc., 1969.

Rest, J. Developmental hierarchy in preference and comprehension of moral judgment. Unpublished doctoral dissertation, University of Chicago, 1968.

Sacrifice. Middletown, Connecticut: Education Ventures Inc., 1971.

Stadsklev, Ron. *Handbook of simulation and gaming in social education.* Part 2: Directory, The University of Alabama: Institute of Higher Education Research and Services, 1975.

Timao. San Diego, California: Pennant Educational Materials, 1971.

Zuckerman, David W., and Horn, Robert E. *The guide to simulations/games for education and training.* Lexington, Massachusetts: Information Resources, Inc., 1973.

10

SIMULATION, VALUES CLARIFICATION, AND NORMATIVE ETHICS[1]

ANTHONY J. LISSKA

ABSTRACT

This paper offers an analysis of the role of normative ethics and moral justification and discusses their incorporation into simulation projects on values and exercises in values clarification. Such an analysis will contribute toward a better conceptual understanding of the philosophical issues involved in values questions as treated in much simulation and values clarification material. Of principal concern is the distinction between a mere descriptive listing of preferences and a justification of moral choices. The final part of the paper discusses a simulation project devised by a team from Denison University. The expressed purpose of this simulation project is to engage the participants in an analysis of normative ethical issues, especially that of moral justification, and thus to transcend the normal descriptive limits of many simulation projects on values and exercises in values clarification.

It is immediately obvious to even the cursory reader of educational literature that much recent pedagogical writing both popular and professional has focused directly on the need to introduce discussions of value theory into the classroom. This refers, moreover, to all levels of education, from the primary grades through the secondary schools and the colleges. Both educational theorists and nonprofessional commentators have decried the pronounced lack of value discussions and moral considerations in the classroom. They perceive this deficiency as an all-too-common and pervasive occurrence in our educational mechanisms.

Speaking quite concretely and directly, my own college, Denison University, sought recently to rework its program of General Education. A central part of that reworking and the resultant proposal centered around the introduction of beginning-level courses in normative ethics for freshmen students and the introduction of a seminar in the field of, for want of a better term, "professional ethics," for senior students in their respective majors. Both of these courses were to be required. Without even going to the level of general educational reform or theoretical articles in educational journals, one need but have read an autumn issue last year of *The New York Times Magazine* (Etzioni, 1976). That issue contains a general discussion of some novel attempts used to confront the apparent "values gap" in American educational practice.

In response to this need, many new, creative, and, in some ways, controversial pedagogical devices and methodologies have been introduced to help students confront the values they hold. Simulation games on values and exercises in Values Clarification are two such items that have attained a degree of wide-spread use and acceptance among teachers at all levels of education. An indication of the widespread use and adoption of values clarification materials is evident in reading Stewart's (1975) quite informative article, "Problems and Contradictions of Values Clarification," which first appeared in *The Phi Delta Kappan* and has been reprinted in Purpel and Ryan (1976). In response to the question that liberal arts colleges more effectively confront the task of stimulating and challenging ethical growth in their students, Ledebur (1977, p. 5) has written that ". . . simulations are a technique of teaching and learning that may prove effective in this task. Their usefulness as devices to generate learning in the affective domain should be carefully evaluated." In this paper I attempt to provide an analysis of some central philosophical issues involved in using simulation games and exercises in values clarification. The expressed purpose of this inquiry is to elucidate the relation between these two pedagogical methodologies and some traditional concepts central to normative ethics. I hope that this analysis will contribute toward a better conceptual understanding of the philosophical—i.e., normative ethical—issues involved in simulation games and values clarification. What I shall be doing in this paper is, in effect, an exercise in what C. D. Broad (1927) called "critical philosophy," by which he meant "the analysis and definition of our fundamental concepts and the clear statement and resolute criticism of our fundamental beliefs." Indeed this is a second-order activity. It is what contemporary analytic philosophers call a "meta" inquiry, whose content is the actual methodologies and processes undertaken in simulation games on value theory and exercises in values clarification. This in a sense illustrates the role for philosophy which the medieval philosopher Thomas Aquinas saw for philosophical activity when he succinctly said: *"Primum vivere, deinde philosophari";* this, roughly translated, means: first you need to have many experiences and only then are you ready to philosophize. The actual methodologies and processes involved in simulation games and values clarification exercises provide the content upon which the activity of critical philosophy is directed in both uncovering the presuppositions and subjecting to analysis and conceptual elucidation the concepts involved in simulation games on values and exercises in values clarification.

Accordingly, insofar as this paper is a second-order analysis it proposes an examination of the presuppositions and concerns involved in simulation games and values clarification programs. It does not pretend to devise a new simulation game or construct another values clarification exercise. Nonetheless, such an analysis will, it is hoped, lead to a better pedagogical use of these materials. For, in the end, simulation games on values and exercises in values clarification are useful and significant pedagogically only if they aid students in the difficult process of confronting values and making ethical decisions.

More precisely, in this paper I shall be doing two things. First of all, I shall discuss what I take to be an important conceptual blur that occurs in many simulations on value questions and value clarification exercises.

Second, I shall discuss a simulation project on value theory devised by a team at Denison University entitled "Values and the Future." The expressed purpose of this simulation exercise was to transcend a deficiency that many philosophers who work with normative ethics perceived as a major weakness in simulation exercises aimed at getting the student to think seriously about moral matters.

Accordingly, while being critical of a pronounced conceptual blur in many simulations and values clarification exercises, nonetheless the general thrust of the paper is positive and constructive. This constructive aspect is especially true of the last part of the paper, during which I shall examine and discuss the Denison University project, attempting to incorporate somewhat sophisticated moral reasoning into simulation exercises.

To my first point. I believe that many simulation games dealing with value theory and exercises in values clarification, no matter how involved and sophisticated or geared for what level, usually conceptually blur a distinction central to normative ethical theory. This is the distinction between a *normative* inquiry and a *descriptive* inquiry. Too often much of this purported value-laden pedagogical material has remained on the level of description. In other words, a mere listing of choices and preferences—which indeed is nothing more than a description—is taken to be equivalent to a complete ethical analysis, i.e., a *normative* account. I submit, however, that while a descriptive listing of preferences is an important and necessary first step in confronting value questions, it is not sufficient for a thorough analysis either of moral values or of moral reasoning. If a moral inquiry is limited only to a descriptive listing of preferences or choices, the important normative element of moral justification and the role of moral theory have been tragically neglected.

On this issue, an important review article by Colby (1975) on values clarification literature appeared in the *Harvard Educational Review.*[2] This article has also been reprinted in Purpel and Ryan (1976). Colby, who is a research associate in Education at Harvard and who works in the area of cognitive and moral development, has written an excellent in-depth analysis of values clarification. I strongly recommend Colby's review article to anyone who works seriously with these materials. While it is true that Colby reviews the values clarification literature and approach from the perspective of Lawrence Kohlberg's schema of moral development and cognitive psychology; nonetheless, I believe that one can profit much from her analysis without being wedded to Kohlberg's theoretical schema for moral development. I found that Colby spelled out in some detail and with much lucidity many of the worries that I had encountered in the process of devising the simulation game at Denison entitled "Values and the Future," to which I referred earlier in this paper.

As Colby notes, often the values clarification approach is less concerned with the content of value judgments than with the "valuing process." Louis Raths once defined a "value" as an area of the human condition that met the following seven process criteria: (1) prizing and cherishing, (2) publicly affirming, (3) choosing from alternatives, (4) choosing after considering consequences, (5) choosing freely, (6) acting, (7) acting with a pattern, repetition, and consistency (in Kirschenbaum and Simon, 1973).

The intended purpose of many of the values clarification exercises is to make each student aware of how he or she actually arrived at a particular decision. The focus is not, however, on defending the content of the choice. Colby comments, from her Kohlbergian perspective, that the values clarification approach, while concentrating on the careful choice of values, lacks any underlying theoretical structure. She notes, again from her Kohlbergian perspective, that indeed Kohlberg's approach to value theory is rooted on a cognitive theory that details how moral development occurs. As many of you know, Kohlberg's theory of moral development has interesting structural similarities—and is probably dependent upon—Piaget's rather developed theory of general cognitive development. For those of you unfamiliar with Kohlberg's work, part of the discussion of the Denison University "Values and the Future" simulation to be discussed later in this paper incorporates Kohlberg's six stages of moral development as one model for moral reasoning. For a most interesting and nontechnical account of Kohlberg's theory, I refer those of you interested to Kohlberg (1967).

As many of you know, Kohlberg uses a "case study" approach in discussing moral development. The important difference between Kohlberg's approach and many values clarification exercises is that Kohlberg attempts to engage the students confronting the moral dilemmas to undertake the process of moral justification. Kohlberg is, I submit, asking the right philosophical question here. Simply put, moral justification means the attempt to support or justify a moral claim or a moral position. In other words, it is not sufficient that a person merely list a set of preferences or discuss alternatives. Indeed the choice itself may be immoral. One need but appeal to explicit instances of racism, sexism, religious bigotry, and so forth, to provide clear cases of immoral choices. Therefore, it is necessary that one attempt to discover if the moral choice itself has clearly reasoned grounds upon which it is based. The issue is not "what *would* you do in situation X," but rather "what *ought* you do in situation X." We must not merely choose; we must justify our choice with clearly reasoned moral grounds. This is the important component of moral justification central to normative ethics.

Many values clarification approaches emphasize qualities of the moral decision-making process like (*a*) independence of deciding, (*b*) thoughtful evaluation of alternatives and consequences, (*c*) commitment to one's beliefs about value propositions, (*d*) action, and (*e*) nondogmatic roles for the teacher. While this is important and probably a necessary propaedeutic step in engaging in value theory, nonetheless it focuses attention on what might be a generic level of decision theory rather than on value-decision-making in particular. The emphasis is on the *process* of independent choosing rather than on the justification of the choice itself. Moreover, in some values clarification exercises, there is a blurring of moral values with nonmoral values. My use of "The TR-4 was a good sports car" and "Tom Dooley was a good person" are indeed different uses of "good." The former is a nonmoral use and the latter a moral use.[3] This conceptual blur between moral values and nonmoral values also bothers Colby in that it hinders and retards the development of moral justification:

> The failure of values clarification to treat moral and non-moral questions as fundamentally different obscures such philosophical issues as ethical relativity (the view that validity of a moral judgment is relative to the values or needs of the individual or culture) and adequacy of justification. (Colby, 1975, 138)

As I mentioned earlier—and Colby concurs—the values clarification approach is limited to the descriptive level (what *would* you do in such and such a situation) rather than going on to the normative or prescriptive level (what *ought* you to do in such and such a situation).

This leads to a fundamental problem. Colby puts it quite nicely when she says that the values clarification approach is:

> . . . interested in having people clarify the values they hold, but once the values are clear, *it is an open question whether these values are good.* (Colby, 1975, 138) (Italics not in original)

Or, as I might say, it is an open question whether indeed these values are justified. Put differently, with emphasis alone placed upon the *process* of choosing values, questions regarding the justification of the choices made and affirmed are not seen as relevant. This totally neglects the element of moral justification. Interestingly enough, Colby speculates why the values clarification approach indeed blurs the important philosophical distinction between normative and descriptive inquiries. She notes that:

> . . . in reacting against the simple-minded, absolutist and traditional moralities foisted upon children, [the values clarification approach] emphasizes the degree to which general moral principles must be tailored to the details of each interpersonal situation. [She suspects that the values clarification approach and its proponents are] . . . insufficiently clear about the distinction between tolerance for differences of opinion and the relativist notion that all opinions are equally justifiable. (Colby, 1975, 138)

The last point bears *repetition!* Too easily the democratic ideal of tolerance in diversity leads down the slippery slope to epistemological and moral relativism and skepticism. My own conversation with a values clarification expert confirms Colby's suspicion. Tolerance was looked upon as the fundamental virtue (moral virtue) and any attempt at moral justification brought the response "Well, maybe you philosophers can do that, but I certainly doubt my capacity to tell another person what indeed is right or wrong." It must be emphasized that the prescriptive level of moral justification is not equivalent to or coextensive with moral dogmatism. To miss this important distinction is to ignore *the* important normative ethical dimension of moral justification. Harmin and Simon, who are generally regarded as principal theoreticians for values clarification, appear to be oblivious to this distinction. Note the following passage from their article "Values," in which they consider the approach of clarifying values:

> [Values are regarded] . . . as relative, personal, and situational. The main task of these approaches is not to identify and transmit the "right" values, but to help a student clarify his own values so he can obtain the values that best suit him and his environment; so he can adjust himself to a changing world; and so he can play an intelligent role in influencing the way the world changes. (Harmin and Simon, 1973)

I believe that a false dichotomy has been drawn when it is assumed that the only way to be nondogmatic in matters of morals is to place the emphasis solely on the *process* of decision-making. In other words, moral justification as practiced in normative ethics does not entail dogmatism. It does entail clear, conceptual analysis of the reasons behind those choices that have been affirmed and those commitments that have been undertaken. To stress the process alone fails to consider the reasons behind the choices affirmed in that process. Stewart (1975) addresses the issues of relativism in values clarification also.

In addition to the above concerns that I share with Colby, my own study of values clarification literature has indicated a further suspicion for the conceptual blurring of normative and descriptive categories. Harmin and Simon note that their values clarification methodology is "built on the positions of pragmatic philosophers and the humanist psychologists" (Harmin and Simon, 1973). In regard to the former, John Dewey is mentioned many times and Carl Rogers is taken as a paradigm for humanist psychology. Philosophically, I suggest that Dewey's form of pragmatism is indeed *methodological* in character, with a strong emphasis on process and development. In a serious theoretical sense, his system lacks any substantive content. Indeed, to use Deweyian jargon, "consummatory experiences" are quite changeable. In fact, Dewey explicitly argues that an experience is educative only if it contributes positively to the process of growth. Nonetheless, he provides no criterion for this process of growth itself. William Frankena (1965, 157) has suggested that an analysis of the criterion of growth is indeed *the central question* in Dewey's philosophy of education.

Furthermore, Frankena suggests that, although Dewey's critics have raised this issue most insistently, neither Dewey nor his followers have provided satisfactory responses. I submit that the same objection can be raised structurally against the methodology of values clarification. Interestingly enough, in his recent article "Beyond Values Clarification," Kirschenbaum (1973) stresses more than ever the process approach to working with values. Given this background, I believe my own work and that of persons like Colby and Stewart is not only theoretically interesting but important constructive criticism for the proponents of values clarification.

In addition, the Rogerian approach to values also places great emphasis on the *process of valuing*. Indeed, one of Roger's most important and widely read articles is entitled "Toward a Modern Approach to Values: The Valuing Process in the Mature Person" (Rogers, 1969). Although some critics have read Rogers's position as one devoid of content, I have argued elsewhere that this is a mistaken view attributed to Rogers (Lisska, 1977). Indeed I submit that Rogers's functional account of values has a strong Aristotelian ring to it; if I am correct, then Rogers's position is a form of ethical naturalism, to use the categories of contemporary metaethics.

Am I suggesting that exercises in values clarification and simulation games on values have no pedagogically significant role to play? Not at all. These pedagogical tools and techniques can be useful if indeed they can sensitize students to values issues and problems and initiate the process of thinking critically about value questions. Nonetheless, these teaching devices must also engage the student into undertaking serious consideration about what counts for a morally relevant and justificatory reason and what does not so count. I agree with Colby when she suggests that a particular choice is ". . . less important than the reason behind the choice." Given this, I must emphasize that the "debriefing session" that follows a simulation program or the discussion component that follows a values clarification exercise must be seen as a necessary condition for the successful use of the game or exercise. Hence, these reflective sessions must never be cut short or seen only as a secondary addition. Indeed, they must be emphasized as an integral part of the process. In the discussion session or debriefing component, the participants must be, to quote Colby, encouraged to do the following:

> . . . to think and talk about why they voted, ranked, or chose as they did; they must also consider whether theirs were good choices and, most importantly, why. (Colby, 1975)

Given this, nonetheless, an important theoretical question remains: Can indeed such a moral development "discussion session" or "debriefing component" become an integral part of a simulation game? I suspect that the introduction of this reflective aspect is probably easier for a values clarification exercise. My colleague, David Goldblatt, has engaged in similar pedagogical activities with some success with a class for freshmen philosophy students. With a simulation game, however, one must ask if the involvement with the game, especially if it is intense, is so engaging that, no matter how good the structured material for discussion might be, nonetheless the discussion session itself is looked upon as an unnecessary "dull" addition that should be run through as soon as possible. Put differently, are the game element and the participant involvement so great that they distract from the debriefing session? I suggest that both more empirical work and more conceptual elucidation needs to be done in this area. As far as I have been able to determine, few simulation games on values have as detailed a debriefing structure as the one devised by Denison's team. We shall consider this next.

Now, to a discussion of the handout sheets (cf. appendix to this paper). A little background material is in order. This is the moral justification segment, which served as the debriefing exercise for a quite involved simulation entitled "Values and the Future," which, as I mentioned earlier, was devised by a team at Denison University in 1975. It has been used by students at Denison and at Albion College. The present form evolved after much time and effort and was presented at the 1975 Lilly Endowment's Continuing Conference for the Liberal Arts. The Denison team based this simulation on an involved exercise developed by Olaf Helmer and printed in Baier and Rescher (1969). We used Helmer's simulation as a model construct and then reworked it so that the choices to be made would unmistakably emphasize value considerations rather than nonvalue-laden proposals.

After the participants had chosen their respective "worlds for the future," we asked them to think about what good reasons they had for making such choices. We introduced them to moral thinking and the justificatory process by using material devised to structure the debriefing session. This material is contained on the handout sheets.

Page one is a conceptual map of moral theories. We found this quite useful in working with students generally unsophisticated with ethical theory. Page two shows Kohlberg's Levels and Stages of Moral Development. This was used as an example of one model for moral reasoning. It must be noted that there was no assumption by us that this is indeed the only model. Pages three, four, and five give examples of various content theories regarding moral justification. We divided these according to (1) an appeal to consequences; (2) an appeal to deed or rule; and (3) an appeal to the basic needs of persons. Page six is an illustration of how we dealt with the problem of moving the participants from the simulation itself to the theoretical stage of considering arguments for moral justification.

With a discussion of the Denison University construct for a structured debriefing session, this concludes my inquiry into the relationship between exercises in values clarification and simulation games on value theory and the central issue of normative ethics, namely, moral justification. Until these new pedagogical devices inculcate a dimension of moral justification as an integral part of their structure, they will lack a necessary condition for a successful analysis of value theory. I trust this lack will soon be recognized and remedied.

APPENDIX 1

A CONCEPTUAL MAP OF TYPES OF MORAL THEORIES

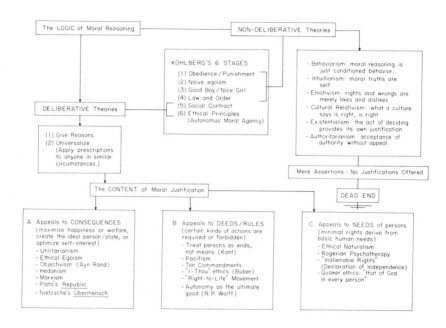

APPENDIX 2

DELIBERATIVE MORAL REASONING (BASED UPON KOHLBERG'S STAGES IN MORAL DEVELOPMENT)

LEVEL 1:	*Basis of Moral Judgment*	*Stage of Development*
Preconventional Level	Moral value resides in external, quasiphysical happenings, in bad acts, or in quasiphysical needs rather than in persons and standards.	*Stage 1: Obedience punishment orientation.* Egocentric deference to superior power or prestige, or a trouble-avoiding set. Objective responsibility.

	Basis of Moral Judgment	Stage of Development
		Stage 2: Naively egoistic orientation. Right action is that instrumentally satisfying the self's needs and occasionally others'. Awareness of relativism of value to each actor's needs and perspective. Naive egalitarianism and orientation to exchange and reciprocity.
LEVEL II: Conventional Level	Moral value resides in performing good or right roles, in maintaining the conventional order and the expectancies of others.	*Stage 3: "Good boy—nice girl" orientation.* Orientation to approval and to pleasing and helping others. Conformity to stereotypical images of majority or natural role behavior, and judgment by intentions.
		Stage 4: "Law and order" orientation. Orientation to "doing duty" and to showing respect for authority and maintaining the given social order for its own sake. Regard for earned expectations of others.
LEVEL III: Postconventional, Autonomous or Principled Level	Moral value resides in conformity by the self to shared or shareable standards, rights, or duties.	*Stage 5: Social contract legalistic orientation.* Recognition of an arbitrary element or starting point in rules or expectations for the sake of agreement. Duty defined in terms of contract, general avoidance of violation of the will or rights of others, and majority will and welfare.
		Stage 6: Conscience, ethical principle orientation. Orientation not only to actually ordained social rules but to principles of choice involving appeal to logical universality and consistency. Orientation to conscience as a directing agent and to mutual respect and trust.

Cf. *Journal of Philosophy*, October 25, *10*(18), 1973, 630-646.

A NORMATIVE ETHICAL THEORY BASED UPON
CONSEQUENCES

Some philosophers and theologians have argued that the locus of value is in the consequences of actions. An ethical theory that places the criterion for evaluation of an action or a moral rule or practice entirely on the consequences is called a TELEOLOGICAL ethic. *"Telos"* is the Greek term for "end." Ends can be evaluated in at least two ways: those relating to the agent alone and those affecting a larger group. When the agent alone is affected, this is a form of ETHICAL EGOISM. When more persons than the agent alone are affected by the action, this is UTILITARIANISM, another normative theory appealing to consequences.

> ETHICAL EGOISM: An action is right if and only if it directly affects the personal well-being of the agent.
> UTILITARIANISM: An action is right if and only if it contributes to the greatest happiness for the greatest number of people.

In the process of justification, some teleological theories focus on each action while others focus on a moral rule or practice governing the action. In the case of Utilitarianism, we have ACT UTILITARIANISM and RULE UTILITARIANISM. In Act Utilitarianism, each time a moral agent is to make a morally justified decision, he or she must calculate the beneficial or adverse effects of that action. Rule Utilitarianism, on the other hand, applies the method of justification to general rules that, when followed, produce the best possible consequences for the society as a whole. Professor John Hospers has described Rule Utilitarianism in the following way:

> . . . [R]ule utilitarianism comes to this: Each act, in the moral life, falls under a *rule*; and we are to judge the rightness or wrongness of the act, not by its consequences, but by the consequences of its universalization—that is, by the consequences of adoption of the *rule* under which the act falls. (*Human Conduct: Problems of Ethics*, 316)

It is important to note that the distinguishing factor with any teleological ethical theory is the dominant *appeal to consequences*.

A NORMATIVE ETHICAL THEORY BASED UPON
DEEDS OR RULES

Some philosophers and theologians have argued that the locus of value is to be found in the moral act itself. Insofar as the appeal for justification is to a feature or features other than the consequences of an action or a rule, this position is called a DEONTOLOGICAL ethical theory. The DEED/RULE position affirms the existence of intrinsic characteristics of actions or rules. These characteristics are such that they render an action morally right or wrong independently of any other circumstances. There is an absolute character to these intrinsic characteristics that determines the theory of value.

An absolute pacifist, for example, would be taking a Deed position in asserting that violent aggression is wrong no matter what the situation or circumstances. Philosophers like Kant have argued that, insofar as human beings have intrinsic dignity, then they must always be treated as ends-in-themselves and never as means for some ulterior purpose. Those who argue the "right to life" position in the debate over abortion often are asserting that destruction of life is intrinsically evil. Buber's affirmation of the "I-Thou" relationship as central to morality can be regarded as a Rule position.

Some ethical theories, like situationalist ethics, focus on single actions that are considered to be intrinsically right or wrong. This is an Act theory. Other theories focus attention on contexts or series of actions. Rules are formed that regulate sets or series of actions and thus are Rule theories. A narrow interpretation of the Ten Commandments would also be a Rule ethic.

It is important to note that the distinguishing feature with any Deed/ Rule ethical theory is the *appeal to an intrinsic moral property of the action or rule.*

APPENDIX 5

A NORMATIVE ETHICAL THEORY BASED UPON
HUMAN NEEDS (FUNCTIONALIST ETHIC)

Some philosophers, theologians, and psychologists have argued that the locus of value is in the fundamental makeup of the human person.

Because the appeal is to some characteristic of the human person rather than to the consequences, this position is called a DEONTOLOGICAL ethical theory. Philosophers like Aristotle and Thomas Aquinas and psychologists like Carl Rogers have maintained that the source of value is the "functioning well" of the human organism in a contextual social setting. The rudimentary content for this position is determined by what some contemporary social scientists have referred to as "basic human needs" or "natural necessities." Minimal human rights are established by the natural necessities common to all human beings. Each person has a fundamental right to the possibility of development and protection from the repression of these natural necessities. As opposed to the Rule/Deed theory, the dimension of process and development are crucial.

Carl Rogers lists the following propositions as necessary conditions for an adequate theory of values.

1. There is an *organismic base* for an organized valuing process within the human individual.
2. In persons who are moving toward greater openness to their experiencing, there is an *organismic commonality* of value directions.
3. These common value directions are of such kinds as to enhance the development of the individual, of others in the community, and to make for the survival and evolution of the species. (*Journal of Abnormal and Social Psychology*, 68, #2)

Thomas Aquinas construed basic human needs in terms of three generic categories: (*a*) basic requirements of human life—survival; (*b*) basic requirements for the furtherance of the human species; (*c*) basic requirements for the promotion of the good of the individual as a rational and social being. These three categories correspond to natural tendencies common to all human persons and serve as the basis for minimal principles of conduct. Aquinas further maintained that any general theory of law (Jurisprudence) that did not consider the demands of these natural necessities was not to be regarded as a legitimate use of legal authority in a society.

Moral rules are determined by the basic natural necessities common to all humans.

APPENDIX 6

EXAMPLES OF MORAL JUSTIFICATION

(The following examples are hypothetical situations drawn from issues discussed in the Denison University VALUES AND THE FUTURE Simulation.)

1. When discussing the potential development of CONTINUED AUTO-MATION IN AMERICA AND INDUSTRY, if the reason for your decision was that automation will increase the level of the general welfare of the whole society, then you made an appeal to consequences. This is an example of UTILITARIANISM.

2. If the reason for your decision was that automation may take away your job, then your appeal was also to consequences, but this time your own welfare was at stake rather than the welfare of society as a whole. This is an example of ETHICAL EGOISM.

3. If the reason for your decision was that you thought automation might help preserve basic human dignity and human rights, then your appeal was to an ethic based upon NEEDS OF PERSONS (MINIMAL HUMAN RIGHT ETHIC).

4. If the reason for your decision was that automation would help preserve basic human autonomy and freedom, then you were making an appeal to a DEED/RULE ETHIC.

5. If the reason for your decision was that automation just *seems* right to you, then this would be an example of INTUITIONISM or EMOTIVISM, depending upon whether you considered your conclusion to be a moral truth or just a preference.

6. If the reason for your decision was that continued automation is the coming thing for the technological culture and whatever a culture dictates is all right with you, then your appeal would probably be to a form of CULTURAL RELATIVISM.

NOTES

1. An earlier draft of this paper was presented at the Annual Meeting of the North American Simulation and Gaming Association, Raleigh, North Carolina, October 16, 1976.

2. I am indebted to my colleague Professor Eric Straumanis for calling my attention to this important review article.

3. For a more developed account of the differences between moral and nonmoral decision-making, Hare (1965) has emphasized the necessity of incorporating both the prescriptive and the universalizable components in moral decision-making.

REFERENCES

Baier, K., and Rescher, N. *Values and the future.* New York: The Free Press, 1969.

Broad, C. D. *Scientific thought*. New York: Harcourt, Brace and Company, 1927.

Colby, A. Review of *Values and teaching* and *Values clarification: A handbook of practical strategies for teachers and students*. Harvard educational review, 1975, 134-143.

Etzioni, A. Do as I say, not as I do. *The New York Times Magazine,* September 26, 1976, *45,* 65-66.

Frankena, W. *Three historical philosophies of education*. Glenview, Illinois: Scott Foresman and Company, 1965.

Hare, R. M. *Freedom and reason*. New York: Oxford University Press, 1965.

Harmin, M., and Simon, S. B. Values. In *Readings in values clarification*. Minneapolis: Winton Press, 1973.

Kirschenbaum, H. Beyond values clarification. In (Ed.) *Readings in values clarification*. Minneapolis: Winton Press, 1973.

Kirschenbaum, H., and Simon, S. B. Values and the future's movement in education. In (Ed.) *Readings in values clarification*. Minneapolis: Winton Press, 1973.

Kohlberg, L. The child as moral philosopher. In *Readings in Psychology Today*. Del Mar, California: CRM Books, 1967.

Kohlberg, Lawerence. The claim to moral adequacy of a highest stage of moral judgement. *The Journal of Philosophy,* October 25, 1973, 10(18), 630-646.

Ledebur, Larry C. Value change in college and the impacts of simulations on value systems of students. Paper read at the Annual Meeting of the American Educational Research Association, New York, April, 1977.

Lisska, A. J. *Philosophy matters*. Columbus: Charles E. Merrill Publishing Company, 1977.

Purpel, D., and Ryan K., *Moral education . . . it comes with the territory*. Berkeley: McCutchan Publishing Corporation, 1976.

Stewart, John. Problems and contradictions of values clarification. *Phi Delta Kappan* (June, 1975), 684-87.

11

THE IMPACT OF SIMULATIONS ON VALUE SYSTEMS OF STUDENTS

LARRY C. LEDEBUR

ABSTRACT

This paper first argues that, generally, several points have been evaluated before any form of simulation was introduced into classrooms at Denison. These questions have concerned whether it was expected that simulation would produce the desired learning outcomes, whether simulation seemed consistent with the learning styles of the students involved, and whether simulation would be expected to impact the values held by participating students. This last question then provides a point of departure for describing some of the criticisms that have been made about what effects simulations might have upon the values structures of students. Finally, a concern for the educational desirability of placing students into simulations where a possibility for values changes exists is discussed in terms of three well-known games, Prisoner's Dilemma, Ghetto, and Diplomacy.

Introduction

Teachers, when considering the uses of simulations in their classrooms, should address four primary considerations:

1. *The effectiveness of simulations in achieving the desired learning outcomes.* This, essentially, is a question of the effectiveness of alternative pedagogical formats or approaches. Educational evaluation is, in general, at a fairly primitive level of development. What data are available to indicate that learning outcomes do not differ significantly regardless of the pedagogical approach utilized?

The Denison Simulation Program is predicated upon the careful evaluation of the learning effectiveness of simulation. Every faculty project funded was required to include an evaluation component. A professional in educational evaluation available to assist faculty in the evaluation of learning outcomes of simulations is a member of the staff of the simulation program. It now would be helpful if faculty not engaged in the use of simulation would undertake equally careful evaluations of the effectiveness of their primary teaching styles in achieving their designated learning outcomes.

2. *The appropriate use of simulations.* Simulation is one pedagogical approach in an array of alternative teaching formats and styles. The Denison Simulation Program carefully avoids the posture that simulation teaching is a preeminent or superior classroom approach. Rather, the program's premise is that every faculty member should have an array or repertoire of teaching techniques. A "needs analysis" should be undertaken to determine the desired learning outcomes for students, and these should be carefully matched with the pedagogical approach that most effectively achieves these designated goals. Therefore, throughout a particular course, a variety of teaching approaches would be used to achieve different learning objectives. The "appropriate" use of simulations would be in those situations in which a simulation would achieve the learning objectives more effectively than other alternatives.

3. *The compatability of preferred learning styles with pedagogical approaches.* To a significant degree, teaching in higher education is based primarily on the lecture-reading class format. This observation would lead one to the conclusion that this is the preferred or most effective learning style of students. If this is the case, it is probably because those whose learning strengths are in other pedagogical approaches either have been selected out, or, to survive, have been forced to adapt to learning in a less preferred style.

All students do not learn "best" in the same manner. They have strengths in some approaches and weaknesses in others. Just as faculty should develop a repertoire of teaching styles in which they are proficient, students should work toward achieving an array of learning styles or strengths. This makes it incumbent on colleges and universities to provide assistance to students in identifying their preferred learning styles or strengths and those in which they are less proficient, and to help the students to develop in their least preferred styles, converting weaknesses to strengths.

However, an effective teaching-learning environment will attempt, particularly in the early stages of the students' college experience, to match the students' preferred learning styles with the teaching formats. Thus, students who learned "in a particular style best" would be placed in a classroom format that emphasized that approach, rather than forcing all students with a variety of preferred formats into a single medium of classroom communication. This approach would improve the student's chances of achieving "successes" in the initial stages of her or his college experience.

The Denison Simulation Program is supporting research into the procedures for identifying preferred learning styles and matching these with classroom formats.

4. *The impact of simulations on the values and value systems of students.* Most types of learning experiences surely impact in some incremental manner on the learner's affective domain, the realm of values, attitudes, and emotions. Yet few teachers in higher education give any consideration to how the learning experiences they design affect students outside of the cognitive outcomes.

Even more infrequently is concern expressed about the impact in the affective domain of alternative pedagogical techniques or the ethical legitimacy of these methods.[1] With the possible exception of the mild furore over authoritarian teaching, the lecture format and passive learning by students, there is not a great deal of sustained and substantial concern about teaching "methodologies" beyond their effectiveness in achieving cognitive outcomes. It would be uncommon to hear discussions of the effects of lecture, Socratic dialogue, group discussions, and independent and self-paced learning on students' values. Where teachers are concerned about values, value questions, and students' growth as "valuing beings," "context" rather than "pedagogy" is considered as the prime vehicle.

One of the major claims of advocates of teaching through simulation is that this pedagogical approach does have significant impact in the affective domain. It places students in contrived situations in which they cannot remain passive and which force "behavioral" and "moral" choices that influence and/or reflect the students' ethical frame of reference and process of valuing.

The questions of evaluation, needs analysis, and learning styles are being addressed in varying degrees within the Denison Simulation Program. The impact of simulations on values and values systems of students is a component of the overall program of evaluation. The related question of the "ethics" of using simulations as a classroom teaching technique has not received attention. The purpose of the paper is to initiate this process.

The Context of the Issue

The issue of the "ethics" of teaching through simulations has been broached in the context of the obedience experiments conducted by Stanley Milgram at Yale University in the early 1960's. In the Milgram experiments, an external volunteer was assigned the role of "teacher," and a second individual was designated as the "learner." In actuality the "teacher" was the subject of the experiment, and unbeknown to him the "learner," rather than another volunteer, was an actor employed by the experimentation staff.

With the so-called learner strapped into a chair, the teacher was told to administer a learning test. Each time the learner answered incorrectly, he/she was to be administered an electric shock by the teacher with the voltage increasing with each wrong answer. While the teacher believed the shocks were administered, they were not actually given. The actor was trained to react in pain to each simulated shock.

The experiment was designed to determine whether the volunteer teacher, in deference to the authority of the experimenter and his instructions, would continue to administer shocks even though he or she believed the learner was experiencing pain and might be injured. The result was that sixty-five percent of the teachers continued to obey the experimenter's authority.

Concern has been expressed about the Milgram experiments, and the ethics of this kind of research, even though the shocks and subsequently expressed pain were only simulated. This, in turn, has raised questions about the "ethics" of simulations *per se.*

It appears that the critical link between the ethics of the obedience experiments and the simulations is whether the experiments were, indeed, a simulation. The confusion arises in part because of the lack of precision in the use of the term "simulation." Because the electrical shocks were not actually being administered, the responses of the persons supposedly experiencing the pain were "simulated." This is very general usage of the term.

The Milgram experiments, however, fail to meet the test of the basic criterion of a simulation. For a project or an experience to be categorized as a simulation *per se,* all participants must know that the "research" or "experience" is "not for real"; that there are no actual costs or risks human, physical, or structural. Therefore, participants can experiment with alternative behaviors or options with complete assurance that any and all outcomes are simulated and not real. Simulated trainers for airline pilots and driver trainees, mechanical and electronic manikins for medical and dental students, simulated urban systems for city planners, and education systems for potential teachers where the process is zero cost in terms of real outcomes are "simulations." Experiments such as Milgram's, in which participants were unaware that the shocks were not actually administered and the expressions of pain "simulated," are not "simulations." However, to dismiss the concern about the ethics of teaching through simulations that was expressed in the context of the obedience experiments by pointing out that the experiments were not simulations does not do justice to the sophistication of the argument. The essence of his concern, as I understand it, is that, even in simulated situations in which the participants fully realize, and perhaps because of this realization, that there are no actual costs or consequences, students may make decisions or behave in ways that contravene their basic values and beliefs. When, in retrospect, they realize what they have done and what they may be capable of doing in real situations, this realization may cause cynicism, self-doubt, and perhaps psychological harm. This is also the crux of the concern about the Milgram experiment. The situational context promotes and encourages behavior or actions that may cause psychological harm to the actor. In the experiment people learn that they have the capacity to hurt another when authority directs them to do so.

The Effect of Simulations on Value Systems of Students

The question of the possible impact of simulations on the affective domain of students, their morals, value systems, attitudes, and emotions is important and deserves close scrutiny. Whether simulation impacts more directly or in greater degree must be answered through careful evaluation of learning outcomes.

The question of whether it is educationally desirable or undesirable for students to be placed in simulated situations that possess the potential for these impacts can be addressed more directly. This task is difficult at the abstract or conceptual level. It is more effectively undertaken in the context of three relatively simple and commonly used simulations. These are described not to provide instructions for use, but to illustrate the underlying dynamics that influence behavior and choices.

1. *Prisoner's Dilemma.* Participants are divided into two groups. The terms "game" and "team" are not used, to avoid placing the exercise in a competitive context in the students' minds. The instructions are simple. In each round, each group passes to the other a slip of paper on which is written either "red" or "black." If both groups pass "black," each receives an equal number of points (+3). If both pass "red," each loses an equal number of points (−3). However, if one group passes "red" and the other passes "black," that group passing "red" receives a number of points (+5) that is greater than that obtained in a black-black combination (+3). The group passing "black" loses a number of points (−5) greater than that that lost in the red-red combination (−3).

The dynamics are obvious. By cooperating, the sum of the points of both groups combined will be the greatest. If, however, one group can pass "red" with the expectation of receiving "black," the potential exists for that group to maximize its total points even though the combined total of both groups is lower (a "beggar thy neighbor" process or policy).[2] Cooperative behavior will work to the benefit of the total population, while competitive decisions benefit only one group but result in lower and often negative net total points for the groups combined.

How should this simulation be evaluated in terms of the potential effect on a student's value system? Almost inevitably, one group begins to act competitively, violating trust and seeking a win-lose solution. Might then participation in this simulation be detrimental or pejorative to a student's growth as a valuing being?

a. Clearly the point allocation system creates an initiative to engage in competitive win-lose behavior, especially for those who do not think through the allocation system and possible outcomes of these actions. The pattern that most frequently emerges is for one group to act competitively, with the other attempting to develop trust through cooperative behavior. Failure to elicit reciprocal cooperative decisions usually results in a change to red-red or lose-lose exchanges. After a few rounds of both groups losing points, groups usually realize the futility of this pattern and tentatively move towards a win-win or black-black pattern.[3] In other words, *the process dynamics have focused the adverse consequences of competitive behavior that results in retaliation and lose-lose outcomes and caused each group to move to a cooperative model.*[4]

b. Yet the simulation has created at least the permissive circumstances for some students to engage in competitively cutthroat behavior. Is this behavior immoral or harmful to the student? In part, the answer to this question depends upon the philosophy and ethical system of the individual making the judgment. Undoubtedly, there are those who would sanction competitive behavior even when it is uncritical and detrimental in the aggregate. Others, with differing value systems and perceptions, are condemnatory of many or most aspects of competitive behavior. Hence, this question, for present purposes, is not explored very fruitfully at this level.

It is pertinent whether the behavior observed is simply a result of the "gaming" situation or really reflects an acculturated behavior pattern of the student. In Western cultures, particularly in the United States, children, especially males, are inculcated with strong competitive drives. It is unlikely that competitiveness would surface in a simulation if this characteristic was contrary to existing cultural mores.

However, even if only gaming behavior, the simulation provides the student with an opportunity to experiment with behavior patterns and provides immediate feedback on consequences. In Prisoner's Dilemma, the point system focuses the shortcomings of "beggar thy neighbor" policies, and the realization and understanding of these consequences can be analyzed in the simulation discussion and debriefing. Careful debriefing is an essential component of teaching and learning through simulation.

The use of a simulation such as Prisoner's Dilemma permits the instructor to observe the behavior of the student. One of the risks that the student realizes is absent from a simulation exercise is that he or she will be evaluated on the basis of his or her interaction and decisions. One of the major "games" played by students in the traditional classroom is providing the instructor with only the feedback they perceive he or she wishes to hear. Where this occurs, the instructor loses the opportunity to analyze and discuss with students their actual attitudes and proclivities. Because simulation provides the opportunity for immediate behavior and feedback, which the instructor can observe, a significant educational opportunity is created. *In other classroom formats, such as group discussion, the instructor may not be able to identify a particular attitude or proclivity and examine it with the student because of students' filtering their feedback.*

It should be evident that the comparison between Milgram's obedience experiments and a simulation such as *Prisoner's Dilemma* is not particularly germane. Student participants realize that the costs in the simulation are not for real. It is unlikely that students will be psychologically affected by the realization that they have contravened their value systems because of the "gaming" aspect of the simulation. Conversely, there appears to be a rich potential for generating circumstances in which value questions can be discussed in a context meaningful and relevant to the students' behavior.

2. *Ghetto.* The simulation is somewhat more involved, although not complex. It attempts to simulate a ghetto environment and the overwhelming difficulties involved in improving the individual's socioeconomic circumstances and earning power, and wider community quality and welfare.[5] The structure of *Ghetto* is difficult to describe in a cursory manner. Each participant is assigned a profile of a ghetto resident, giving sex, age, number of children, education, and earning power. Earnings are determined by education level achieved and time available for work or education. For example, a female with children has fewer hours to work or go to school unless she has the resources to pay for child care.

In each round participants allocate their resources (time or hours of the day) among school, work, community development, or "hustling." "Hustling" is any criminal activity. It has a relatively high payoff, but also a risk of getting caught and penalized. Residents can increase the probability of hustlers getting caught by investing in community welfare. These investments, however, entail the necessity of sufficient resources being mobilized from residents. To contribute these resources to cooperative community development efforts, participants must reduce their individual effort at personal advancement.

For every individual who hustles in a round, there must be a victim. Victims are identified on a random draw basis. The consequences of being victimized range from a loss of resources to loss of jobs and education advancement because of injuries.

Finally, there are a series of random events that affect outcomes. Women in each round may have additional children. This is determined on a probability basis and the roll of a die. Other random events are either adverse or beneficial.

It is extremely difficult to succeed in this simulation or even to make significant progress because of the low payoffs to education and work, the improbability of achieving sufficient cooperation for the necessary community development, and the frequent setbacks that are encountered. In short, it is a good simulation of some aspects of the ghetto environment.

The dynamics of *Ghetto* follow a predictable pattern. Participants quickly become frustrated. The options are limited, the obstacles formidable, the setbacks frequent. They become angry at a system that forces them into hustling simply to survive, although some go into crime because of the higher returns.

The level of emotion generated is often quite high. A high degree of empathy for ghetto dwellers and an understanding of their circumstances develops, which is extremely difficult to replicate through other types of educational experiences. The simulation is effectively debriefed both at the level of feelings and attitudes and the alternatives available to inner-city residents.

The empathy, the effect on attitudes, and the emotions generated by *Ghetto* are highly positive educational attributes. But are there negative features? One, and perhaps the most serious, is the level and quality of humor that can develop if not carefully monitored, although this, in part, is a means of relief from the tension that is created. Also the dynamics and structure of the simulation force participants into "hustling" and activity that, it is hoped, is antithetical to the value systems and moral precepts of those involved in the experience. It is unlikely that this has a negative impact on their development as moral, valuing beings. On the other hand, the empathy and understanding that result would seem to contribute to their growth in personal and social values.

3. *Diplomacy.* This is a simulation of the historical preconditions of World War I and the dynamics that detemined the course of the war. It examines the military power and geographical features of the countries of Europe that generated coalitions, determined strategy, and influenced the nature of diplomacy prior to and during World War I. It is particularly useful in focusing the effects of geographical access, natural barriers, and contiguity and propinquity of countries.

The simulation does not replicate necessarily the actual conditions and dynamics of World War I. Rather, it illustrates the forces that were at work, the exercise of international power politics, and the national need for establishing geographical buffers to protect a country's boundaries.

The decisions that are made and the behavior generated in the course of *Diplomacy* are nationalistic, emphasizing vested interests, imperialistic and aggressive. Once war has broken out, the primary emphasis is upon becoming victor.

The behavior induced is self-serving and productive of the tensions and mistrust that create and sustain war as a solution to international conflicts of interest. The question then becomes pertinent whether participants are affected adversely in their growth as moral "beings."

The benefits to the participants are a level of understanding of and a sense and feel for the dynamics and preconditions of World War I that would be difficult to achieve in other contexts. The simulation has reflected actual historical processes, if not actual circumstances. In a sense the participants have relived, in some degree, the historical context. It would seem difficult for an educator then to argue that participation in the simulation has an adverse impact on the student. The realization of the consequences of these actions and the instability of world order should contribute to the education of a "moral" person who can function realistically and idealistically in an imperfect world and imperfect society.

Perspective and Conclusions

Liberal arts colleges should differentiate their mission and goals from those of the large university. If they attempt only to fulfill the functions that larger educational institutions can accomplish more economically, and perhaps better because of greater resources, it is inevitable that liberal arts colleges will suffer in the competition to attract students.

A frequent assertion for distinctive education in the small college of liberal arts is that students' lives are enriched through growth in their value systems and development of their capacity to live and function as ethical beings. Most teachers in these colleges accept as an article of faith that the liberal arts experience has a "liberalizing" (in the historical sense of the word) effect on the ethics and value systems of students. Yet studies of the effects of a liberal arts education on students' values indicate that little or no change occurs during these years.

Few faculty seem aware that this claim to distinction is not validated in fact. Most appear reluctant to explore ways in which learning and developing in the affective domain can be stimulated and encouraged.

One strong hope for simulation as a teaching technique is that it can impact meaningfully in the realm of value, attitudes, and emotions. Refined and careful evaluation of simulations is needed to determine the degree of "affective" learning that can result from their use in the classroom. Noting, however, that the potential exists and that the actual learning outcomes have not been validated through careful evaluation, the question of attendant "risks" or detrimental consequences to the student is appropriately raised.

Not all simulations are good. Many suffer from flawed design and faulty dynamics. Others are simply frivolous, addressing inconsequential subjects, and oriented more to the fun and excitement of play rather than meaningful learning outcomes. Some are "bad" in the sense that what they teach is incorrect and not in correspondence with reality, or are unethical and detrimental to students' development as persons capable of "liberated" ethical reasoning. This is not unique to simulation. The same is true of all forms of educational materials and classrooms. Judgment must be used in the selection of all teaching materials.

Given the use of judgment in the selection of simulations, a tentative conclusion can be registered that "good" simulations will not affect negatively the student's ethical development; rather, simulation may represent a potential pedagogical approach for focusing some part of the student's education on value questions in a manner that may generate at least incremental change in their value systems, a "liberalizing" experience in the affective domain. This judgment is a personal one, based primarily on my own experience in using teaching simulations. I have attempted, in an imperfect manner, to identify the basis for this conclusion by examining the structure and dynamics of the three simulations, *Prisoner's Dilemma, Ghetto,* and *Diplomacy.*

This conclusion, however, is not unqualified. There appears to be some basis for concern about the impact of even "good" simulations on students. The observation of behavior and decisions in simulations may result in a degree of cynicism and a tempering of idealism about human motivation and goals. To the degree that this serves to generate realism and increase the student's effectiveness in working to improve the world in which we live, this is desirable. But to the degree that this tempering of idealism diminishes motivation to work for the goals the student believes desirable, it is unfortunate. The risk of working with students to achieve greater realism and perspective is that of encouraging a cynical pragmatism. Experience beyond college often has this effect as well. Perhaps it is better that students confront this in a controlled environment in which the influence of the teacher can be helpful in achieving a sense of balance and perspective. This again points to the importance of careful debriefing as a component of simulations.

NOTES

1. The term "ethical" is used here to refer to systems or principles of morality. "Moral" refers to the concern for "right conduct" in behavior.
2. The question at issue is not whether Prisoner's Dilemma is effective relative to other approaches for illustrating particular points or

concepts. I personally feel it is and have used it as a technique of raising such issues as aculturated competitiveness, mutuality and cooperation, trust and trust building, as well as the dynamics of groups. Obviously, the simulation raises a number of questions germane to economic systems.

3. With the exception of the last round, when students tend to engage in end-game strategies. This is easily handled by not announcing that it is the last round and terminating the simulation unexpectedly.

4. In most cases, movement to a win-win strategy results because of recognition of self-interest rather than idealism or humanitarianism. This is a merit of the simulation for those who wish an approximation of reality in the learning experience. For those who wish to focus on moral behavior and idealism in the learning experience, the simulation provides an excellent focuser, and value questions can be extensively examined in the debriefing period.

5. In many ways this is one of the most effective simulations I have used in the classroom.

Part VIII
GEOGRAPHY

The paper that follows summarizes an interesting and unusual approach to simulation. The technique, developed by Robert E. Nunley, involves the use of an analog field plotter which allows graphic representations of three-dimensional processes. The applications described in the paper are for geographic phenomena, but the possible generalizations to other kinds of phenomena are myriad. The authors invite those who are interested in this form of simulation to inquire for further information.

12

DYNAMIC, MULTIDIMENSIONAL EDUCATION AND THE ECSTASY OF FIELD PLOTTER SIMULATION

Larry K. Laird
Robert E. Nunley

ABSTRACT

This paper will introduce an analog modeling technique developed by Robert E. Nunley, of the University of Kansas, to describe geographic and historical phenomena.[1]

Using visual simulations, television weather forecasters attempt to explain national, regional, and local weather patterns. Forecasters describe dynamic processes (changing centers of high and low pressure) moving over a curved, two-dimensional surface. Thus, they anticipate weather changes at different scales, or levels. Weather forecasters must communicate the dynamic phenomena they observe to an essentially untrained audience. More specifically, they have the task of describing a multidimensional, dynamic process to people accustomed to dealing primarily with one-dimensional, static situations. They use a weather map with changing symbols and an occasional satellite photograph and hope for viewer understanding. The forecaster's weather "simulation" would be better understood by all if our educational systems emphasized discovery learning about multidimensional, dynamic processes.

One of the largest areas of study available to us involves graphic simulations of multidimensional processes. Some academic disciplines have extensive experience using multidimensional processes. Sculptors, silversmiths, and architects work primarily with three and four dimensions. Painters, weavers, earth scientists, and civil engineers work primarily with two or three dimensions. Perhaps the disciplines achieving the most comprehensive understanding have been the more art-oriented ones, where neither words nor formulae are used to describe the processes depicted. The works of art speak for themselves. In contrast, architects, earth scientists, and civil engineers tend to take partial and specialized views that utilize words and formulae to describe "rational" process. Both academic approaches have merit and we can get much needed guidance from both.

To achieve multidimensional education effectively, we need more than guidance—we need concepts and simulation equipment that can serve as intelligence amplifiers, freeing our minds from the mathematical computations involved in order to concentrate our attention on the overall processes depicted. Such concepts and equipment also need to have the ability to combine several individual and apparently different multidimensional processes and treat them as more general cases.

The present article treats one such concept and a related piece of equipment—field theory and the analog field plotter.[2] The simulations completed in module two of the workshop were predicated on this theory and equipment—field theory and the analog field plotter. Its application to a large variety of multidimensional processes in the earth sciences is demonstrated, including speculation as to how it might be applied to disciplines other than earth sciences. Our goal is to involve you in playing around with these kinds of concepts and equipment, feeding back to us your experiences; that way the application can be made even more general. We would also like to encourage the development of similar concepts and devices.

I. *What Is a Field Plotter?*

A field plotter is a very simple-to-operate analog computer. The field plotter under discussion here might more properly be referred to as an electrically conductive sheet analog. It involves representing a two-dimensional surface by a sheet of carbon-impregnated paper that permits the flow of electrons as readily in any one direction as any other. The sheet can be grounded at the margins or at any point on the sheet. At up to nine input points (15 on the larger model) electrons can be fed into the sheet.[3] The relative number of electrons fed in at each point can be controlled very accurately.

The movements of electrons set up a pressure (potential) that varies from place to place on the sheet. The plotter can be readily calibrated for diverse arrangements of locations and strengths of inputs in such a way that the maximum pressure in the sheet is set to 100. The pressure at the ground, by definition, is always 0. Therefore, the pressure anywhere other than at a ground or the point of maximum pressure on a calibrated configuration will be between 0 and 100 and is, thus, an expression of the percentage of the pressure found at that point of maximum pressure.

Thus, on a sheet of paper 13″×16″, one is permitted to make inputs of various strengths, generate a pressure (potential) surface, and then probe that sheet to find the relative value of pressure (potential) at any point or to draw contours that connect points of the same value. The field plotter permits various techniques to be used either to retard or expedite the flow of electrons, offering a very powerful instrument for simulating diffusion over nonuniform two-dimensional space.

II. *What Can Be Simulated on a Field Plotter?*

If one desires a perfect simulation without any error whatsoever, the only process that can be simulated by the field plotter is electrons flowing through a conductive sheet of paper. That is, it is a perfect simulation only of itself. But, at that level, it is very much worth studying. After all, at a most general level we are concerned with the behavior of energy in space and this is a special case of energy (electrical) diffusing over a two-dimensional space, under very complete operator control. We can draw an initial potential surface; make a change in the input, ground, or conductive pattern; draw the altered potential surface; and compare the initial surface with the altered one and know that the difference is due to the change we induced. We can repeat the experiment for verification, we can have others replicate the experiment, and we can observe the results in a maplike form without having to describe them with one-dimensional written language. There is no "Society for the Prevention of Cruelty to Electrons" so we are free to move them about with almost complete abandon and, in the process, learn an enormous amount about one kind of energy diffusing through one form of multidimensional space.

The field plotter can be used to simulate a large number of processes with very little error in an almost perfect analogy. These include processes already well enough studied scientifically to be demonstrably capable of being simulated. Many ground water problems, for example, have a perfect analogy with the field plotter. That is, we can demonstrate that the mathematical description of the behavior of each parameter of the ground water problem is matched by one and only one parameter of identical mathematical description in the electrically conductive sheet (Mack, 1957). Consequently, the analogy is one to one. For those interested in the mathematics, the field plotter turns out to yield a solution to the Poisson equation[4] or, in the special case of inputs and ground being at the margins of the paper, the Laplace equation.[5] Because of this strict mathematical interpretation every time the probe indicates the percentage of pressure at a point it is yielding the answer to a very complex mathematical solution without the operator's having to be even conscious of the mathematics. Also, there are numerous physical processes that are described by the same math and, thus, can be directly simulated—heat transfer, fluid flow, electrostatics, electrodynamics, mechanical statistics, mechanical dynamics, electromagnetics, magnetics, gravity, and electricity (Nunley, 1971).

By going one step further and relaxing insistence on a strict analogy, the kinds of processes that can be simulated by the field plotter become virtually unlimited. It requires a Kierkegaardian "mad leap of faith" into the world of analogy but it is exciting and rewarding. While solving a given problem one may not attain the accuracy desired for pure research purposes, but one will surely create an heuristic device that gives considerable insight into the problem being studied. One may start exploring how electrons move around the sheet of conductive paper and how that process relates to how people move about the surface of the earth (Nunley, Sabol, and Youngman, 1969). Such processes are not described well enough mathematically to permit a strict analogy to be established in any event. And such processes are not limited to the social sciences; we are not able to describe glacial flow well enough to establish a strict analogy, but the conductive sheet analog has been used to simulate glacial flow (MacKay, 1965). It can be used to simulate the height and pattern and waves that are generated by dropping stones in a pool of water and, consequently, can be used to simulate any of the processes that have been simulated by the dropping of stones in water—trade areas of cities, gravitational attraction, and rural land use (Morgan, 1967).

III. *In What Form Must Processes Be Stated for Simulation?*

The field plotter simulates "systems of energy on a two-dimensional surface," which we call here "Cartesian processes." It turns out that virtually all such Cartesian processes may be described in terms of three concepts: (1) the propogation of influences from one or more discrete sources, (2) as modified by properties of areas surrounding the sources, .and (3) to produce a varied pattern of effects throughout the area. These three basic concepts are difficult to state in more rigorous terms, so your indulgence is required. If you find this more rigorous statement too boring, just skip to the next section and, perhaps, come back and give it a try later on. "The *first* concept is the influence(s) that relate(s) some point(s), line(s), area(s), or combinations thereof to all or part of the surrounding area and/or other areas. The *second* concept is the characteristics of the surrounded area and/or areas that act as barriers or expediters to the influence(s). The *third* concept is that of variation in the resulting effect on all or part of the surrounding area and/or other areas. Each concept, to be appreciated adequately, needs to be considered separately.

"1. The influence(s) that relate(s) some point(s), line(s), or some combination thereof to all or part of the surrounding area and/or other areas is the primary of the three concepts. If every aspect of a phenomenon is passive, it can have no . . . (significance in terms of Cartesian processes) . . .—effect on anything located elsewhere. If any aspect of a phenomenon exerts an influence, then that phenomenon possesses . . . (significance in terms of Cartesian processes) . . .—it must have some effect on something elsewhere. The phenomenon that has . . . (significance in terms of Cartesian processes) . . .—may still be insignificant in any practical problem. The task is to define for a given problem the principal aspects of phenomena under study that exert influence at a distance. . . .

"2. Once the influence(s) is (are) identified, the characteristics of the surrounding area and/or other areas that act as barriers or expediters must be studied. Distance by itself is always something of a barrier to any influence, and it, therefore, is the basic ingredient in the uniform-plane assumption, which is another way of saying 'other things being equal.' But, in real life the uniform-plane never exists: therefore the principal barriers and expediters should be isolated and studied. . . . Once the barriers and expediters have been simulated, it is desirable to return to the uniform-plane assumption to gain a grasp of the fundamental pattern.

"3. Wherever there is motion, there are barriers and expediters; therefore, variation will occur in the resulting impact of the motion on all or part of the surrounding area and any other area affected. The variation may be expressed in terms of potential. *Potential* is here defined in terms of mathematics and physics—any of certain functions from which the intensity (or, in some cases, the velocity) at any point in a field may be readily calculated. If the motion and the barriers and expediters are known, then it is possible, at least theoretically, to compute the potential. For even simple problems, however, an analytical solution is difficult. For any set of motions, barriers, and expediters simulated on the field plotter, a potential surface is produced that is accurate with a negligible error factor. That is, if the influence(s), barrier(s), and expediters are properly simulated, then the potential (spatial variation in impact) will be accurate" (Nunley, 1969).

Needless to say, not all Cartesian processes can be simulated effectively on the field plotter. Many are too complex. Some are understood only in a probabilistic way and the field plotter yields a deterministic solution. Still others are poorly understood and more detailed understanding must be achieved before effective simulation can be achieved. Nevertheless, many Cartesian processes can be simulated effectively.

In general, the field plotter may be used to simulate effectively some aspects of most Cartesian processes, most aspects of some Cartesian processes, and all aspects of some. First, the parameters of any problem need to be grouped into the three concepts of motion, barriers and expediters, and potential (either intensity or velocity). Then, within any one concept, the parameters may be treated individually or collapsed into a smaller number; often into a single parameter. Parsimony is especially significant in simulation—the smaller the number of parameters used to achieve effective simulation, the easier it is to accept and learn from the results.

IV. *Nine Groups of Models*

The following conceptual and theoretical models provide an adequate explanation of field theory and field plotter operations to give you an idea of how changes in inputs, grounds, barriers, or expediters cause changes in the potential surface. They begin very simply and then get more complex.

1. *One Central Input with Four Different Grounded Barriers*

Potential, in the vicinity of the largest inputs, depends almost exclusively on the value of the input, but, in the rest of the field, it varies with the type of boundary condition employed. The simplest model has one input in the middle of a conductive sheet and a grounded boundary around the margins of the rectangular sheet of conductive paper (see Figure 1-a). The 10% line (connecting all points that have a potential 10% of the potential at the main input) tends to conform to the shape of the outer grounded boundary; the 20% and higher contours tend to form concentric circles. The cross-sectional profile beneath each model should help you visualize the distribution of values across the potential surface. The ground wire around the whole field under study simulates an absolute boundary that permits no influence to go beyond the boundary, permits no influence to come in from beyond the boundary, and forces values to be low in the vicinity of the grounded boundary. Contours tend to run parallel to grounded boundaries.

When some sides of the rectangular sheet of conductive paper are left ungrounded the total pattern is much affected. When three sides are grounded and one not (Figure 1-b) the values will remain much higher at the ungrounded margin. When the top and left margins are left ungrounded (Figure 1-c) the energy is even less efficiently dissipated and, consequently, potentials are even higher. When all margins but the bottom one are ungrounded (Figure 1-d) low values (10% or less) are found only in the immediate vicinity of the grounded bottom margin. Observe how the profiles below 1-b and 1-c indicate increasing values

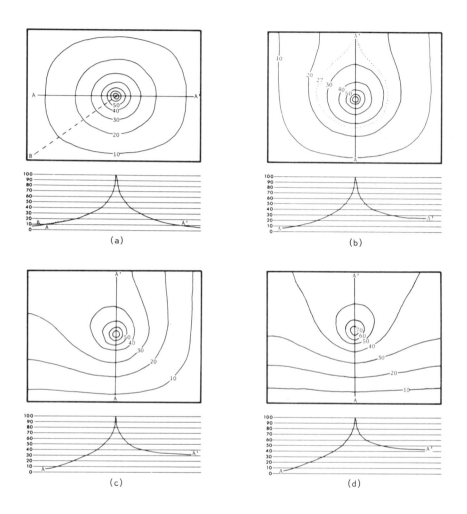

FIGURE 1

One Central Input With Four Different Grounded Barriers. Figure 1-a is grounded on all four sides; 1-b is ungrounded at the top; 1-c is ungrounded at the top and left side; and 1-d is grounded only on the bottom margin. The cross-sectional profile should facilitate the visualization of the form of the potential surface.

183

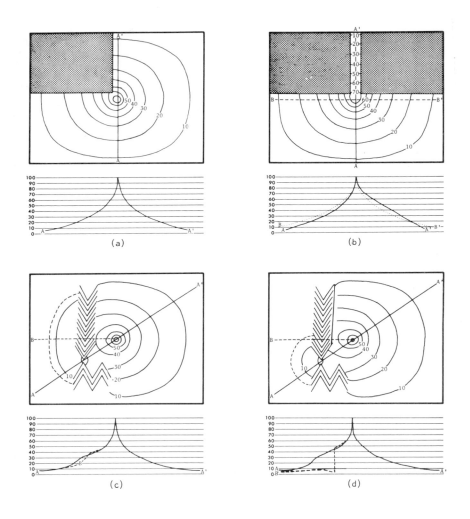

FIGURE 2

One Central Input With Four Different Sets of Barriers. Figure 2-a has an absolute barrier blocking out most of the upper left quadrant; 2-b has an additional such barrier in the upper right; 2-c has two partial barriers—a single one and a double one; while 2-d has the single partial boundary of 2-c converted into an absolute barrier.

with fewer grounded margins. Note also on these last three models that contours intersect ungrounded boundaries at right angles. Look back over the first four models and observe how the patterns of potential are affected by changes in exterior boundary conditions.

2. *One Central Input with Four Different Sets of Barriers*

Absolute barriers may be made in the models just by cutting the paper. If most of the upper left quarter of a sheet were removed while leaving one central input and grounded margins (Figure 2-a), the values would not be much changed along the cross-sectional profile. But when a similar such block is removed from the upper right quarter as well (Figure 2-b), then the change is quite significant. Because the energy in the bottom of the model (2-b), as well as the energy in all previous models, can diffuse over a two-dimensional surface, the potential values fall off as of the inverse of distance squared (d^2)! In the top of model 2-b, however, beyond the 70% contour the energy can diffuse only along a one-dimensional strip and the potential drop is linear $(d^1 = d)$. From B to B' the energy can diffuse more readily than at the top but less readily than at the bottom and so it has a distance decay function to $(d^{1.5})$. The profiles tell the story.

Partial barriers may also be erected. By cutting "V-shaped" slits in the paper (as in Figure 2-C) it is possible to lengthen the path that electrons must take. Note that the 10% potential contour in the left part of the model is roughly where the 15% contour would be if the partial barrier were not there. Also note how the "M-shaped" slits in the lower part of the model are a more effective barrier than the inverted "V-shaped" slits because they are longer and because they are not oriented directly in the path of electron flow (which is always at right angles to the potential contours). The effect of the partial barrier is made clearer if the paper is cut along the right-hand side of the inverted "V-shaped" slits (Figure 2-d). That is now an absolute barrier and the potential extending through the gap between it and the "M-shaped" barrier is quite conspic-uous. The smaller area included within the 10% contour line on the left side of 2-d, in comparison with the larger amount in 2-c, is due completely to the barrier erected to the right of the "V-shaped" slits. Observe on the profiles how in 2-d the potential actually increases at one point with straight-line distance away from the center.

3. *One Central Input and Four Different Sets of Expediters*

Expediters can be erected that extend the higher potential values a greater distance from the inputs. Carbon paint adds the conductive element (carbon) to any part of the paper where it is applied. One coat of carbon paint not reaching ground (expediter A in Figure 3-a), causes the values to increase slightly (the dotted line in the profile of 3-a). Two coats of paint extending all the way to ground (expediter B) cause an even greater increase in potential along its route. Three coats of carbon paint extend-

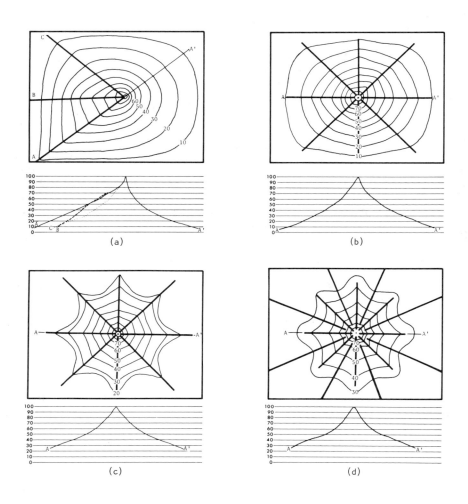

FIGURE 3

One Central Input and Four Different Sets of Expediters. Figure 3-a has a weak expediter (A) not reaching ground, one (B) reaching ground, a moderate one (B) reaching ground, and a strong one (C) reaching ground; 3-b has eight weak expediters; 3-c has eight strong expediters; and 3-d has eight strong expediters interspersed with expediters extending in from the ground.

ing all the way to ground (expediter *C*) cause the electrons to flow along
it so effectively that the spacing of potential is almost perfectly linear.
That means that it behaves almost like the strip in the top of Model 2-b.

Eight expediters radiating from the center but not going all the way
to ground (Figure 3-b) produce a pattern not greatly different from our
initial pattern, Figure 1-a. Yet there is a tendency for the contours to be
straight lines between the expediters. The nonsymmetrical nature of the
potential pattern is owing to the unevenness of the carbon paint; it is
difficult to apply a perfectly even amount of such paint. When additional
coats are applied to the expediter the contours between expediters get
straighter and straighter and the 10% contour becomes concave (Figure
3-c). When the eight expediters are made to straddle partial grounds,
even the higher value contours become concave (Figure 3-d). By changing the location, number of coats, grounding, and other conditions of
expediters it is possible to produce a wide variety of patterns of potential
(2-a,b,c, and d). Such changes can be made primarily on the basis of
intuition; in almost every instance a modification to the model will do
what you intuitively feel it will do.

4. *Four Cases of Multiple Inputs*

Up until now we have looked only at models with a single input;
we now turn our attention to multiple inputs. Two inputs of the same
strength located the same distance from the four grounded margins
(Figure 4-a) produce a nice symmetrical pattern. What pattern have
we already seen that looks most like it? Look only at the left half.
Compare the left half only with Figure 1-b. The 41% supplementary
contour occupies a similar position on 4-a to that which the 27% contour occupies in 1-b. The ungrounded boundary is a "reflective" boundary that throws back onto the field the energy it would receive if the
field were extended in area and the potential beyond the boundary were
mirrored back and added to the normal potential. Four inputs of the
same strength greatly increase the amount of energy in the system
(Figure 4-b). The slopes are steeper and the lowest potential value on
the plateau between the inputs is over 40%, whereas on 4-a it was less
than 40%.

Inputs do not have to be of the same value and they do not
have to be symmetrically located. Two randomly located and randomly
sized inputs (Figure 4-c) produce a pattern that should correspond to
what you would expect intuitively. If Figure 4-c, or any other model,
produces an output that does not agree with your intuition, ponder it
for a while. Most who ponder this come to recognize the error of thought
that led them to disagree. The cross-sectional profile is particularly helpful. In addition to permitting the plotting of the contours for potential,
the field plotter also permits the delimiting of gravity fields or spheres of

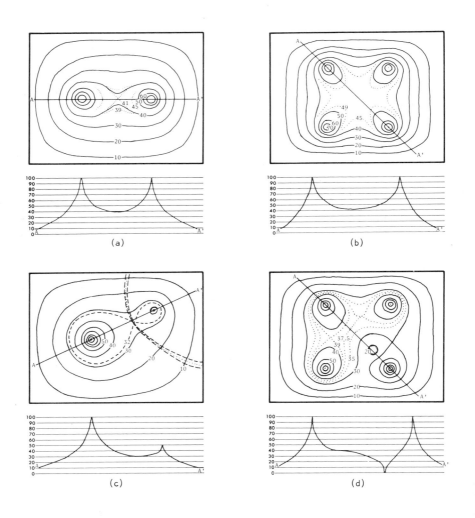

FIGURE 4

Four Cases of Multiple Inputs. Figure 4-a has two inputs of equal strength; 4-b has four inputs of equal strength; 4-c has two inputs of unequal strength, with the demarcation of the region of dominance of each; while 4-d is identical to 4-b except a point ground has been added.

188

influence, assuming that we are looking at two heavenly bodies and that the inputs are proportional to the mass.

Another modification of the inputs is to model places that not only do not attract but actively repel. By adding to the inputs of 4-6 a point ground (Figure 4-d) we force a zero potential in the center of the surface. Notice that it pulls a lot of energy from the overall model, as you would expect. The 30% contour barely encompasses all four inputs, whereas the 40% contour easily encompasses all the inputs on 4-b. Compare the two profiles.

5. *Flow Phenomena*

Inputs to the sheet of conductive paper do not have to be points; they can be lines or areas and they can be located at the margins. A line input all along the left margin and a line ground along the right margin produce a simple flow problem. The cross-sectional profile has a different interpretation than that of our first four sets of models. Now the slope of the line reflects the velocity of flow—steep slopes represent rapid flow, while gentle slopes represent slow flow. Because there is very little change of slope in this profile we are modeling flow of uniform velocity.

In addition to velocity, the models can reveal the most likely paths of flow around obstacles. By putting a line input all along the top, a ground all along the bottom, and a grounded strip all along a barrier to flow (Figure 5-a), the potential lines can be interpreted as the most likely paths of flow, or streamlines. Notice how the streamlines run parallel to grounded barriers in the interior of the field just as they did with grounded boundaries at the margins.

The barriers affect the velocity of flow, obviously, and that, too, may be modeled. By making the inputs the same as Figure 5-a, and cutting the conductive paper at the site of the barriers that we grounded in 5-b, we can simulate streamlines (see Figure 5-c). Remembering the interpretation of the profile, trace paths *A, B,* and *C.* Notice how the flow along *A* slows as the two barriers are approached and then speeds up as it moves between them. Path *C* is even more pronounced in that way, while path *B* is less affected. Note that the potential lines intersect the ungrounded boundaries at right angles as in previous models.

By combining the two previous models we create a most significant set of curvilinear squares (5-d). In a purely electrical sense, each of the squares will contain approximately the same number of electrons. Because the number of electrons is constant, then any variation in size of the square is a direct indicator of variation in the density—the large squares have few electrons and thus low density, and vice versa. The analogy holds for any other phenomena as well.

A wide variety of flow phenomena can be modeled. By making the width of the paper proportional to the width times the average depth

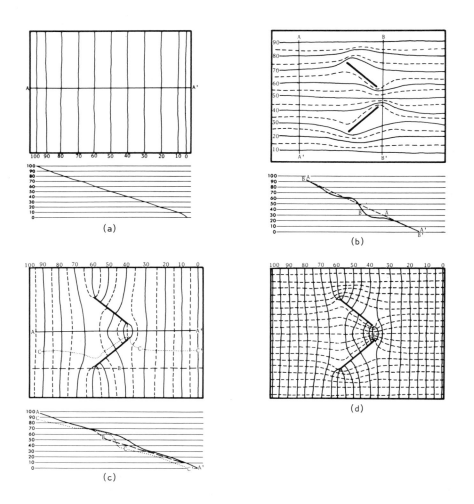

FIGURE 5

Flow Phenomena. Figure 5-a has an input all along the left margin with the right margin grounded; 5-b has the input along the top, a ground along the bottom, and two grounded barriers; 5-c is like 5-a except the two barriers are cut out of the conductive paper; and 5-d combines 5-b and 5-c to form curvilinear squares that permit a potent density interpretation.

190

of the stream and its tributaries, very realistic stream simulations can be achieved. Wind tunnels with obstructions and numerous other such flow processes can be modeled in this fashion.

6. *Gravity Models and Dominance Regions*

Figure 4-c touched upon gravity models and dominance regions; we now take a closer look. Theory suggests that, if heavenly bodies were lying in a plane, all of them the same size and distributed according to the closest-packing principle (the same way you rack pool balls or space bowling balls), the resulting dominance regions, except near the boundary (where the closest-packing principle does not hold), would be in the shape of hexagons as in Figure 6-a. (Notice that on these kinds of models each point is solved in relation to its closer neighbors and the limits of nine to fifteen inputs do not hold.)

By leaving sizes the same and changing spacing, some interesting changes result. By moving alternate rows up one inch (Figure 6-b) the hexagons become less regular. Further departures from the closest-packing principle (6-c and 6-d) lead to highly irregular hexagons and, finally, pentagons, and octagons. By further change, aligning most along a straight line (Figure 6-e), rectangles emerge for the first time. Removing a few inputs from the straight line (6-f) causes the rectangles to drop out. All the boundaries remain nearly straight lines as long as the size of the bodies is kept constant.

By leaving the spacing the same and varying the size of only one body a different set of changes results. Returning to the closest-packing principle and a hexagonal pattern of twelve neighboring bodies (six in an inner ring and six in an outer ring) around one central body, when all the bodies are considered to be the same size we get perfect hexagons once again (6-g). When the neighboring bodies are considered to be only three-fourths as large as the central one (6-h), then the central body extends its boundaries to a minimum amount along a straight line from it to any one of the inner six neighbors, while extending a maximum amount along a line from it to one of the outer six that runs midway between two inner neighbors. The result is a hexagon with gently arching boundaries instead of the straight boundaries of models 6-a through 6-f. As the neighboring bodies are considered to be one-half and then one-fourth as large as the central body (6-i and 6-j), the central body extends its gravitational influence over more at the expense of the inner ring of neighbors. As they are considered to be one-tenth and then one-twentieth as large as the central body (6-k and 6-l), the inner ring at first no longer has a common boundary with each other and, then, no longer has a common boundary with the outer ring; the inner ring ends up being embedded in the dominance region of the large central body. The dominance regions of the outer ring are also being separated.

By leaving the spacing the same and varying the size of several

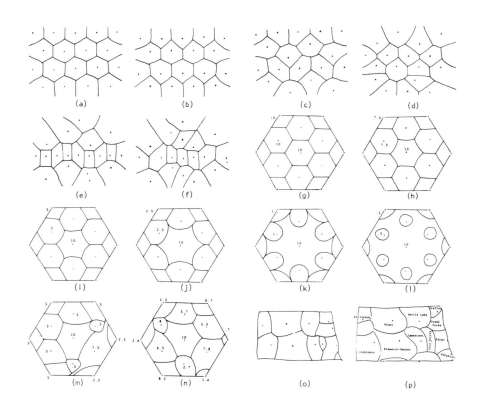

FIGURE 6

Gravity Models and Dominance Regions. When the centers are the same size and spaced according to the closest packing principles (6-a), the pattern is a hexagon. As size is held constant while spacing is varied (6-b through 6-f), other forms appear. As spacing is held constant and size is varied (6-g through 6-n), curved boundaries emerge. Varying size and spacing (6-o) permit real-world simulation (6-p).

bodies the pattern of dominance is most instructive. By assigning sizes to the neighbors of one-fourth, one-half, and three-fourths that of the main body (6-m), the regions of dominance take on quite varied shapes. When the neighbors are assigned random values (6-n), even more varied shapes result.

By varying both location and size at the same time, a complex set of shapes results. To think of the principal cities in a state as if they were heavenly bodies and to consider their areas of dominance in, say, retail trade as being analogous to those gravitational regions we have been developing, the area can be readily modeled. If, for North Dakota, we were to space the inputs according to the eleven largest towns and set the strength of each input proportional to the size of the town, a pattern of such urban dominance would result (6-o). When compared with a map of trade centers and trade areas derived from field studies (6-p) (Borchert and Adams, 1963), the similarities are striking. The main deviations were a result of the influence of towns outside the state not considered in model 6-n. Even so, our own limited checking of the discrepancies indicated that the theoretical model was right and the empirical study may be wrong!

In any event, the simulation of such complex gravity models and the resulting dominance regions is a giant step in the direction of dynamic, multidimensional education. To be able to hold all but one set of theoretical assumptions constant while varying that one, then to vary another while holding the first constant, then to vary both combined to give one a thorough understanding of the complex dynamics, then to be able to apply this to a real-world situation and compare the results of the theoretical model with those derived from empirical measures is a potent set of thought constructs.

7. *Four Analysis and Two Synthesis Models*

The types of real-world models that can be thus simulated are seemingly endless. They basically can be divided into two categories—analysis models and synthesis models. In analysis models we know the relative location and strengths of the inputs and we solve for the potential patterns as in the preceding models. The synthesis models are those for which we know the patterns we wish to simulate but we determine the location or strength of the inputs by trial and error until we reproduce the pattern; we then go back to measure the relative strengths required to reproduce the pattern.

The analysis models are the more straightforward of the two. Knowing the relative sizes of St. Louis and Kansas City and the location of the major highway routes of the state of Missouri, it is relatively easy to cut out the areas more than (say) ten miles from major routes to form a resistance network and compute the breaking-point that divides the potential spheres of influence of the two cities (7-a). Likewise, knowing

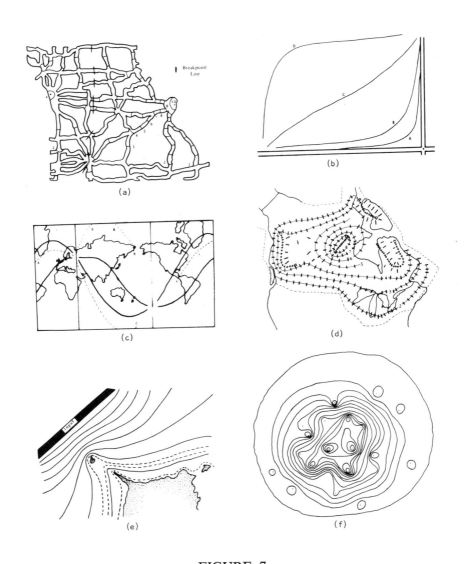

FIGURE 7

*Four Analysis and Two Synthesis Models. The four analysis models
are of the regional dominance of St. Louis and Kansas City along the
major highways of Missouri (7-a), the lines of equal accessibility to two
lines of unequal length (7-b), great circle routes (7-c), and continental
glaciation (7-d). The two synthesis models are of wave refraction along
an irregular shoreline (7-e) and atmospheric pressure of the northern
hemisphere (7-f).*

the relative lengths of a north-south street and a longer east-west street, it is possible to produce lines of equal accessibility to those streets as a determinant of urban land use (7-b); uses requiring maximum accessibility will locate within *A*, while those requiring least will, eventually, be pushed to *D*. Apparently quite different from any of the preceding models is one of great circle routes; that is, if we put a Mercator projection on a piece of conductive paper, ground the meridian running through the point of interest and the meridian 180° around the earth from that point, plot two great circle routes and excite them with current, and then place the probe anywhere on the map and calibrate the model, it will draw the great circle route (the shortest surface route) between that point and the point originally chosen (Figure 7-c is based on Moscow). As already indicated, knowing the center of ice accumulation and relative strengths, it is possible to simulate potential patterns and then draw at right angles to the potential lines the direction of ice flow in continental glaciation (Figure 7-d).

For synthesis models we offer two examples. The first is the reproduction of lines of wave refraction along an irregular shoreline (7-e). The lines to be simulated were taken from an aerial photograph, as were the shoreline and island that were to be grounded to reproduce the retraction pattern. It turned out that one series of small islands had to be treated as a peninsula, rather than as islands, to reproduce the pattern; that tells us something about how those islands were functioning in relation to wave processes. In a more complex way, we have simulated atmospheric pressure at the 500-millibar level for the northern hemisphere (7-f). In order to get a good simulation we had to have some additional controls; the low-pressure centers were simulated by regular current input controls, but the high-pressure centers were simulated by partial grounds that required the same degree of control used for regular inputs. We used some extra controls (potentiometers) to handle the problem. Around every college there are ham radio operators or other electronic buffs who are happy to rise to the challenge of building such special apparatus. That only helps to increase the involvement of more and more points of view in the simulation process.

V. Summary and Some Conclusions

In summary, field theory and the analog field plotter represent the kinds of concepts and instrumentation that we need in order to move more effectively into dynamic, multidimensional education. There is an enormous amount of work to be done to develop the capabilities inherent in these and similar concepts and instrumentation. The best approach is probably not to develop the concepts and instrumentation and put them into the hands of the students, but rather to recruit students *as part of their normal learning process* to develop such concepts and instrumentation. Almost all the projects presented, Figures 1 through 7, were designed and carried out by students in a freshman course; these figures represent only a small percentage thus developed by them. We need to find out how to recruit them and how to build the learning environment that will let them experience the ecstasy of learning (Leonard, 1965). For us, the field plotter is a synergetic sandbox that forms one of the nuclei of our efforts. We would welcome you and your students as collaborators.

NOTES

1. Illustrations in this section are reproduced by permission from the Association of American Geographers' Commission on College Geography Technology Paper Series, 1971, R. Nunley.
2. The present article is primarily a brief form and more general version of Living Maps of the Field Plotter: Analog Simulation of Selected Geographic Phenomena, Commission on College Geography Technical Paper Number 4, Washington, D.C., 1971, 177pp.
3. The present article is based on instruments available from CHILD, Inc., P.O. Box 764, Lawrence, Kansas 66044. They are the only ones available that we know of, which can be operated by untrained and non-technical students.
4. $V = f(x, y)$ where x and y relate the two-dimensional distribution of system components and where V is the potential variable and is related to the vector variable by the following: Force, Flux, Current $=$

$$V = \frac{2_v}{2_x\, y} + \frac{2_y}{2_y\, u_y} \text{ where } u_x \text{ and } u_y \text{ are unit vectors along the } x$$

   and y axis.
5. $2_v = 2_{v/}\, x^2 + 2_{v/}\, y^2 = 0$

REFERENCES

Borchert, J. R., and Adams, R. B. Trade centers and trade areas of the upper midwest. Upper Midwest Economic Study Urban Report Number 3, September, 1963.

Leonard, G. B. *Education and ecstacy.* New York: Dell Publishing Co., 1968.

Mack, L. E. Evaluation of a conductive paper analogy field plotter as an aid in solving ground water problems. Lawrence, Kansas: *Kansas Geological Survey Bulletin,* 1957, *127,* Part II, 27-47.

MacKay, J. R. Glacier flow and analog simulation. *Geographical Bulletin,* 1965, 7(1), 1-6.

Morgan, M. A. Hardware models in geography. In (Eds.) R. J. Chorley and P. Hagget, *Models in geography.* London: Barnes & Noble, 1967.

Nunley, R. E., Sabol, J. S., and Youngman, C. E. People and electrons: An analogy. *Proceedings of the Association of American Geographers,* 1969, *1,* 126-129.

Part IX

HISTORY

There has been considerable interest on the part of historians in using gaming simulations in the classroom. In the paper that follows, written by historians Bigelow, A. Gordon, and M. Gordon, there occurs a discussion of how simulation can be used well in teaching history, and areas where it might better not be used. The authors pivot around discussions of simulation and history that were held at the 1976 Denison Simulation Workshop.

13

HISTORY, VALUES, AND SIMULATION

BRUCE E. BIGELOW
AMY G. GORDON
MICHAEL D. GORDON

ABSTRACT

Our purpose here is to treat both the theoretical and practical aspects of the use of simulations as a means for understanding value questions in history. We begin, therefore, with a discussion of three basic approaches to history, and the ways in which these approaches do or do not lend themselves to the use of simulations. We also consider the importance of helping students to confront values, their own and those of the past, and the ways in which simulations can be useful for this purpose. We then go on to discuss the workshop itself, which was in essence based on our theoretical understanding of the relationship between simulation and values in history, and which was organized around the dual theme of the historian's own values, and that of understanding the values of the past. Finally, we conclude with a theoretical discussion of the strengths and weaknesses of simulation as a teaching tool for historians, with particular emphasis on those areas where simulation is especially effective as a means for better understanding the past.

I. *Approaches to the Past*

Historians have never been able to agree on a common definition of their own profession, and the opinions about the nature of history and approaches to the study of history are nearly as prolific as the number of practitioners of that discipline. But generally, these perspectives fall into one of three broad categories.

First, there are those who claim for historical study no special judgmental ability. In fact, they consciously eschew analysis of the events they describe, asserting instead that the only valid task for historians is to report, as faithfully as they can, the facts of what happened in the past. To go beyond the description of events and the chronicling of occurrences is, these historians contend, to distort history and to betray the trust that the world has placed on their shoulders.

Others are less dogmatic about their views of history and argue that analysis does not preclude objectivity, but rather that true objectivity requires analysis, demands the asking of why things happened as they did. Simply to describe events is to distort, these persons note, because no chronicler can possibly know everything that happened and is forced, therefore, to rely upon extant sources that may be incomplete, or, worse yet, he chooses himself what to include in his description and therefore leads his readers in a predetermined direction. He is distorting without admitting doing so. Much better, these historians argue, to ask one's critical questions directly and admit to one's reader the emphasis that one hopes to give to the study of history. Besides, history is relevant only when it asks questions of why. Only under these circumstances can one learn from history as well as learn about history. Only in that way can one draw the continuities from the past to the present and understand how and why societies have moved as they have and what the recipe has been for the social stew in which we now find ourselves.

There is a third school of historians who have become more and more open in recent years, a school that admits much of the validity of these foregoing arguments, but that argues that no historian, regardless of the perceptiveness of his analysis, can avoid making value judgments. History is filled, these students of history contend, with value choices and it is value choice that has not only determined much of what has happened in the past but also that guides our approach to the study of that past. The job of the historians is, therefore, from this perspective, not only to relate the facts of the past or to try to analyze why the past developed as it did and how it led to the present; they are also obligated to ask critical value questions. They must articulate right from the start the values and biases with which they themselves approach history, and they must try to extrapolate from their factual knowledge about the past to get at the values of other societies in other times. Such extrapolation requires a certain leap of faith, which many historians have heretofore balked at making, but, so argue the defenders of this view of history, by so doing they have not fulfilled their total responsibility either to their profession or to the general public.

This criticism is based upon the assumption that the historians have a duty to do more than simply dig out obscure facts from archives or write in greater detail for their own colleagues; rather it makes historians into servants of a larger constituency who, through the careful explanation of the past and its relationship to the present, can help people understand each other better and overcome the barriers to communication that have marred human intercourse. Gordon Dickson (1969), in his recent science fiction novel *None But Man,* describes the importance of just such uses of history, by arguing that societies, especially in an age of nuclear weaponry,

> . . . cannot exist side by side . . . without eventually either cooperating or destroying each other. And the key to cooperation is the responsibility upon both to accept the other on the other's terms, and judge them by their other standard. . . . For we need not embrace, only accept, each other—in order to survive as friends and neighbors. . . . And the choice is simply that: between mutual acceptance of a way not one's own; or blind misunderstanding and misinterpretation, leading to mutual annihilation. (Dickson, 1969, p. 222)

And history—value-laden history—is, according to Dickson and according to this third school of historical interpretation, one of the principal tools for creating the ability to understand and, therefore, to accept the fact that other societies do not always reason on the same basis as we and that words and concepts may have meant or may now mean totally different things to different societies.

It is upon the arguments set forth by this third school that the use of simulation is built. While simulation may be useful also to those for whom history is "objective" chronicling or analysis, it is particularly apropos in the questions of value, either to point up the perspectives of the historian or to understand better the values of the society or time he is studying.

There are two principal reasons that simulation is particularly appropriate to the study of history. First, historians, whether they realize it or not, simulate all the time. That is, they all try to recreate a setting in which they do not actually live, either in order to determine what that setting was like or to ask why it was like that. Usually the overt tools with which historians perform these tasks are words, whether written or spoken, but words can at best only approximate the situation being discussed, and, by so approximating, the historian is, in effect, simulating.

Second, in the direct task of determining values of the past, simulation—and here we mean simulation either of the verbal or the active variety—lets one ask questions without facing the real consequences of answering those questions. Simulation, that is, is the primary laboratory tool of the historian. It is the technique whereby he varies his experiments, isolates his variables and is able to ask those critical questions, "What if . . . ?" Simulations may, of course, produce tension, stimulate emotions, or engage attention and curiosity, but in the long run historians can always step back from the simulation and ask, "What has been going on here?" "What are the value assumptions I/we have been making?" "What can we learn about ourselves or about this other society or other time period by simulating the conditions of that society or time?" These are the most important questions for historians to ask, and simulation enables them to ask these questions more directly and to receive more satisfying and more convincing answers because simulation brings not only cognitive understanding but also greater empathy with people in other situations and consequently greater affective understanding.

Simulation is, while compatible with teaching of history as a general discipline, especially appropriate for history courses at the college level. Four reasons stand out.

First, students in college are, or should be, in the process of forming and articulating their own values. That is, as most of us are well aware, not an easy task and one that often continues well past college years. But it is in college that the values and norms with which many students enter are challenged and forced to be either confirmed or replaced by values of greater meaning. Most college instructors see part of their task in the classroom to be to challenge unexamined values, but most have no wish for the student to leave college having rejected all values or refusing to think as an ethically motivated human being. Insofar as college history courses address the questions of values and examine the ways in which people have, over the centuries, tried to come to terms with the issues of truth, meaning, and the goals of human existence, so they are a critical part of the college student's education. And, by enabling the student to risk making choices without having to face the total consequences of his choices, by allowing the student to experiment with various possible answers to these value questions, simulation plays an important role in the student's growing ability to make intelligent, humane value choices.

Second, students in college are often faced with the sudden realization that "Truth" is a relative concept. Students have all too often been trained prior to college to accept "Truth" as an absolute, and they demand absolute answers in college too. They are frustrated when such answers are not forthcoming and sometimes feel cheated by the university system. No one is ever completely immune from these feelings of frustration, and each of us longs at times for the certainty of absolute answers—in history and in life in general. But we also learn that, even though such answers are difficult, if not impossible, to obtain, we can, nonetheless, differentiate good from bad answers. Just because history offers few absolutes does not mean that it presents no insights. And it is often through the use of simulation that that insight becomes most apparent, because simulations allow students to discover for themselves what is most meaningful to them.

Third, college is a time when students learn to relate to one another and to the world as adults, no longer dependent upon their parents to support them or to dictate to them how to deal with the world. This process of becoming adult requires an ability to judge others not by our standards but by the standards of those others. We need not accept those standards as our own but neither can we assume that our standards are totally acceptable to those around us. This is true in personal relations and true in our confrontation with other cultures. History lets us reflect on the impact of different standards upon human values and behavior, and simulation helps us to do so with greater total involvement.

Finally, the college years are a time when students should be learning how better to communicate with the people with whom they come in contact. This may involve the more basic skills of writing and oral communication, but verbal activity is not sufficient by itself. Unless it is constructed upon a solid foundation of understanding the meaning of the words and the concepts inherent in the words, it becomes no more than playing with sounds. Intelligent communication demands using language that means the same thing to both parties. History helps to point out how failure to do so may result in disaster or how miracles may be performed by the ability to convey the right message at the right time. And again simulation may serve as a critical tool of the historian's trade. As before, students can test various ways of communicating in the course of a simulation to discover for themselves the possible consequences of misunderstanding.

History is, as we have said, many things to many people, and each historian or student of history has his or her own subtle definition of history. But, insofar as history serves to clarify and explicate the values of the past and insofar as it helps people formulate and articulate the values with which they will confront the future, it is a critical aspect of the college curriculum. And, insofar as simulation facilitates history's confrontation with these value questions, it too is critical and can play a vital role in making college the important testing ground for values and value choices that it ought to be.

Given this belief that it is a part of the historian's task to confront the issue of values in history, and that simulation is a valid method of approaching this task in the teaching of history, our aim throughout the workshop was to explore a variety of ways in which the teacher might use simulations to raise with students critical value questions. In examining these values as they relate to history, there are two levels on which the problem needs to be raised. In the first place, students—and teachers— need to be aware of their own values, so that they will be more fully able to recognize the ways in which they are looking at, and perhaps distorting, the past. In the second place, students need to be sensitized to the ways in which the values of the past—and of other, non-Western societies—may either differ from or form a continuum with their own values.

II. *The Historian's Values*

In order to approach both of these levels relating to values in history, we designed our workshop course so that we could begin by confronting our own values—as human beings and as historians—and then move on to the ways in which we might hope to understand the values of times and/or cultures other than our own. In preparation for the task of using simulations to understand our own values, we had assigned the participants two articles by historians dealing with the issue of how historians' values affect their judgment of the past, and whether it is, in fact, desirable or even possible to examine the past without distorting it with present values. Beard (1934), in effect, argues that value-laden history is the only kind possible and that each generation thus alters the interpretation of the past given by the generation preceding it. Krieger (1957), on the other hand, points out some of the ways in which historians, through the awareness of a variety of approaches, can, to some degree, hope to understand the past on its own terms. While Beard and Krieger disagree on the desirability and indeed the necessity for value-laden history, both imply a difference between the values of the historian and those of his subject.

The questions thus raised are "What are our values?" "How can simulation help us see them?" Exercises directed toward these issues are of great benefit to the historian beginning to approach the issue of values in history. A value-clarification exercise designed to deal with both personal and sociopolitical values can be helpful. We designed a variation on the coat of arms, in which participants are asked to draw up his/her own coat of arms, divided into six areas. The questions, which are to be answered in symbols or pictures rather than words, in order to simulate more closely an actual coat of arms, are: (1) What do you do best; (2) biggest success (past year); (3) biggest failure (past year); (4) meaning of freedom; (5) role of the state, and (6) morality and the family. After having completed the coat of arms, participants spend some time interpreting them for one another, and talking about and comparing what they reveal about beliefs and general outlook. One interesting result of this exercise can be to reveal, often, a great similarity in values, which is revealed upon discussion, yet a widely varying choice of symbols to illustrate these values.

The coat of arms can be useful for helping students to understand their personal beliefs on a variety of issues, yet there is need as well to focus more specifically on values related to our professions as teachers of history and/or political science. To approach our more properly "professional" values, a forced-choice exercise revolving around four rather extreme definitions of history, posted at intervals around the room, can be quite successful. Four definitions might be (1) "History is useless but fun"; (2) "History is moral philosophy teaching by example"; (3) "History is a testing ground for examining theories of human behavior," and (4) "History is a pack of tricks we play upon the dead." The participants align themselves under the definition with which they feel most compatible, then are given time to talk with others who have made the same choice and to modify the definition so that it more nearly meets with their own personal views on the nature of history.

There is then discussion of the original definitions and reasons for choosing a particular one, and of the modifications made by groups. In the end, with modifications, all the definitions are likely to come much closer together, revealing a common ground in the various approaches to the study of history; in the workshop it became evident that we all believed that there were indeed lessons to be learned from the past, but that part of our dedication to its study was not solely for its utility but because we enjoyed learning about the past for its own sake.

Another method for determining one's own values might be the use of a continuum, an exercise we discussed without actually running through it. For the continuum, a statement is posed and participants are asked to line themselves up according to whether they strongly agree or strongly disagree with the statement, or rather find themselves somewhere in the middle. They then are asked to articulate their reasons for taking their own particular positions on the continuum, both literally and figuratively. To approach the question of what one's values are and how they affect one's attitudes toward the past, a possible continuum might be framed around whether one believes the individual can effect change or rather is a helpless pawn in the hands of forces far greater than himself. Once the participants have taken their position on this question, they can then be asked to line up according to their views on certain specific historical events involving the ability of the individual to effect change. Certain possible choices might be the 1968 Democratic Convention, the *sans-culottes* (working class) in the French Revolution of 1789, or Martin Luther and the Protestant Reformation. There is, of course, an infinite variety of similar circumstances or events that can be selected according to the background and interests of participants. Once they have taken their positions, discussion should follow, both about why they have taken a particular position, and, as well, how their positions on specific issues correspond with the stance taken on the more general statement about the role of the individual in effecting change. This can then lead to a discussion of whether they are, in fact, applying their own values—as evidenced by the response to the general statement—to particular historical situations, or whether they have tried to assess each historical situation within its own particular context.

There are then a number of ways in which simulations can be used to clarify one's own values, particularly as these relate to the study of history. These types of exercises have the additional advantage of being, for the most part, exercises in small group dynamics as well as in value clarification, and this can make them particularly useful in the classroom, as they encourage students to interact with one another, and in particular, to interact on the very important level of trying to understand their own values and the values of the others in the group. In turn, learning to deal with values of their classmates that may be different from their own helps to prepare students for an understanding of the values of other eras and other cultures.

III. *Values in History: Historical Simulations*

Simulations can thus be used to move naturally from an examination of the historian's values to the study of the past itself. The second and third days of the workshop course were devoted to exploring a variety of historical simulations that might be used to further an understanding of the past and its values. The emphasis was on the approach, rather than on any one particular game or model in and of itself. Rather, we were concerned with how the general goals of a particular simulation, and its general methodology, could be applied to a whole variety of historical situations and issues. To fulfill this purpose, we actually played some games, and discussed others, always with the emphasis on flexibility and applicability—or lack thereof—to a broad spectrum of teaching areas in history.

One extremely flexible approach to values in history, which can be most effective, revolves around relatively simple forms of role-playing. For example, after reading Georges Lefebvre's (1967) *The Coming of the French Revolution,* students can use role-playing as a way of better understanding the desires and goals of the various groups involved in the Revolution of 1789. The class can be divided up into small groups representing some of the participants in the Revolution, such as the king, the aristocracy, the bourgeoisie, the peasants, and the *sansculottes.* Each group is asked to agree on what its particular goals were in May-June 1789. The teacher then records the goals of the various groups and discusses with the class the accuracy of the goals represented and what these goals show us about why the Revolution progressed as it did. Questions can also be raised as to why certain groups, whose goals seem to have been similar, were not able to work together.

Such a role-playing has a number of advantages. It encourages students to examine and identify various groups, to argue for the position of a particular group, and to see more clearly the differences and similarities among the groups because of differing political, social, and economic goals. It involves them directly in the issues of what people wanted at a particular time in the past and why they were able, or unable, to fulfill their aspirations. It is a simulation technique that can be applied to any number of students, and any number of historical situations, and it serves the purpose of involving students both with the past and with each other.

Another, more complicated use of role-playing can be in combination with a gaming situation. As an example of this, there is a game based upon the European Revolution of 1848, designed by Donald Schilling, Associate Professor of History at Denison University. In this game, which is generally played over a period of about two weeks, the students, having done reading on the actual Revolution of 1848, are presented with the prerevolutionary economic, political, and social situation in the imaginary European country of Germance in 1848. The students are assigned roles, with descriptions of their aspirations, social position, and so on, and then go on to try to fulfill these aspirations according to a calculated number of points for achieving certain aims. The player who most successfully achieves the realization of his/her goals is declared the winner. The actions taken must be consistent with the historical period and the social class of the player. Players may negotiate with one another, but with certain restrictions. The king, for example, can converse directly only with aristocrats, the banker, the capitalist, and the lawyer. The game is played in rounds, and players record the course of action decided upon for each round. As the situation in Germance changes through the actions of the players, the facilitator releases information on changing conditions, to which players then adjust their strategy in the next round.

In such a game, students are involved in assuming the roles, and thus the values, of various groups in society. Using these values, they must try to act within a historical context to achieve certain ends. They are thus confronted with the values of another age, and with a better understanding of why certain people acted the way they did and why certain events occurred as they did. The game can be applied to other revolutionary situations and, indeed, to any historical situation where one wishes to examine the interaction of various social groups working for— or against—change. Again, as with less complicated forms of role-playing, it helps students to identify with the values and aspirations of another age and thus to understand better why people have behaved in certain ways and why historical events have had a certain outcome. It does involve a fairly substantial commitment of time on the part of the instructor and students, but such time is well spent in a course that has such social interaction as one of its primary interests.

One additional game, designed to develop understanding of the dynamics involved in diplomatic history, is the *National Decision Game*. For this game, participants are divided to represent three imaginary countries, Camelot, Sidon, and Ergoland. During the course of the game, which generally consists of seven rounds, each nation seeks to maximize its power relative to that of the other two nations. Power is symbolized by the points the citizens of the nation get by making a strategic decision to maintain the status quo or to attack. Furthermore, the payoff of a nation's strategic decision is contingent upon the strategic decision of the other nations. Thus, if one nation decides to maintain the status quo while another decides to attack, that nation, the status quo nation, loses 25 points while the attacker gains 100. If, however, each attacks the other, each gets 5 points, while if each decides to maintain the status quo, each gets 25 points.

During each round, each nation makes two decisions, determining its behavior toward the other two nations in the game. Thus, Sidon may decide to attack Ergoland but maintain the status quo with Camelot. The decisions are based both on the general decision the group has made about its strategy and posture on the international scene, and upon the way it believes the other nations will behave. At the end of each round, decisions are recorded, and points then allotted depending on the success or failure of the nation's strategy. Negotiations between nations are possible after the first round, but nations are not bound by any statements or promises made during the course of the negotiations.

Having played the *National Defense Game,* participants then debrief by talking about what it reveals with regard to international relations and about how it can perhaps be applied to a variety of historical situations. It was noted in the workshop class that, as a game dealing with international relations, it perhaps fails to meet twentieth-century conditions, in that mutual attack under present-day conditions ought to cost points rather than adding them. There is also the question of whether the game could be used to meet historical situations where factors other than power are involved in international relations, as, for example, with the wars of religion in sixteenth-century Europe and other situations where commitment to an ideology might override considerations of power politics.

Yet, with all its limitations, such a generalized game can still offer students an opportunity to put themselves into the position of decision-maker in any number of historical situations, helping them to understand more fully the pressures that operate in such a situation and often enough raising the point that, despite their own disclaimers of aggressive behavior as a satisfactory means for solving problems, when put in a position of making such situations they often act aggressively. Discussion can then proceed as to why this is and has been so in the past and whether such behavior can be avoided in the future. In such a way, the question of values in history and in our lives is thus raised and the interrelationship among values past, present, and future is emphasized.

There are other types of historical simulations that can be applied to a whole variety of historical situations, but our particular illustration was the choice of two board games—of differing complexity—used to demonstrate the dynamics involved in the collectivization movement in the Soviet Union. These games themselves are adaptations of other games and could be easily adapted to other historical events, where one wished to emphasize the hopes and frustrations of a given situation, particularly a historical climate wherein people were trying to organize or cope with changes in their way of life.

To prepare for these simulations, participants were assigned excerpts from *A History of Soviet Russia* by George von Rauch (1967), and *Russian Peasants and Soviet Power* by M. Lewin (1968), because some knowledge of the historical facts and issues involved is essential. The simple board game is basically a Monopoly type, centering on collectivization. Each player throws the dice and proceeds around the board, gaining or losing points depending on the square upon which he/she lands. One can, for example, win points for a good harvest, but lose points—and all too frequently does—through crop failures, policy failures, actions of the state, and so on. One can also land on "Chance" or on "Communist Chest" and then must pick a card from a central pile. As the players soon learn, too, as the game goes on, losing points is far more common an experience than winning them and, furthermore, one can do nothing to affect one's fate. The player is at the mercy of the dice, and, generally, the roll of the dice brings misfortune rather than good fortune.

The player, then, is put into the position of the Russian peasant during the period of Soviet collectivization in the late 1920s and early 1930s. As he travels around the board, he becomes more and more aware both of his own helplessness and of all the things that could go wrong and adversely affect his life. Most players become angry, and then discouraged and finally apathetic, because there seems to be no way to win with any degree of consistency. One may pile up points for a while, but almost invariably, as the game goes on, one loses everything one has gained.

Once the game ended, participants talked about these feelings, and related them to the situation of the peasants in Russia, who were helpless, frustrated, and at the mercy of forces that seemed unable to understand them and that the peasants could not control in any meaningful way. The game thus gets at a certain historical reality—the reactions of the Russian peasants undergoing collectivization—and brings out the ways in which the peasant felt threatened, felt his values to be under attack.

A similar board could be constructed to bring out the frustrations and aspirations of almost any social group caught up in the process of change. It thus offers a valuable—and relatively uncomplicated—form of simulation that might be applied to a whole range of historical situations, from ancient to modern times, and in non-Western as well as Western cultures. One could, for example, construct a board dealing with industrialization rather than collectivization, and apply this industrialization model to Western countries in the nineteenth century, and to non-Western countries in the twentieth, in order to show the reactions of people caught up in the processes of industrial change.

The simple collectivization board game focuses on the reactions of the peasants to a collectivization process that was, by and large, imposed on them from above. It thus gets at only one aspect of collectivization: peasant response. The second board game, adapted by Bruce Bigelow from the commercial game *"They Shoot Marbles, Don't They?"* also revolves around the theme of collectivization, but it is constructed to elicit the reactions of broader strata of Russian society, and most particularly to elucidate the hopes and frustrations of the planners as well as those for whom they were planning. Thus, this second game includes members of Gosplan and of the Communist Party Central Committee as well as members of the peasant community.

The game revolves around a large board, divided up into areas to represent more or less desirable croplands. Around the board stand people assigned the role of "shooters" (peasants), and their goal is to collect for themselves as many marbles as possible by hitting marbles scattered about the board. The reward (in marbles) increases according to the desirability of the cropland in which the shooter hits a marble. Observing the "shooters," and part of the peasant community, are players assigned roles in this community, such as the local party official or the head of the village commune. Outside, in two separate rooms, are players assigned the roles as Gosplan or the Central Committee. They cannot communicate directly with one another or with the peasant community; they must rely on couriers to bring them information and to relay their orders. Thus, they have the task of developing and implementing policies for the peasant community, but have very little direct evidence of what is happening in the community. They can issue orders, but cannot go along to implement orders. They must hope that the courier delivers the orders properly and that those in the village assigned to carry out their orders do so. The two planning agencies also must hope that their orders do not contradict one another, and that they see eye to eye on the goals for which they are working.

The game then begins with very few rules. The participants make up the rules as they go along, in the form of orders issued by Gosplan and the Central Committee, and responses to these orders by the peasants and local officials. Gosplan, for example, may order that the shooters (peasants) turn in half of their marbles (crops). The courier relays this message and, it is hoped, collects, although the shooters may foil him by hiding their marbles, etc. As the game continues, with orders going back and forth, and with the local villagers doing what they can to hold on to their marbles, the facilitator from time to time introduces new elements, such as tokens representing fertilizer and so on, which may be used as bargaining points by Gosplan, the Central Committee, and the local officials. The game continues so long as the participants remain actively involved. It produces great feelings of frustration for all players: Gosplan and the Central Committee are so removed from the local scene and thus are not always aware of how large the supply of marbles is, of what local officials are doing, of whether orders are being obeyed, etc. In the village, on the other hand, shooters and local officials receive orders that often seem senseless in the light of actual conditions and thus have the tendency to ignore or disobey orders whenever possible.

The debriefing session after the game is used to explore these feelings of frustration and compare them with actual conditions and emotions, because there was, in fact, a lack of communication and understanding, which in turn produced more and more regulations as well as efforts on the part of the peasants to avoid or sabotage government decrees. While the first board game simulated the feelings of the peasants, this second game provides the student with an insight into the problems of the government as well as the peasants, and helps to create an understanding of why collectivization of Soviet agriculture proved to be such an extraordinarily painful and difficult process. The second game is more complex and time-consuming, but provides a more nearly complete picture of the process of collectivization and the problems involved.

As with the simpler board game, there are other situations for which this game could be adapted. Again, the examples of societies undergoing industrialization or modernization come to mind, but these are not the only possibilities. One could, perhaps, adapt the game to deal with the growth of the central government in early modern European society and the frustrations and difficulties it created both for local society and for the newly developing centralized government bureaucracy.

IV. *Values in History: Nonhistorical Simulations*

Simulations dealing directly with historical situations are clearly one way of using simulation to get at certain issues, particularly those centering on the critical area of values in history. The historian, however, may find other approaches to value questions to be extremely fruitful. When one is dealing with the effort to comprehend the values of another society, other disciplines may offer to the teacher and student of history an insight not found in most historical works. Yet, surely, the historian trying to come to a better understanding of the values of the past is not asking questions fundamentally different from those asked by the anthropologist about contemporary societies and the science fiction writer about societies of the future.

There is, thus, value for the historian in exploring the use of nonhistorical simulation. Participants in the workshop class were assigned an excerpt from Claude Levi-Strauss's (1963) *Structural Anthropology,* on "History and Anthropology," and a science fiction novel by Arthur Clarke (1975), *Rendezvous with Rama,* both works having been selected to raise some of the problems involved in confronting an alien culture and trying to understand its values. A simulation that illustrates these problems is the commercially available game "Bafá, Bafá," which explicitly speaks to the issue of comprehending another society's values.

In "Bafá, Bafá," participants are divided into two teams, the Alphas and the Betas. These two represent fundamentally different cultures, each with its own set of rules, its own lifestyle, and its own values. Each group goes off to learn and practice the rules of its culture, and neither culture knows anything about the rules of the other group.

The Alpha culture is a rather relaxed, friendly, noncompetitive culture, yet at the same time has rather rigid rules governing social relationships. As we played it, the Alpha society was a matriarchy, with contacts initiated by women. The Alphas have a card game that they play among themselves, but the purpose of the game is not to win; rather it serves as an excuse for social interaction.

The Beta culture, on the other hand, is fiercely competitive, yet has very few rules governing social interaction; indeed, it has very little social interaction except for the purpose of trading cards in order to accumulate points and win. The Betas have their own language, which is used to express what cards a person wants to gain. It cannot communicate anything else.

Once the two teams have familiarized themselves with their respective culture, each sends an observer to the other, to try to learn the rules. The observers then return to their own cultures and tell what they have perceived. Then each culture begins to send participants, who try to enter into the alien culture. Participants in turn report back, and then new participants are sent, until all have visited the other culture.

During the debriefing session, each culture offers what seems to it to be an explanation of the rules of the other, as gleaned from observation and participation. As well, participants discuss their own feelings at being placed in a culture where they do not understand what is happening, where the values are alien to their own. In our debriefing, we found that we had not understood the other culture, and that, for the Betas in particular, we were so caught up in our own value system that we kept trying to perceive the rules of the other culture as if they were some form of our own rules. The Betas, for example, kept focusing on the Alpha card game and trying to learn how to win it—where, in fact, it was not a game where one could win or even desired to do so. We all became dramatically aware of how value-laden our judgments about others were, even when we were trying to understand as fully as possible, and, we thought, without bias or prejudice.

Although "Bafá, Bafá" is a nonhistorical simulation, there are many ways in which historians could adapt such a game for use in the teaching of history. For historians dealing with the non-West, the applications are obvious, and could be used to elucidate the difficulties of the non-Westerner in trying to understand the Western world, and, as well, the failure of Westerners to come to grips with the values of non-Western societies. Moreover, such a simulation could also be adapted to help further an understanding of the values of past societies, societies from which our own values may indeed have developed but which were, nevertheless, in many ways very alien to our own age. One example might be medieval society, but certainly there are many more such possibilities.

V.   *Designing a Simulation*

Throughout the workshop, our emphasis was on how participants might adapt some of the techniques discussed and utilized to their own teaching situations. Participants themselves suggested simulations that they had used with success and that could be used by others at other institutions.

One interesting possibility is a classroom technique developed by Eugene Lubot of Wheaton College, Norton, Massachusetts, which is a simulation of the Chinese civil service examination, designed to capture the spirit of the examination and emphasize its role in Chinese society. Students take an actual examination, and are expected to behave in accordance with the situation. The simulation recreates an atmosphere and provides students a very real insight into the values of a society very different from their own. Again, it offers a technique that might be adapted by other historians to meet their own particular needs and subjects.

Robina Quale of Albion College, one of the members of the workshop, shared with the other participants a rather simple form of role-playing that she has used most successfully to initiate her students into a better understanding of traditional Asian societies. In this "Name Game," students rename themselves in the fashion of a caste-oriented society. Thus, for example, in a version of the game applied to South Asian society, a student whose parents are professional people—teachers, doctors, dentists, ministers—becomes "John Learned Smith" or "Mary Learned Smith," a student whose parents work for the government at any level becomes "John Ruler Smith" or "Mary Ruler Smith," a student whose parents are neither professionals nor government workers becomes "John Trader Smith" or "Mary Trader Smith." Thus, students are made aware of a society where a person's name immediately reveals something about his/her family and status. Quale has also developed versions of this game for Chinese society, and for Arab or Arab-influenced societies.

The device of name-changing is not complex, yet it can initiate students into an understanding of societies whose values are different from their own and also show them that differences in values can affect a society on every level, including that level of the names by which people are identified—and by which they in turn identify themselves. It can very successfully give students a sense of what that other society might be like to live in, and how differently they might feel about themselves in such a society.

Another interesting approach is found in two rather complicated simulation games developed by Bruce Bigelow for use in courses taught at Denison. One, worked out in conjunction with Donald Schilling for a jointly taught course on imperialism, is called "Trading Empire" and is designed to simulate the expansion of Europe overseas and the development of worldwide domination of trade by European nations. Players are part of a complex trade network, moving the products of the Empire Continent to the markets of Gondoland, Fezia, and the Cinnamon Islands and bringing the valued spices of the Cinnamon Islands to the people of the Empire Continent. Each player is a decision-maker in one of six trading companies, and each company tries to make the biggest possible profit. The company that makes the most money is the winner, and the ability to drive a hard bargain, an awareness of market conditions, and profit margins are all important. The game builds in risk factors, to recreate the atmosphere of an age when a trading voyage was a risky undertaking yet potential profits were great enough to make people willing to venture into unknown seas. A dartboard is used to determine the cost of the trip, as well as potential loss of cargo. Other than that, action is determined by strategy and bargaining among the players.

Such a simulation can be successful in recreating the atmosphere of another age, the spirit that makes men willing to explore, to trade, to gamble and expand. At the same time, it can make more meaningful to students the actual processes involved in mapping out trade routes, buying and selling, trying to secure markets and raw materials, and thus makes more comprehensible to them the reasons why Europeans, beginning with the pursuit of trade, ended up by establishing Empires.

The second game of Bigelow's, "Mid-East Muddle," is a simulated peace conference on the modern Middle East used in the context of a course on Middle Eastern history. The purpose is to simulate some of the dynamics of international relations and national perspectives in the Middle East today. Its goal is both to remain true to the genuine interests of the countries or interest groups involved and to try to reach, insofar as possible, some common solution to the problems of the Middle East. In so doing, participants become aware of the complexities of the Middle East as well as some of the possible potential for future change.

There are eleven teams, each representing a country or interest group concerned with the Middle East. Each team submits a set of priorities or goals for itself, and, on the basis of these priorities, the game director assigns possible points that may be gathered by the teams. Each team tries to get as many points as possible, to satisfy, that is, its own priorities at the conference.

To prepare for this simulation, students do extensive research on the "country" or "interest group" they are representing. They thus learn about that country or group, and then at the Peace Conference have the opportunity to learn about the other groups' needs and desires, while defending their own position and at the same time learning about the extreme difficulties that occur when groups with separate interests try to develop a common policy or understanding. The basic agenda for the conference deals with the Palestinian refugees, the borders of Israel, and the creation of an independent state of Palestine, but these questions have so many ramifications and touch on so many contradictory goals that they serve as a focus for all the complexities of the Middle Eastern situation, beyond the related questions of Israel and Palestine.

A simulation such as this one obviously requires a great deal of time spent in preparation and thus becomes a focal point for the course in which it is used. But this in itself need not limit the usefulness or feasibility of such a simulation, because most of the time is spent in doing research outside of class and thus it is no different from requiring a term paper, with research to be done over a period of a semester or quarter. The actual conference itself can be a culminating experience for the course, bringing together what has been accomplished by the students themselves. Such a combination of outside research and some sort of classroom simulation could be used to recreate and elucidate a whole variety of historical situations, from revolutions to peace conferences.

There are, then, a number of types of simulation that may be used by historians to illuminate for their students the values of other times and other cultures, and thus give students a fuller understanding of the historical moment. Simulations developed for one historical situation can frequently be adapted to meet the needs of another situation and another historical era. What about, however, taking a particular historical theme, one that has recurred at various stages of history, and developing a simulation that could be applied to any historical era where the theme was applicable? Our discussion in the workshop led us to the point of considering the possibilities of just such a "frame game," one that would focus on a theme and provide the framework within which various historical examples of the theme could be viewed through the use of simulation. Political integration, because it is an area of some interest to political scientists and economists as well as historians, is a good possibility for a "frame game," and it is a theme that has relevance for western and non-Western societies, and for the past as well as the present. One would need to isolate those factors involved in political integration that are consistent in any situation involving such integration.

The possible factors to consider might be the role of the leader, as a positive or negative force, outside pressures, types of regions to be integrated, religion or common ideology, languages and/or culture and heritage, economic integration as a precursor to political integration, integration imposed from outside, war as a step in integration, geographical compactness, racial determinants, military and strategic considerations, social stratification, the complementary character of regions within the system, and the presence or absence of nationalism. This list is by no means exhaustive but rather an indication of the types of common factors to look for. It would need a group of interested people, working in particular areas of expertise, to isolate the factors that seem to operate in cases of political integration. Then those factors common to all could be pulled out, used to construct a simulation that could be applied to any historical instance of political integration, and used for purposes of understanding any one particular instance, and at the same time for a comparative study of various instances.

Our workshop, then, beginning with the attempt to understand our own values as a necessary preliminary to the understanding of value questions in history, and then moving on to consider simulations designed to raise such value questions, concluded with the topic of designing simulations, especially the idea of a simulation that would get at the issues of values in history and, at the same time, facilitate the understanding of history as an ongoing and unified process, rather than the fragmented study of isolated moments within the past.

VI. *Conclusion*

Simulation can facilitate historical understanding, but only if it is properly used. Moreover, even when properly used, the utility of simulation—though real—is limited. It is limited in that it is not an end in itself. Rather, it is a means, a teaching device that can perform a role similar to that which the use of audiovisual technique plays in the classroom. Simulation will not replace the usual techniques of lecture and discussion, nor will it replace the usual activities of reading and writing. Rather, it will complement and supplement these techniques and activities.

Clearly, the utility of the several simulation techniques will depend upon the type of course in which they will be used. For a survey course, particularly an introductory one, which cannot devote a great deal of time to any individual topic, simple board games and especially role-playing can be a pleasant way for students to internalize information of various types. For a more narrowly focused course, which can devote a substantive amount of time to a particular topic, more sophisticated and complicated games may be appropriate. It is in these situations—particularly those where the student consciously prepares before engaging in the simulation— that the utility of simulation techniques reaches its maximum level. Clearly, the proper choice of techniques in light of the use they will be put to is crucial to the utilization of simulation in the classroom.

The use of the simulations discussed above has produced not only a sense of their effectiveness on the part of the instructors but also some data about their impact on students. Several of the more complex games used by Bigelow and Schilling have been carefully evaluated, as students were asked to submit both written evaluations and a completed questionnaire on their reactions. In all cases, the students responded overwhelmingly that the simulations were more motivating than a lecture might have been and that they prompted the students to think in ways different from those they had previously used. The overall conclusions were that the simulations added considerably to the courses involved and helped the students to appreciate the complexity and ambiguity of the situations on which they focused. There was on occasion some concern expressed that the simulations did not approximate the real life situation as well as they might have and that the students, therefore, had some difficulty generalizing from their experiences. In some cases, this problem can be corrected by modifying the game. In others, the distortion is deliberate and built into the game in order to stress certain points while allowing others to be dealt with later. In the game on the revolution of 1848, for example, the game does not take fully into account the role of religion or of developing national aspirations, but the instructor handled these issues later through readings, lectures, and discussions, thus permitting the class to focus more directly on the social interaction of the 1848 disturbances. Similarly, the Mid-East game described above did not include the complexities of the international oil market, but instead held that issue in abeyance while the simulation dealt with the diplomatic and national issues of the Middle Eastern conflict. In both these and other games the distortions did not destroy the effectiveness of the exercises, but only because the instructors were careful either to explain the distortions beforehand or to deal extensively with the distortions in the debriefing. In fact, it is sometimes most effective to leave it up to the students to discover the distortions for themselves and then let them analyze how the addition of these outside factors might have influenced the outcome of the simulation.

These data, as well as the instructors' intuitive sensitivity, underline the critical role of the debriefing process in all simulation activities. All techniques, whether simple or complex, whether role-playing, gaming, or in combination, should be followed by as extensive a debriefing as possible. It is difficult to overemphasize this point. It is in discussion, and often criticism, of the activity that the most valuable insights into the historical realities being simulated often appear. No game, no matter how sophisticated it be, can reproduce precisely the complexities and subtleties of an historical reality. Without a proper debriefing, the student may feel that the game does in fact represent the reality; hence, he may be led to a simplistic and naive view. With a good and careful debriefing, on the other hand, the student's understanding of the complexities and subtleties of any historical event can be significantly enhanced and developed. One component of the debriefing should be to expose the complexities behind, and thus the inadequacies of, the simulation used and, indeed, of all historical generalizations.

The utility that historians will find in the classroom use of simulation techniques will depend, ultimately, on how they view their task. More precisely, it will depend on how clearly they define their activities as compared with those of the antiquarian and the social scientist. If the historian's taste is only, or even primarily, to recapture a specific event in all its minutiae and complexity, then simulation will be of no, or little, value. No game, indeed no construct or model, can recreate *everything* that went into the storming of the Bastille. But historians do not attempt such a task. On the other hand, if the task of the historian is to uncover general laws of human behavior, then simulation would be of obvious and primary value. But few historians try to uncover general laws; indeed, most would argue that such laws do not exist. Hence, historians would distrust a game designed to illustrate "the dynamics of revolution," for they would question the very existence of such dynamics.

Historians are not engaged in empirical research, nor are they engaged in the formation of general laws. Rather, they are concerned with both the general and the particular, and view each in the context of the other. Simulation techniques are but one means of expressing the generalization in which all historians must engage. Like all such generalizations, they must be viewed with reference to the specific reality that they hope to describe. In turn, the specific reality cannot be viewed without the aid of generalizations. In the words of Erich Heller (1959, pp. 184-5), ". . . all historical generalizations are the defeat of the empiricist; and there is no history without them."

REFERENCES

Beard, C. "Written history as an act of faith." *American Historical Review,* 1934, XXXIX, 219-231.

Clarke, A. *Rendezvous with Rama.* New York: Ballantine, 1974.

Dickson, G. *None but man.* New York: Pyramid, 1969.

Heller, E. *The disinherited mind.* Cleveland: World, 1959.

Krieger, L. The horizons of history. *American Historical Review,* 1957, LXIII, 62-74.

Lefebvre, G. *The coming of the French Revolution.* Princeton: Princeton University Press, 1947.

Levi-Strauss, C. *Structural anthropology.* Garden City, New York: Double-day, Anchor Books, 1963.

Lewin, M. *Russian peasants and Soviet power: A study of collectivization.* New York: Norton, 1975.

von Rauch, G. *A history of Soviet Russia,* Fourth Revised Edition. New York: Praeger, 1964.

Part X
INTERNATIONAL RELATIONS

The paper in this section, written by political scientist Sorenson, briefly overviews some examples of the heuristic use of simulation in international relations. Sorenson discusses a simulation on Mideast conflict, developed by Feste, the "Inter-Nation Simulation" (Guetzkow), and "Nuclear Deterrence," developed by the author. He then briefly concerns himself with the problems of evaluating the teaching utility of these kinds of simulations, emphasizing the fact that such evaluation has thus far yielded ambiguous conclusions, and that further work in evaluation is necessary.

14

SIMULATION IN
THE TEACHING OF
INTERNATIONAL POLITICS

DAVID S. SORENSON

ABSTRACT

This paper discusses the development of the pedagogical use of international relations simulations over the past twenty years, and provides three
examples of such simulations. It is noted that the use of simulation in
international relations studies was originally research-oriented, and teaching applications followed from these efforts. A wide variety of teaching
simulations has resulted from the pioneering work of Guetzkow, Coplin,
and others, and these simulations range from simple board games to
complex all-machine games.

The paper contains three examples of simulations currently in use.
The first is the well-known INS ("Inter-Nation Simulation"), originally
developed in 1963 and modified several times since then. INS provides
a macroview of global conflict and cooperative relations. The second
simulation is "Conflict in the Middle East," which is designed to demonstrate conflict theories as applied to that particular part of the world.
The third example is "Nuclear Deterrence," which demonstrates the application of deterrence theory with respect to the five nations currently
in possession of deliverable nuclear weapons.

The paper concludes by noting that systematic evaluation of international relations simulations has shown mixed results, but overall the findings tend to be more negative than positive, at least in terms of cognitive
changes. Further research is necessary in the evaluative area.

For over a decade and a half, simulation has been used as an integral
part of the study of international politics. While simulation was initially
utilized primarily as a research tool, it was not long before the pedagogical
advantages of this method became apparent. Instructors at both the college

225

and the secondary level were becoming familiar with simulation as a teaching device by the mid-1960s, and a variety of simulation exercises have been developed for this purpose. But adoption of simulation in this fashion has been accompanied by questions that have been raised by both users and developers concerning such wide-ranging problems as validity, student acceptance, the cost in time and resources, and the general ability held by students to transfer the learning experience from simulation to the real world of international politics. The sheer number of classroom simulations currently available has also posed a problem for instructors who must choose the simulation or simulations that best suit the goals of both the teacher and the course. The problem may be even more basic than this—should one use simulation at all?

The initial development of international relations simulations began in the late 1950s, with several projects originating at about the same time. In California, work was being done at the RAND Corporation by Herbert Goldhamer on the Political-Military Exercise (Goldhamer and Speier, 1961; Smoker, 1973), and the basic design of PME was later adopted and modified by Lincoln Bloomfield and Norman J. Padelford at MIT (Bloomfield, 1960; Bloomfield and Padelford, 1959). The late 1950s also saw development of Project TEMPER, funded by the Department of Defense, and created primarily by the Rayathon Company (Abt and Gordon, 1969). About the same time Harold Guetzkow at Northwestern began work on the Inter-Nation Simulation (INS), basing his initial model on an exhaustive propositional inventory of the international relations literature that existed at the time. While Guetzkow did not originally perceive INS as a pedagogical device, several of his graduate students, including Robert Noël and William Coplin, saw such possibilities, and later developed their own classroom simulations. Guetzkow himself, along with Cleo Cherryholmes, did develop a teaching version of INS, INSKIT, 1966, and this simulation remains in wide use today.

During the mid-1960s, interest in simulation in international politics grew, partially in response to the work by Guetzkow and others, and partially in response to the growing interest in the subject shown by the federal government, and particularly the Defense Department. While gaming has long been a part of military training and planning, advances by social scientists were causing the military to become more aware of the advances in simulation that, among other things, integrated "political" and "military" variables and concepts together in a single exercise. The Defense Department thus began making arrangements for cooperation with social scientists in the development of simulation-related exercises, and funding was provided by both the Air Force and the Navy. The Navy's participation in particular led to Project Michelson, which was conducted at the Naval Ordnance Test Station at China Lake, California, between 1959 and 1966, and led to a large number of studies produced by scholars such as Charles and Margaret Hermann, Harold Guetzkow, Thomas Milburn, J. David Singer, Thomas Schelling, Richard C. Snyder, and many others (Milburn, 1969).

This initial work in simulation was bound to spill over into pedagogical applications, and the early work by Guetzkow and Cherryholmes, Bloomfield, and Coplin, has been joined today by a large number of classroom-oriented simulation devices, which vary in complexity from simple board games to complex, computer-based interactive models that require some degree of sophistication on the part of the participants.

One of the more prolific developers of pedagogical simulation exercises in the area of international politics has been Professor William Coplin of Syracuse University. Coplin has developed, for example, the State System Exercise, which, because of its very simplicity, is a good simulation to use in classroom situations where the students are relatively unfamiliar with the technique. This simulation is also useful as an integrative device to combine macro and micro theories of international politics at a basic level. Coplin has also developed PRINCE, a more complex simulation, and his most recent effort is Everyman's PRINCE, a simulation that allows the student insights into the resolution of a variety of political problems.

Another simulation exercise that has attracted quite a bit of attention, especially on the West Coast, is POLIS, developed by Robert Noël (another Guetzkow student), along with William Hyder, both currently at the University of California at Santa Barbara. POLIS (which stands for *POL*itical *I*nstitutions *S*imulation) allows students to play a variety of crisis and noncrisis situations derived from real-world situations. While Noël developed his own elaborate POLIS laboratory at UCSB, it is possible for students at other institutions to play POLIS via interactive terminals in an interuniversity setting, with members of each participating university taking the role of a specific nation and its decision-makers (Dickinson, 1976). These teams interject actions into the POLIS network based on position papers programmed into the simulation. So far, more than 35 colleges have participated in POLIS in this manner, and, while this number is expected to grow, the problems of communications costs for schools outside California ($500 in some cases) may limit the expansion of the system.

STARTREK, an interactive simulation designed to simulate nuclear strategy and the effects of nuclear weapons capacity, has been developed at the University of Michigan. STARTREK is played via a programmed interactive television, and the player may introduce various options in a man-machine setting, and the program will respond to changes in both strategy and capacity. While the Michigan version of STARTREK is programmed in FORTRAN, a version of the simulation written in BASIC is now available at Dartmouth College.

From this brief description of the development of simulation in international politics, we may now turn to three specific simulations for a more detailed examination. The three are "Conflict in the Middle East," "INS," and "Nuclear Deterrence."

I.   *"Conflict in the Middle East"*

"Conflict in the Middle East: A Public Policy Simulation," was developed by Professor Karen Ann Feste of the Graduate School of International Studies at the University of Denver. This simulation is one of a series entitled Supplementary Empirical Teaching Units in Political Science (SETUPS), and the series itself is the result of a project authorized by the American Political Science Association and funded by a grant from the National Science Foundation. The actual work on the SETUPS projects was done in cooperation with the Inter-University Consortium for Political Research at the University of Michigan. The Test Edition of "Conflict in the Middle East" was published by the American Political Science Association in September, 1975, and the revised edition for actual classroom use expected to be ready for publication in the fall of 1976.

The actual simulation is designed to give students an understanding of both the situation in the Middle East (current and projected), and also to provide some understanding of how theories of international relations commonly found in the literature may aid in explaining the various political outcomes found in the region. The simulation thus introduces a number of salient issues found in the area that require students to accumulate some degree of knowledge about the area itself and about the interests held there by major powers, before actually playing the simulation. The first section of "Conflict in the Middle East" is devoted to a summary of major events and political interests in the region, and exercises are available that require some library research on the student's part. The simulation is based in part upon a data set collected by Barry M. Blechman (now of the Brookings Institution) on the countries of Israel, Egypt, Jordan, Syria, Lebanon, and Iraq. These events are categorized by the following questions (Feste, 1975):

1.   Which country in the Middle East is identified as initiator of the action?
2.   What type of action occurs?
3.   Which Middle East country is the target of the action?
4.   What is the issue of the action?
5.   When did the event happen?

A classification system for actions between countries was also established, with actions coded into 22 basic categories where such actions as registering a complaint, threatening another nation, and the establishment or rupture of diplomatic relations are characterized by a basic key word like COMPLAINT, THREAT, WARN, etc. (Feste, 1975, 52). These data are provided by the Inter-University Consortium for Political Research and can be used simultaneously with the simulation, but they are not necessary to the central purposes of the game. It is possible to use the data set in conjunction with the student exercises contained in the SETUPS manual.

The simulation is actually played through the assignment of students into country teams, and the first assignment of each team is to write a policy position paper outlining the positions that the nation will take in the first round of the game. The teams consist of:

1.	Israel	9.	United States
2.	Egypt	10.	Soviet Union
3.	Jordan	11.	United Kingdom
4.	Syria	12.	France
5.	Lebanon	13.	Palestinians
6.	Saudi Arabia	14.	United Nations
7.	Iraq	15.	Rest of the World (ROW)
8.	Iran	16.	Press

Some of these actors may be excluded if the number of students is insufficient.

After the policy papers are completed, they are turned over to the Press, and communications between the teams commences, with the Director serving as the communications channel. Either bilateral or multilateral negotiations may occur, and alliances or joint sponsors of resolutions become common. The nation-state players have the most flexibility, but the nonnation players hold important roles. The team representing the United Nations has the task of outlining and playing the various situations that the organization may find itself involved in in the Middle East, specifically, as a peacekeeping force, or by provision of envoys to negotiations. The team that plays the Press may in itself be divided into teams representing the *New York Times* and *Pravda* if there are sufficient players; otherwise it may be a unitary actor. Each country team submits a series of news releases to the Press along with their policy papers (unless classified), and the Press compiles a report on the day's activities. The Press is the only means by which all players get the total picture of the events taking place. Finally, a team composed of the rest of the world (ROW) provides input from other nations or organizations (including multinationals) that may hold interests in the area. ROW participation must be called for only by request of the national teams in the area.

The major objectives of the game are to have all teams enact the position outlined in their position papers. The game is divided into move periods of about 30-60 minutes, with four moves as the recommended minimum. The actual control of the game is provided by the Simulation Director, who, in addition to faciliating communication between players, performs such functions as ensuring the representative nature of moves and disallowing moves that are unrealistic or invalid. In addition, the Simulation Director assigns a probability of success or failure to each move, calculated as follows:

Nature of Decision	Probability of Success
Routine	100%
Moderately routine	80%
Serious, nonroutine	60%
Moderately extreme, drastic	40%
Extreme	20%
Unrealistic	0%

In the event of a war occurring, a War Outcome table is provided for the calculations of the probability of success or failure for any given move, or moves. The sequence of play is as follows:

1. Newspaper distribution
2. Country strategy session
3. International conference
4. Country session—form move
5. Move submitted to Control
6. Move submitted to Press
7. Press constructs newspaper

As the moves are made, the probability of success or failure is assigned.

Before the final version of "Conflict in the Middle East" was published, the test versions were used in a number of classroom situations during the 1975-1976 academic year. Feedback from the evaluation forms that accompanied the simulation was to be used in making any necessary changes in the final version. From preliminary test results, several things emerged. First, students appeared to be enthusiastic about the simulation and, in most cases, were willing to do the necessary background preparation. Second, the simulation seemed to work best when preceded by other, simpler exercises during the course, such as the Coplin State System Exercise mentioned earlier. Professor Feste has used SSE and one other simulation in her own course in international politics before introducing the students to SETUPS, which was played during the last few weeks of the quarter. Finally, it is interesting to note that the students playing the simulation showed a high reluctance to engage in military conflict, preferring strategies of negotiation and cooperation below the war threshold, and this factor was also observed during a run-through of the simulation during the module. But it seems that once the simulation is played past three turns, the probability of conflict becomes much higher. A similar phenomenon, incidentally, has been observed in the use of POLIS, mentioned earlier, where, in more than two thousand hours of gaming, war took place only once (Dickinson, 1976, 58).

II. *The Inter-Nation Simulation*

As noted earlier, the Inter-Nation Simulation (INS) was originally developed for research use, and in this guise the simulation has produced a number of interesting studies. Margaret Hermann (1966) used INS to measure the effect of psychological stress on crisis decision-making, and has produced several follow-up studies to this one since then, with work in progress on further research. Daniel Druckman applied INS to test the hypothesis of ethnocentrism as a universal characteristic of nations (Druckman, 1968), and studies of conflict have been done by the Hermanns (Hermann and Hermann, 1967), on the outbreak of World War I, by Richard Brody to simulate the effects of a multinuclear future (Brody, 1963), by John Raser and Wayman Crow to study nuclear deterrence (Raser and Crow, 1964), and these cited studies represent only a small sample of INS as a research tool.

Although INS has been used as a teaching device since 1958, the Inter-Nation Simulation Kit (INSKIT) was not published until 1963. The kit, in its original form contains:

> Instructors' Manuals
> Participants' Manuals
> 350 Main Decision Forms
> 250 Inter-Nation Agreement Forms
> 100 Statements of Goals and Strategies
> 300 Official Advisory Forms
> 150 Force Utilization Plans

INS players are divided into teams of nations, and either fictional or real nations may be used. Each nation is assigned certain characteristics, such as Overall Satisfaction with Foreign Affairs, Domestic Satisfaction, Decision Latitude, Basic Resources, Population, and so forth (see Guetzkow and Cherryholmes, 1966, 8-10, for complete list). These characteristics are organized along three systems: political, economic, and military. The values for these characteristics are either assigned by the Simulation Director (i.e., changes in satisfaction characteristic), calculated by the players, or drawn from standard sources of political, economic, and population data, such as the World Handbook, the World Almanac, etc.

The nation-teams are divided into subcategories, such as Head of State (HS), Foreign Policy Adviser (FPA), etc., and, as Guetzkow and Cherryholmes state, "The central driving mechanism of the INS is the need for decision-makers to hold office to remain in control of their government" (Guetzkow, 1968, 17). This requirement is important, as INS has opposition forces built into it, and internal political change can come about through several means.

International relations are carried out in the INS in several ways. Nations may communicate directly through written messages, and bilateral and multilateral conferences may be held. International organizations may also be formed, as may alliances. Nations may also trade with each other, issue threats, and go to war with other nations. The INS routine includes "free," or unprogrammed, behavior that allows for the distribution of various messages by nations in the world press, which may be either truthful or deceiving, but in any event allow for students to create their own forms of inter-nation behavior (Guetzkow, 1968, 17).

For Guetzkow and Cherryholmes, the purpose of the INS is to give "the participants the experience of making decisions in a miniature prototype of the complicated international world" (Guetzkow and Cherryholmes, 1966, 2). But INS has not been without its critics. Alker and Brunner (1969, 108) discuss "fallacies of misplaced variables and relationships" and note that problems arose when players were not always able to transfer the experience with fictional nations to their real-world referents. Edwin H. Fedder (1969) suggests that INS is mistaken in its assumption that alliance formation adds to the power of any individual member and, further, that the "war" option in INS lacks constraints against such an option that exists in the real world. Coplin (1966, 569) notes that "many verbal theorists could not agree with the neglect of the impact of domestic restraints on the actual processes of negotiation" and, further, that ". . . the simulation does not provide the sets of specific issues which, according to some theorists, characterize the international environment." And, finally, Smoker (1973, 445) has reviewed the validity studies of INS, and claims that ". . . the reality performance of INS leaves much to be desired." In addition, at least one study has questioned the value of INS as a teaching device (to be discussed later in this paper). But criticism of the original INS has not gone unnoticed by its developers and by others, and several revisions are now either available, or will become available shortly. One such revision is now being developed by Guetzkow and W. Ladd Hollist. This version updates data in the original INS with CREON data and data collected by Professor Edward Azar of the University of North Carolina. The revised INS also substitutes Richardson process equations for some of the original equations for the calculation of parameters, and this is particularly true in the case of competitive arms interactions between dyads of nations, and real test data has been generated and examined with Richardson equations to measure the amount of interaction between:

USA/USSR
Israel/Egypt
Iran/Iraq
India/Pakistan

The submodels used to measure dyadic reaction are the Reaction Model, the Rivalry Model, the Submissiveness Model, the Explicit Cost Constraint Model, the Reaction/Technology Model, and the Consolidated Arms Race Model (two trials) in order to assess such reactions (Hollist, 1976; Hollist and Guetzkow, 1976). The revised INS will also include a set of hypothesized relationships between and within an arms expenditure module, an economic development module, and an inter-nation cooperation and conflict module. In addition to the variables and parameters specified in the arms race model, this relationship will include variables for an economic development model, such as education, expanding GNP, and tax revenue; and variables for cooperation and conflict, such as inter-nation trade, foreign investment, and foreign aid (including both grants and loans). Such additions will add richness to the original INSKIT, and this version should be available once publishing arrangements are complete.

Another version of INS is now available in draft form, developed by Dr. Bahram Farzanegan at the University of North Carolina (Asheville) and R. J. Parker of the North Carolina Educational Computing Service. While the basic structure of INS remains similar, the NCESC version is fully computerized, and time-consuming calculations that students had to make are now done for them by machine. The NCESC version (called INS2) is currently undergoing evaluation, and should be ready for distribution shortly.

The final simulation in this paper is NUCLEAR DETERRENCE, developed by the author with assistance through a grant from the Lilly Endowment, Inc. This simulation involves an effort to simulate nuclear deterrence in both theoretical and applied form. The simulation itself is designed for several purposes, and the first involves the need to organize pedagogically the complex factors required for a thorough understanding of nuclear deterrence. Such factors include deterrence theory itself, capacity analysis, measurement of intent, perceptual variables such as perception and misperception, the impact of technology, alliance structures, cost and risk analysis, and so forth. It is one purpose of NUCLEAR DETERRENCE to enhance student understanding of the interrelationships among these factors as they are organized into a cohesive framework. NUCLEAR DETERRENCE is also designed to demonstrate the difference between theoretical and applied approaches to deterrence. It may be noted that much of the contemporary literature on deterrence relies on assumptions of "rationality" (George and Smoke, 1974, Ch. 4; Schelling, 1960), and these assumptions have been primarily derived from game-theoretic models. But in NUCLEAR DETERRENCE it is possible for students to opt for either "rational" or "nonrational" choices, where nonrational implies the presence and effect of certain modes of behavior that may lead to nonmaximalizing responses. NUCLEAR DETERRENCE also allows comparison of the "maximalist" versus the "minimalist" approach to deterrence. The "minimalist" approach is practiced by nations that cannot afford to achieve nuclear parity with the superpowers (the U.S. and the USSR), and thus rely on attempting to convince a potential superpower attacker that even a small number of successful nuclear shots will cause unacceptable damage. The "maximalist" approach, practiced by the U.S. and the USSR, seeks to convince an opponent that unacceptable damage will be wrought upon him in the event of a nuclear attack, but differs in that the target for the initial strike will be the opponent's nuclear force, made in an effort to minimize damage from the use of such a force. This approach thus implies nuclear parity as a requirement for a maximalist approach, and thus questions about comparative nuclear capacity become much more important with this approach.

There has been an important debate in the discipline of international politics about the meaning and measurement of nuclear capacity, and such questions are partially addressed in the simulation. Nuclear capacity will be measured in at least two ways: number of warheads, number of launchers (land-based intercontinental ballistic missile submarines), and the total effect of these measurements will be combined with measurements of accuracy. This is done through the calculation of K (kill capacity) as expressed by

$$K = \frac{NY^{(2/3)}}{(CEP)^2}$$

where NY stands for nuclear yield (the capacity of deliverable megatonnage) and CEP means circular error probability, defined as the radius of a circle within which 50 percent of nuclear shots will fall. All nuclear-equipped nations will be provided with K factors, which will correspond to real estimates of K held by the nations involved. Because decisions about the size of K and its advantages and limitations are affected by (and in turn affect) strategic choices, each nation's K will serve as a parameter on the choices available. For example, K is affected much more by quantum increases in accuracy than through increases in throw weight (launch vehicle payload capacity) and megatonnage, and thus advantages in K normally reflect advantages in accuracy over nuclear yield. This advantage may be translated into a relatively higher probability for a successful counterforce strike (against hardened ICBMs) for those who hold it, and lower Ks may compel either an attacker or a responder to an attack to target softer targets such as cities, with less military advantage. The advantage in K that the United States is expected to hold by 1980 over the Soviet Union (approximately 8:1) will ultimately give the U.S. a first-strike capability over Soviet ICBMs, and the USSR is not expected to overcome this advantage until 1990. Information such as this will be given to students, and they will be able to plan their strategies accordingly. This information will be supplemented by a calculated probability of success for various combinations of nuclear attack. The probability of a single-shot kill probability (SSKP) and the chances of a single nuclear warhead achieving a hit within the lethal radius (LR) and scoring a kill will be provided, as will the calculated errors involved in a multiple firing of a nuclear system. Each step of the missile flight holds a certain error of failure attached to it, and these error probabilities are multiplicative—thus more complex systems are more prone to error than are simple ones, and consequently students may make choices along this direction as well. They may calculate the error probabilities attached to both opponent and alliance nuclear forces as well as their own systems. It can be noted in passing that K factors are now being used by both the United States and the Soviet Union to calculate nuclear capacity, so the measure does approximate reality.

Students will also have the option of choosing between strategic and tactical nuclear weapons. While the actual distinction between strategic and tactical weapons is admittedly blurred, strategic weapons will be operationalized as land-based ICBMs, submarine-launched ballistics missiles of over 1,000-mile range, and manned strategic bombers. Weapons below this threshold will be labeled "tactical," and will be seen as limited primarily to limited battlefield situations. In order for this choice to approximate reality, students will be introduced to the concept of a "firebreak" between nuclear and nonnuclear (conventional) forces, so that this latter option will be available as well, with its lower risk factor. Students may decide on their own whether the threat is sufficient to warrant the crossing of the firebreak to tactical nuclear weaponry, and finally may ascertain whether this crossing will ultimately lead to the use of strategic nuclear weapons in an all-out conflict. Such choices will provide a real assessment of the costs and risks involved in deterrent choices where nuclear weapons are concerned.

The first trials of NUCLEAR DETERRENCE will involve only the U.S. and the USSR, but subsequent trials will include the other nuclear-equipped nations as well, specifically, Great Britain, France, and the People's Republic of China. India is not presently included because she lacks a deliverance capacity. These other nations will allow some interesting possibilities, especially with respect to alliance formation. One such situation may arise if the Soviets engage in a simulated attack on Western Europe, and the French become faced with the choice of either using the minimalist (Gallois) approach unilaterally, or allying themselves with either the U.S. alone or with NATO. A Soviet attack on the People's Republic of China also poses interesting alliance possibilities for alliance formation between the PRC and the United States.

As noted above, students will have the option of employing "non-rational" responses to the various actions in the simulation. This will allow the students to become more aware of the effect that emotions and other personality factors have on crisis decision-making. In addition, the concept of "national character" will be programmed into the play. This concept is controversial among international relations scholars, and it is being used here only to approximate the national goals that the various national actors in the simulation may hold, as well as the means used to obtain such goals. For example, the Chinese concept of defense policy has been characterized as defensive in nature, with little attention paid to expansion beyond Chinese national borders, or areas that have not been a part of China in some period of history. On the other hand, the Soviets have shown themselves willing to engage in expansionary behavior when it suits their national interests, and when the risks and costs are not perceived as excessive. Similar characteristics may be identified for the other nations in the simulation based on their foreign policy behavior, although they may not be as precise as those indicated for the Soviets or the Chinese. The purpose of this concept is simply to constrain student players in their choice of options.

III. *Evaluations and Conclusions*

At this point, it is apparent that the use of simulation in the teaching of international politics has been widespread, and appears to be growing rapidly. But is such a development justified in terms of the effort and expenditure of resources? What is the opportunity cost involved in substituting simulation for lecture and class discussion? If it can be shown that the use of simulation increases student motivation and interest in studying international politics and, further, that students learn as much or more through simulation as through the more traditional methods of teaching, the use of simulation may well be justified. But the available evidence of this is not very conclusive. When INS was originally developed at Northwestern University, the developers and their associates reported that the simulation raised the interest and motivation of the students involved, and this occurred in part due to the student's enjoyment of the simulation runs (Alger, 1963). Similar results were reported on the use of the Political Military Exercise at MIT (Bloomfield and Padelford, 1959, 1112). But these claims were not accompanied by empirical data to verify them, and it was not until 1966 that an empirical evaluation of INS appeared that did not exactly support the earlier enthusiasm seen above. Robinson, *et al.*, compared the use of case studies and INS in international relations courses, and found that, in terms of learning differences, levels of motivation, and amount of interest shown, there was no significant difference between the two approaches (Robinson, *et al.*, 1966). Such findings, which the authors indicate have been supported elsewhere by Charles McClelland (p. 65), are troublesome when one considers the amount of time and cost involved in preparing case studies for teaching compared with the much greater allocation of such resources involved in purchasing, preparing, and running INS, or some other simulation. It would, in fact, lead users or potential users of simulation in search of more recent evaluations that might disconfirm these earlier findings, but one of the original authors (Margaret Hermann) has indicated to this writer that these results remain confirmed by later tests. It must be noted, of course, that the findings pertain directly to INS only, as it was the simulation used in the experiment, but it is not unrealistic to generalize these findings to other simulations as well, although it may be surmised that the tedious calculations involved in INS and the problem of identifying with the fictional nation-states in that simulation may have detracted from the learning experience.

Why use simulation in the classroom at all, then? Perhaps several reasons may be offered by way of conclusion. First, despite the impressive and complete nature of the Robinson, *et al.*, findings, clearly more research needs to be done on the effectiveness of international simulations before any final verdicts may be rendered. Second, questions may be raised about whether motivation and interest are things that a simulation should be able to generate by itself in the first place. Granted, if a simulation produces only boredom or frustration, it should either be abandoned or at least revised. But, in this writer's opinion, the principal purpose of any simulation should be to instruct students in the complexities of international politics, and the interest and motivation should come from an involvement in the topic itself, and not simply from a supplemental simulation. The ultimate success or failure of any simulation may well rest, then, as much on the course itself, the quality of the lectures, discussions, and reading material, as it will upon the simulation itself. This implies that previous preparation in the topic is vital, and that simulation may well work best if used toward the latter part of any course. Alternatively, simulations should at least be well integrated into any course, with adequate time devoted both to preparation and debriefing. A number of instructors have found, in fact, that the debriefing sessions are often the most useful parts of the total simulation exercise, for it is here that the transfer of the learning experience from the simulation itself to the more generalized world of international politics may take place.

Finally, much more work needs to be done in the area of evaluation.

Fortunately, such evaluational work is now being done, and is now becoming available, for example, through the American Political Science Association's News for Teachers of Political Science and through various activities of the International Studies Association. As this work progresses, the task of selecting and using simulation effectively will, it is hoped, become much easier.

REFERENCES

Abt, Clark C., and Gorden, Morton. Report on project TEMPER. In Dean G. Pruitt and Richard C. Snyder, *Theory and research on the causes of war.* Englewood Cliffs, New Jersey: Prentice-Hall, Inc., 1969.

Alker, Hayward R., and Ronald D. Brunner. Simulating international conflict: A comparison of three approaches. *International Studies Quarterly* 13, 1, 1969, 70-110.

Bloomfield, Lincoln P. Political gaming. *United States Naval Institute Proceedings LXXXVI,* 9, 1960, 57-64.

Bloomfield, Lincoln P., and Padelford, Norman J. Three experiments in political gaming. *The American Political Science Review LIII,* 4, 1959, 1105-15.

Brody, Richard. Some systematic effects of the spread of nuclear weapons technology: A study through simulation of a multinuclear future. *The Journal of Conflict Resolution, VII,* 4, 1963, 663-753.

Coplin, William D. Inter-nation simulation and contemporary theories of international relations. *The American Political Science Review, LX,* 3, 1966, 562-578.

Dickinson, Jean. Games political scientists play. *Change, 8, 6,* 1976, 56-59.

Druckman, Daniel. Ethnocentrism in the inter-nation simulation. *The Journal of Conflict Resolution, XII,* 1, 1968, 45-68.

Fedder, Edwin H. On the use of models in simulations and games. *International Studies Quarterly,* 13, 1, 1969, 111-116.

Feste, Karen Ann. *Conflict in the middle east: A public policy simulation.* Washington, D.C.: The American Political Science Association, 1975.

George, Alexander, and, Smoke, Richard C. *Deterrence in American foreign policy—theory and practice.* New York and London: Columbia University Press, 1974.

Goldhamer, Herbert and Speier, Hans. Some observations on political gaming. In James N. Rosenau (ed.), *International politics and foreign policy.* New York: The Free Press, 1961, 498-503.

Guetzkow, Harold. Simulation in international relations. In William D.

Coplin, *Simulation in the study of politics.* Chicago: Markham, 1968, 9-30.

Guetzkow, Harold, and Cherryholmes, Cleo. *Inter-nation simulation kit.* Chicago: Science Research Associates, Inc., 1966.

Guetzkow, Harold; Alger, Chadwick; Snyder, Richard C.; Brody, Richard A.; and Noel, Robert C. *Simulation in international relations.* Englewood Cliffs, New Jersey: Prentice-Hall, Inc., 1963.

Hermann, Charles F., and Hermann, Margaret. An attempt to simulate the outbreak of World War I. *The American Political Science Review, LXI,* 2, 1967, 400-416.

Hollist, W. Ladd. Comparative empirical analysis of alternative explanations of competitive arms processes: The United States-Soviet Union, Israel-Egypt, Iran-Iraq, and India-Pakistan pairs of nations, from 1948 to 1973. Northwestern University (mimeo).

Hollist, W. Ladd, and Guetzkow, Harold. An empirical analysis and computer simulation of arms processes in the United States and the Soviet Union in the 1950's and 1960's: An illustrative use of a cumulative strategy for research in international affairs. Northwestern University (mimeo).

Milburn, Thomas W. Intellectual history of a research project. In Dean G. Pruitt and Richard C. Snyder, *Theory and research on the causes of war.* Englewood Cliffs, New Jersey: Prentice-Hall, Inc., 1966.

Raser, John R., and Wayman, J. Crow. A simulation study of deterrence theories. In Dean G. Pruitt and Richard C. Snyder, *Theories and research on the causes of war.* Englewood Cliffs, New Jersey, Prentice-Hall, Inc., 1966.

Robinson, James; Anderson, Lee F.; Hermann, Margaret G., and Snyder, Richard C. Teaching with inter-nation simulation and case studies. *The American Political Science Review, LX,* 1, 1966, 530-65.

Schelling, Thomas C. *Arms and influence.* New Haven: Yale University Press, 1963.

Smoker, Paul. International relations simulation: A summary. In Hayward R. Alker, Karl W. Deutsch, and Antoine H. Stoetzel, *Mathematical approaches to politics.* Amsterdam: Elsevier Scientific Publishing Co., San Francisco and Washington: Jossey-Bass, Inc., 1973.

Sorenson, David S. Nuclear deterrence. Granville, Ohio: Denison University, Department of Political Science, 1976. (Mimeo)

Part XI
PSYCHOLOGY

The first paper that follows, written by William Bewley, describes six computer-based experiments in cognitive psychology. They are designed to allow students to run themselves as subjects and to run a simulation of an information-processing model. Our use of these experiments at Denison has proven highly successful in demonstrating the dynamic and often complex processes underlying many contemporary models in cognitive psychology. Because the programs were written to allow manipulation of several parameters in each model, they encourage students to construct and test their own hypotheses against either simulated data or actual data they collect themselves. The package includes the six experiments, a student's manual, and an instructor's manual.

The second paper in this section follows Bewley's nicely, in that author Snyder describes a computer simulation designed for physiological psychology that is not too dissimilar from Bewley's programs. Snyder also, however, elaborates upon why she chose to turn to computer simulations for supplemental course work, as well as how she designed the simulation so as to meet those particular needs.

The final psychology paper, also written by Snyder, briefly overviews simulation-gaming approaches, as techniques for the college psychology classroom. Again, Snyder is analytic in discussing what considerations should be taken into account when deciding whether or not to use gaming, and then, once the decision is made, what kinds of games are available at the college level.

15

A COMPUTER-ORIENTED INTRODUCTION TO COGNITIVE PSYCHOLOGY

WILLIAM L. BEWLEY

ABSTRACT

This paper describes a laboratory manual for psychology called *Cognitive Psychology: A Computer-Oriented Laboratory Manual.* The material in the manual is presented by means of six experiments, each of which is run on a time-shared computer system using the BASIC language, and a teletype terminal as the input/output device. In each experiment, a computer program presents a task to the student and a simulation of a model of human information processing relevant to the task. Most of the programs are designed so that features of the tasks and the models can be changed by the student, allowing the running of experiments on the model or on other humans.

The present paper is divided into four sections. The first is concerned with technical details of the computer program and with the question of transportability to different systems. The second section describes the organization of the manual. Section three briefly describes the six experiments that can be run with the manual. The fourth section presents a rationale for the instructional use of the computer, discussing what students should learn from the manual and why the computer is needed to help them learn.

I. Technical Details and Transportation

As mentioned in the abstract, the computer programs on which the manual is based were written for a time-shared computer and use a teletype terminal for input and output. CRT output would be desirable because of its speed and silence, but all of the experiments require that the student obtain a "hard copy" of the output.

The programs were originally written in BASIC for the PDP-11 RSTS System. They were later translated into Dartmouth BASIC for use on the Dartmouth Time-Sharing System and to KRONOS BASIC for use at the University of Colorado. They are presently being installed on the UNIVAC 1110 time-sharing system in Minnesota. No insurmountable problems have been encountered in these translations, most of the difficulty being related to idiosyncratic system functions for measuring clock time. CONDUIT has recently standardized the programs, making them even more transportable.

Each of the programs requires at least 8K of storage and from 30 to 60 minutes of terminal time to run.

II. *Organization of the Manual*

The manual is really two manuals, one for the students and one for instructors. Each is approximately 100 pages long. The main body of the student manual consists of material relating to the six experiments. The material for each experiment includes a brief abstract, a description of the experimental procedure, a description of the model, a set of study questions designed to encourage critical evaluation of the model and independent experimentation, and a general discussion that briefly describes alternative models and suggests further reading. In addition to material on the six experiments, the student manual contains an introduction describing the relation of each experiment to a general information-processing model, and two appendices, one dealing with a suggested format for lab reports and the other with the minimum chi square procedure for goodness of fit.

The instructor manual contains program listings and documentation, remedies for a few potential transportability problems, and answers to the study questions contained in the student manual.

III. *The Experiments*

The six experiments were chosen to cover the range of cognitive activity represented in current general conceptions of the human information-processing system, e.g., Atkinson and Shiffrin (1968), Norman and Rumelhart (1970), and Atkinson, Herrmann, and Wescourt (1974).

Each experiment is conducted using a computer program that presents a student with both an experimental task and a simulation of an information-processing model. The task and model associated with each experiment are summarized below.

EXPERIMENT 1. PATTERN RECOGNITION

Task: The task is a partial replication of the visual search experiment of Neisser (1963). Students search through 50 6-letter lines for the presence or absence of 1 or 2 target letters in a context that is visually similar to or different from the target. If, for example, "Z" was the target, a line with visually similar context might be "EXIMZW"; a line with visually different context might be "CDGOZU."

The student is allowed to specify the target, the number of targets, and the context from a standard set of alternatives (those in Neisser's experiment). He or she can also specify nonstandard target and context letters and choose to run a subject and the simulation or the simulation alone.

The program records search latencies for both the student and the simulation.

Model: The model is a nonlearning version of the Selfridge (1959) Pandemonium. It has a memory that associates visual features, e.g., straight lines, curves, and angles, with letter names. It assumes feature extraction with hierarchical and parallel processing of features. These assumptions lead to certain predictions about search latencies. The student is asked to evaluate the model by comparing his or her search latencies with those of the model. The student also evaluates the model by comparing its capabilities with those of template matching and scene analysis models, (e.g., Guzman, 1969; Winston, 1970, 1973).

A more detailed description of this experiment can be found in Bewley (1974).

EXPERIMENT 2. SHORT-TERM MEMORY

Task: The task is based on the continuous memory experiment of Atkinson and Shiffrin (1968). Students are presented with a series of paired-associate trials in which they are first asked to recall the response most recently paired with a stimulus and then to study the pairing of a new response with that stimulus. The independent variable is the "lag" or time between study and recall. The dependent variable is the probability of correct recall at each of the six lags. These data are recorded for both the student and the model.

The student can choose to run the standard experiment, in which the stimuli are six two-digit numbers and the possible responses are all letters of the alphabet, or he or she can choose to specify any even number of stimuli from two to twelve. The sequence of stimulus presentation can also be specified. The student can choose to run a subject and the simulation or the simulation alone.

Model: The model is the buffer model of Atkinson and Shiffrin (1968). This model assumes that incoming information passes through three different memory stores: a sensory register, the short-term store, and the long-term store. The short-term store is assumed to contain a limited capacity rehearsal buffer.

There are four model parameters that can be manipulated by the student: (1) *r,* the capacity of the rehearsal buffer; (2) *a,* the probability that information in the sensory register enters the rehearsal buffer; (3) ϕ, the rate at which information is transferred from short-term store to long-term store, and (4) *T,* the rate at which information is lost from long-term store. The student runs experiments with the simulation, manipulating parameters in an attempt to make the model's behavior match the student's and to determine the effect of each parameter on the model's behavior.

The manual's discussion of this experiment suggests that rehearsal is an information-processing strategy evoked by the nature of the continuous memory task. The Reitman (1970) queuing model, which has no rehearsal mechanism, is presented as an example of a short-term memory model appropriate for tasks in which rehearsal is less appropriate, e.g., the memory span task.

Experiment 3. Long-Term Memory

Task: The task is the Palermo and Eberhart (1968) paired-associate task. Subjects learn a list of number-bigram pairs, e.g., "61-VM," by the study-test method. Most of the pairings follow a rule that relates a particular number to a letter; e.g., if "6" is the first number in the stimulus, "V" is the first letter in the response. A few of the pairings, the "irregular pairs," violate the rule. Of the pairs that follow the rule, some are not presented during the study phase. These are called "omitted regular pairs." In order to respond correctly to these pairs, the student must learn the rule. The regular pairs that are presented during the study phase are called "presented regular pairs." Each of the presented regular pairs is presented once during the study phase; each irregular pair is presented twice.

The dependent variable is the proportion of correct responses for irregular pairs, omitted regular pairs, and presented regular pairs.

The purpose of the experiment is to provide an experimental analogy to children's learning of morphological rules. Ervin (1964) found that children tend to learn the past tense inflections of the more frequent irregular verbs (verbs for which there is no rule for forming past tense, e.g., came, went, did), before those for regular verbs (verbs for which there is a rule for forming past tense inflections, e.g., kissed, hugged, loved). When children learn how to inflect the regular verbs, however, they begin to make mistakes on irregular verbs, e.g., comed, goed, doed. The nature of the mistakes suggests that they are "overregularizing"— applying the rule too broadly. If the same thing happens in the paired associate experiment, students should learn the irregular pairs first and then, when they learn the rule for the regular pairs (as indicated by correct responses on the omitted regular pairs), they should make over-regularizing errors on the irregular pairs.

Model: The model is the Hintzman (1968) discrimination net model. This model, which is a modification of the Feigenbaum (1963) EPAM model, assumes that stimulus discrimination is the primary process in learning. Long-term memory is represented as a discrimination net consisting of a hierarchy of test nodes that look for the presence of particular items in particular positions of the stimulus. The net for the pair "61-VM" is shown below. The test mode in line 1 is looking for the presence

Line	S/R	Position	Positive	Negative
1	6	1	2	3
2	VM			
3	?			

of "6" in the first position of the stimulus. If a "6" is found (the outcome of the test is positive), control is transferred to line 2, where the response is stored. If the outcome of the test is negative, control is transferred to line 3, which indicates that the correct response is not known.

The model learns by adding new test nodes or by changing stored responses. These are three parameters: (1) *A,* the probability that a new test node is added following an incorrect response; (2) *B,* the probability that, if a new test node is not added following an incorrect response, the stored response is changed, and (3) *C,* the probability that a new test node is added following a correct response.

There are two computer programs associated with this experiment. The first, which is called PAL, presents the paired associate task to the student and the model but provides for no changes of the task or model parameters. The second program, SAL, allows the student to manipulate parameter values, to run either a subject and the simulation or the simulation alone, to specify the number of simulations to be run, to define list length and stimulus-response pairs, and to specify the maximum number of trials allowed. The student uses PAL to compare human behavior with model behavior on the Palermo and Eberhart (1968) paired associate task. SAL is used to run experiments with the model and with other paired associate tasks.

The manual's discussion of this experiment points out the weaknesses of the discrimination net as a model of long-term memory (e.g., it has no rule-learning strategies) and points to Anderson and Bower (1973), Kintsch (1972), Rumelhart, Lindsay, and Norman (1972), and Quillian (1969) as alternative models.

Experiment 4. Concept Learning

Task: The task is the blank trials concept identification task of Levine (1966). Students are given a series of concept-learning trials, each consisting of a pair of four-dimensional stimuli, e.g., a large black *T* on the left and a small white *X* on the right. They are told that one of the two stimuli is an example of the concept they are to learn. Some of the trials are "blank" trials in that the students receive no feedback on their response. The purpose of the blank trials is to provide information on the student's hypothesis about the identity of the concept.

The dependent variables are those employed by Levine (1966): the percentage of blank trials showing one of the possible hypotheses, the probability that the current hypothesis is retained following positive and negative feedback trials, and the number of hypotheses in the subject's pool of possible hypotheses.

Model: There are really four models associated with this experiment: (1) the sampling with replacement model of Restle (1962); (2) the local consistency model of Gregg and Simon (1967); (3) the consistency check model of Trabasso and Bower (1966), and (4) the focusing model of Levine (1966). All are "hypothesis models" in that they assume that the subject selects hypotheses about the correct concept from a pool of hypotheses. They differ primarily in the strategies used to select hypotheses.

The student can choose to run either a subject or one of the four models. If one of the models is chosen, the student can specify the number of replications to be run and the level of detail in the output. Level of detail ranges from the printing of summary statistics at the end of the simulation to the printing of the stimuli, the model's current pool of hypotheses, hypotheses selected by the model, and the model's response. If the computer system has more than 8K storage, it is also possible to install an attention mechanism that allows a choice of the number and identity of stimulus dimensions to be attended to. This mechanism requires only 14 additional lines.

The manual presents S-R theory, e.g., Hull (1920), and mediated S-R theories, e.g., Kendler and Kendler (1962), and Zeaman and House (1963), as alternatives to hypothesis theories. It suggests that S-R theories and hypothesis theories might represent alternative concept learning strategies, with strategy selection being controlled by factors such as the nature of the task and instructions.

EXPERIMENT 5.   DECISION-MAKING

Task: The task for this experiment is a game similar to the famous Prisoner's Dilemma Game. There are two players, the student and the computer. To play the game, each player makes one of two possible choices. The outcome of the game is determined by the payoff matrix shown below:

Computer

		1	2
Student	1	4,4	1,3
	2	3,1	0,0

If both players make the same choice, both receive an equal number of points—4 for choice 1 and 0 for choice 2. If the players make different choices, the player making choice 2 receives 3 points and the opponent receives one point.

The experiment involves playing 75 of these games. There are two independent variables. The first is the type of feedback the student receives after each game. With OWN feedback, the student is told the number of points he or she received in the last game and his or her total points. RELATIVE feedback tells the student the number of points he or she received in the last game and the *difference* between his or her total points and the computer's total points.

The second independent variable is the pattern of the computer's responses. There are two patterns, U and inverted U. The pattern refers to changes in the frequency of "1" choices by the computer over the 75 games. In the U pattern, the frequency is high in the early and late games and low in the middle games. This is reversed for the inverted U pattern: the frequency is low in the early and late games and high in the middle.

The student can set values for these variables and has the option of running a subject and a simulation of the associated model or a simulation alone.

Model: The model is a combination of the social motives model of Messick and McClintock (1968) and a stochastic learning model of choice behavior described by Rapoport and Chammah (1965). The social motives portion of the model assumes that there are two possible motives in the game: (1) a motive for own gain, in which the player attempts to maximize his or her own points, and (2) a motive for relative gain in which the player attempts to maximize the difference between his or her points and those of the opponent. The motive for own gain leads the player to make choice 1; the motive for relative gain leads to choice 2.

The probability of a player holding one of the two motives is determined by the opponent's response, using a linear operator equation taken from scholastic learning theory:

$$P(g+1) = AP(g) + (1-A)\text{L}$$

$P(g)$ is the probability of a motive at the beginning of game g. $P(g+1)$ is the probability at the beginning of game $g+1$. A and L are parameters that determine the rate and direction of probability change, respectively.

The model plays against the computer with its preprogrammed responses (determined by the response pattern variable) just as the student plays against the computer. The student can specify values for the A and L parameters in attempting to obtain the best fit of the model's behavior to student behavior and to determine the influence of the parameters on the model's behavior.

Prescriptive decision models for game situations, e.g., Rapoport (1967), and the descriptive models described by Rapoport and Chammah (1965) are presented as alternative decision-making models. Material on nongame decision-making is also mentioned, e.g., Coombs, Dawes, and Tversky (1970), Edwards and Tversky (1967), and Raiffa (1968).

EXPERIMENT 6. PROBLEM-SOLVING

Task: The task is the missionaries and cannibals problem. In a typical problem, there might be three missionaries, three cannibals, and a boat that holds a maximum of two people at the bank of a river. All six people and the boat are to be transferred to the opposite bank without ever having the cannibals outnumber the missionaries on either bank.

The program allows the student to specify any number of missionaries and cannibals and any boat capacity. It also allows the student to choose between running a subject or a simulation. If a subject is run, the program records errors and response time at each step of the solution. Errors at each step are recorded for a simulation.

Model: The model is the General Problem Solver (GPS) of Ernst and Newell (1969). The model uses means-end analysis as an heuristic to choose from among several operators appropriate to the missionaries and cannibals problem, e.g., "move one missionary and one cannibal to the river bank." Operators are chosen and applied by using three recursively connected procedures: TRANSFORM, REDUCE, and APPLY. TRANS-FORM attempts to transform the current problem situation into the desired problem situation. In order to do this, it calls on the REDUCE procedure to reduce the difference between the two situations. REDUCE calls on APPLY to apply an operator judged appropriate for reducing the difference.

As the simulation of the GPS model attempts to solve the problem, it prints a trace of its activity, including the current procedure and operator. If the model solves the problem, the program prints the number of errors at each step of the solution. The student uses the trace and the error data to compare the model's behavior with student problem-solving behavior.

The manual suggests that means-end analysis and the operators are information-processing strategies and discusses the influence of a person's perception of the task and his or her past experience on strategy selection in problem-solving. Functional fixedness and habitual set are used as examples.

The S-R theory of Maltzman (1955) and Gestalt theory (Kohler, 1925) are presented as alternative models.

IV. *Rationale*

A legitimate and important question to ask about any computer-oriented curriculum is whether the computer is really needed. Can students learn anything from the computer-oriented curriculum that could not be learned from a traditional curriculum? Does the new learning, if any, balance the added cost?

NEW LEARNING

A cognitive psychology course must include some discussion of the models relevant to the field. In most courses, presentation and analysis of models and associated data are the primary activity. This manual, it is hoped, includes at least some of the models most frequently discussed.

As usually presented by lecture and written description, these models can be extremely difficult for the student to comprehend. They are abstract and complicated. They are also dynamic; they represent processes rather than static structures. It is difficult to capture this feature in a verbal description.

The manual's use of the computer helps students comprehend the models and their behavior by representing them in a concrete and dynamic form. The students learn by experimenting with the models. They can manipulate parameters and tasks and then observe the effects of their manipulations. The effects that can be observed include the operation of the model because the models are presented as "glass boxes" rather than "black boxes." Students can see Pandemonium analyze the visual features of input letters and watch items enter and leave the rehearsal buffer; they can observe trial-by-trial changes in the contents of the hypothesis pool and, in the probability of holding the "own gain" motive, they can follow the sequence of GPS procedure and operator activation. The result of all this is that the student will learn more about the models and about cognitive psychology.

The computer may also help students learn how to learn and think.

The computer allows the student to evaluate the adequacy of models and to tinker with the models in an attempt to test hypotheses about the causes of their behavior. While testing hypotheses and trying to solve problems with the models, the students should be learning something about how to test hypotheses and solve problems.

In addition to providing an opportunity for students to test hypotheses and solve problems, the computer may be providing models for learning and thinking. College students have no doubt mastered rehearsal as a memory mnemonic, but have they all discovered the power of focusing or means-end analysis as problem-solving strategies? Are they even aware of the fact that they can use strategies and that some are more appropriate for certain tasks than others? Have they ever thought about the use of critical tests in drawing conclusions from partial evidence as suggested by Pandemonium and the discrimination net? This idea, that the computer may provide models for learning and thinking, has been developed further by Bewley, Holznagel, and Klassen (1975).

Cost

Whether the value added by the use of the computer outweighs the cost of requiring the computer is a judgment that will have to be made by potential users of the manual. As you might expect, I believe that it does.

I also believe that, at some institutions, the cost of requiring the computer may be insignificant. When I developed the manual, I was teaching at Lawrence University, a small (1,500 students) liberal arts college in Wisconsin. I had little laboratory space and no equipment suitable for a cognitive psychology course serving 60 students. There were eight terminals and a PDP-11 sitting around, though, and I found I could run the laboratory on the terminals free of charge. If there had been a charge, the cost would have been at least partly offset by savings on lab space and equipment. A description of my experience with this course, using an early version of the manual, can be found in Bewley (1973.)

REFERENCES

Anderson, J. R., and Bower G. H. *Human associative memory.* Washington, D.C.: V. H. Winston, 1973.
Atkinson, R. C., and Shiffrin, R. Human memory: A proposed system

and its control processes. In K. W. Spence and J. T. Spence (eds.) *The psychology of learning and motivation: Advances in research and theory,* Vol. 2. New York: Acadamic Press, 1968.

Atkinson, R. C., Herrmann, D. J., and Wescourt, K. T. Search processes in recognition memory. In R. L. Solso (ed.), *Theories in cognitive psychology: The Loyola Symposium.* Potomac, Maryland: Lawrence Erlbaum Associates, 1974.

Bewley, W. L. The use of time-shared terminals in a human-learning course. *Proceedings of the Fourth Conference on Computers in the Undergraduate Curricula,* Claremont Colleges, 1973.

Bewley, W. L. Computer-based experiments in cognitive psychology. *Creative Computing,* November-December, 1974, 36-42.

Bewley, W. L., Holznagel, D., and Klassen, D. L., Toward a cognitive-developmental rationale for the instructional use of computer simulations. *Proceedings of the 2nd World Conference on Computers in Education,* Marseilles, France, September 1975.

Coombs, C. H., Dawes, R. M., and Tversky, A. *Mathematical psychology: An introduction.* Englewood Cliffs, New Jersey: Prentice-Hall, Inc., 1970.

Edwards, W. and Tversky A. (eds.) *Decision making.* Harmondsworth, Middlesex, England: Penguin Books, 1967.

Ernst, G. W., and Newell, A. *GPS: A case study in generality and problem solving.* New York: Academic Press, 1969.

Ervin S. M. Imitation and structural change in children's language. In E. G. Lenneberg (ed.), *New directions in the study of language.* Cambridge: The M.I.T. Press, 1964.

Feigenbaum, E. A. The simulation of verbal learning behavior. In E. A. Feigenbaum and J. Feldman (eds.), *Computers and thought.* New York: McGraw-Hill Book Co., 1963.

Gregg, L. W. and Simon, H. A. Process models and stochastic theories of simple concept formation. *Journal of Mathematical Psychology,* 1967, *4,* 246-276.

Guzman, A. Decomposition of a visual scene into three-dimensional bodies. In A. Graselli (ed.), *Automatic interpretation and classification of images.* New York: Academic Press, 1969.

Hintzman, D. L. Explorations with a discrimination net model for paired-associate learning. *Journal of Mathematical Psychology,* 1968, *5,* 123-162.

Hull, C. L. Quantitative aspects of the evolution of concepts. *Psychological Monographs, 28,* Whole No. 123, 1920.

Kendler, H. H. and Kendler, T. S. Vertical and horizontal processes in problem solving. *Psychological Review,* 1962, *69,* 1-16.

Kintsch, W. Notes on the structure of semantic memory. In E. Tulving and W. Donaldson (eds.), *Organization of memory*. New York: Academic Press, 1972.

Kohler, W. *The mentality of apes*. London: Routledge and Kegan Paul, 1925. 2nd ed., available in paperback from Vintage Books, New York, 1959.

Levine, M. Hypothesis behavior by humans during discrimination learning. *Journal of Experimental Psychology*, 1966, *71*, 331-338.

Maltzmann, I., Thinking: From a behavioristic point of view. *Psychological Review*, 1955, *66*, 367-86.

Messick, D. M. and McClintock, C. G. Motivational bases of choice in experimental games. *Journal of Experimental Social Psychology*, 1968, *4*, 1-25.

Neisser, U. Decision-Time without reaction-time: Experiments in visual scanning. *American Journal of Psychology* 1963, *76*, 376-385.

Norman, D. A. and Rumelhart, D. E. A system for perception and memory. In D. A. Norman (ed.), *Models of human memory*. New York: Academic Press, 1970.

Palermo, D. S., and Eberhart, V. L. On the learning of morphological rules: An experimental analogy. *Journal of Verbal Learning and Verbal Behavior*, 1968, *7*, 337-344.

Quillian, M. R. The teachable language comprehender: A simulation program and theory of language. *Communications of the ACM*, 1969, *12*, 459-476.

Raiffa, E. *Decision analysis: Introductory lectures on choices under uncertainty*. Reading, Massachusetts: Addison-Wesley, 1968.

Rapoport, Amnon. Optimal policies for the prisoner's dilemma. *Psychological Review*, 1967, *74*, 136-148.

Reitman, J. S. Computer simulation of an information processing model of short-term memory. In D. A. Norman (ed.), *Models of human memory*. New York: Academic Press, 1970.

Restle, F. A. The selection of strategies in cue learning. *Psychological Review*, 1962, *69*, 320-43.

Rumelhart, D. E., Lindsay, P. H., and Norman, D. A. A process model for long-term memory. In E. Tulving and W. Donaldson (eds.), *Organization of memory*. New York: Academic Press, 1972.

Selfridge, O. Pandemonium: A paradigm for learning. In *Symposium on the Mechanization of Thought Processes*. London: HM Stationery Office, 1959.

Trabasso, T. and Bower, G. H. Presolution dimensional shifts in concept identification: A test of the sampling with replacement axiom in all-or-none models. *Journal of Mathematical Psychology*, 1966 *2*, 163-173.

Winston, P. H. Learning structural descriptions from examples. M.I.T.

Artificial Intelligence Laboratory Project. AI-TR-231, 1970.

Winston, P. H. Learning to identify toy block structures. In R. L. Solso (ed.), *Contemporary issues in cognitive psychology: The Loyola Symposium*. Washington, D.C.: V. H. Winston, 1973.

Zeaman, D., and House, B. J. The role of attention in retardate discrimination learning. In N. R. Ellis (ed.) *Handbook of Mental Deficiency*. New York: McGraw-Hill, 1963, 159-223.

16

DESIGNING COMPUTER SIMULATIONS FOR CLASSROOM USE: AN EXAMPLE FOR PHYSIOLOGICAL PSYCHOLOGY

RITA E. SNYDER

ABSTRACT

Many authors have suggested that simulations provide a useful tool for teaching at the undergraduate level. The present paper provides an example of how the teaching of traditional course material may be aided by the use of computer simulations. The paper describes how an evaluation of the weaknesses perceived in a traditional course, physiological psychology, was used to formulate objectives for the use of computer simulations. An in-depth description of how one computer simulation, NEURON, was developed to meet such objectives is also provided.

I. *Formulating Educational Objectives*

Inbar and Stoll (1972) point out that there are three general areas in which simulations are useful: in model-building, in experimentation, and in teaching. The present discussion focuses on the use of simulation, particularly computer simulation, in teaching.

Many claims for the usefulness of simulations as a teaching device have been made, but, in general, such claims have little evidence either to support or refute them. The approach outlined below suggests that, at the present time, one may view such claims with the question: to what extent are the weaknesses perceived in a particular course addressed by the claims made by those using simulations in the classroom? If it appears that simulations may meet some of the needs perceived by the instructor, it could be of general interest to try to develop simulations to meet these needs, and then proceed with careful evaluation of this effort.

What are some of the claims for the usefulness of simulation as a teaching device? Inbar and Stoll (1972) present the following points for simulations games:

> First, games come under the category of settings known as "responsive environments" (Moore and Anderson, 1969). These environments are structured to encourage the learner to find a question and then seek the answer to it. . . . The game is fully structured to provide answers because it is a representation of the system, not a set of descriptive statements about the system. . . . Secondly, responsive environments are also characterized as self-pacing. . . . Another feature of a responsive environment is the opportunity it offers for discovering or uncovering a series of interconnected relationships. . . . Not only is the feedback from simulated environments more lucid and faster than provided in other educational settings, it is also perceived less arbitrarily. . . . Simulations bridge the reality gap by bringing a miniaturized version of some sphere of real-life activity into the classroom. . . . Finally, games are autotelic activities (Inbar, 1970) in the sense of having the reward for engaging in them built into the activity itself. Being ends in themselves, games generate a motivational force of their own, from within. (pp. 259-262)

In deciding whether to incorporate simulations into classroom activities, the first step should involve specifying the particular needs of the course as it is currently taught, and the goals that might be met through the use of simulation. Thus, one might simply ask the following questions: "What are the weak points in teaching this material? What are the points that the students have the most difficulty learning? Can simulation address these points (see claims listed earlier)? If so, in what manner might simulations best be implemented in (this) course?" By articulating answers to these questions, the first, and probably the most important, step in utilizing simulation as a teaching device is taken: the instructor has specified the goals to be met by these activities and has begun the careful process of restricting the use of simulation to the attainment of particular intellectual skills not otherwise successfully developed in a particular course of study.

II. *General Considerations for Designing Simulations*

The next step involves making the choice of topics for simulation, organizing these into a sequence most likely to reach the specified goals, and then briefly describing each simulation, with emphasis on stating how each contributes to these goals.

Finally, after needs and goals have been stated, and a clear picture of the manner in which simulations will be implemented in the classroom is developed, the specification of particular simulations for classroom use may be made. This step may involve selecting simulations developed in other contexts, or designing new simulations. The former point is addressed in the next essay (simulation games in psychology); this discussion will suggest the critical points in designing new computer simulations for classroom use.

The critical points in designing a computer simulation involve addressing the following set of questions:

1. What specific points or knowledge are to be communicated? Which of these points can be made by the simulation and which can be made by discussion of the simulation or by accompanying materials? To what extent can these points be made by each vehicle?
2. How similar must the model represented by the simulation be to the actual (physical) process under study in order to teach most effectively and to learn the targeted points?
3. What particular input choices should be allowed to the student to meet most effectively the specified goals?
4. What specific outputs should be provided to meet the specified goals? (This includes both the number of things that outputs will be provided for, and the range of values for each output that is seen as useful.)

An example of the implementation of these points will be provided in the next section of this paper.

III. NEURON: *An Example of the Development of a Computer Simulation for Physiological Psychology*

In the discussion that follows, an example of the implementation of the more general points made earlier will be provided. It should be noted that the simulation, NEURON, is in its first stages of development: it has not yet been put to the test of actual use in a classroom setting, and undoubtedly some changes will be necessary based on the experiences of both the instructor and the students who use it; however, it should serve to illustrate the manner in which one may begin to operationalize the more general considerations suggested as important in the process of designing simulations for classroom use.

The first step outlined earlier involves specification of needs and goals. In evaluating my course in physiological psychology, I identified the following weak points. First, I was unable to characterize and communicate the view of the nervous system as a complex interactive system, where any one "action" had multiple ramifications; indeed, to present any one topic clearly, such as a sensory system, I felt the need to present it in isolation in order to guarantee that students could understand the essential features of sensory activity. As a consequence of this method of presentation, students were quite adept at describing a principle in isolation, but did not seem able to take the next crucial step of "carrying through" with the multiple ramifications of any one principle.

Second, as the semester progressed, students clearly exhibited a compartmentalization of their knowledge through a failure to carry over principles discussed for one topic to others presented later in the course. The students' class discussion and answers to exam questions pointed to oversimplification and a lack of generalization of the course material.

Third, a related point centers on the lack of time in the typical classroom setting to integrate material presented early in the course into the discussion of topics presented later in the course.[1]

Given these weaknesses, in what ways do computer simulations appear to be able to address these points? First, computer programs appear to provide an excellent vehicle for meeting the first criticism above: computers are ideal for executing complex iterative procedures, as are seen in the nervous system, and, when a program is initiated, all steps are executed and all specified outputs are provided. When the student then views the output, it is apparent what all the ramifications of the inputs were, thus guaranteeing that the student does not miss any of the consequences of any particular input features. Also, in order to account for the particular outputs, the student will soon recognize the need to draw on principles learned earlier in the course, and thus get some practice with generalizing the applicability of the principles of nervous system operation.

Second, through use of a set of computer simulations, all based on the same principles of action, the need to guarantee that the basic principles of nervous system activity are reapplied to each new topic will be met. Thus, the simulations themselves can serve to provide important threads of continuity through the course material and help the student integrate important principles throughout the course. This feature of information presentation can save time for classroom discussion of new principles by demanding and carefully directing more individual work from the students.

In summary, the goals for the use of computer simulations in physiological psychology are: (1) to allow the student to observe principles of nervous system activity in specific simulated contexts; (2) to guarantee that the student will be exposed to the multiple ramifications of certain changes in nervous system input, and (3) to guarantee that students integrate information about basic principles with more complex models in physiological psychology.

The next step taken in developing these simulations involved the choice of topics. It was decided to select one subtopic from each major area covered in the course for simulation. These areas included: basic nerve physiology, sensory processes, arousal, motivation and emotion, and learning. Each subtopic was to be chosen by the following criteria:

it should lend itself to the use of iterative procedures on multiple-outcome situations; it should clearly illustrate feedback principles, and it should share several principles of operation in common with other areas also chosen for simulation.

The manner in which the choice of a simulation for the general topic of basic nerve physiology was made should serve to illustrate these points. My first idea in this area was to develop a simulation of the electrochemical events governing neural activity. This was soon rejected as I realized that it would be most cumbersome to include this type of simulated activity in other simulations of more complex nervous system features. Thus, I selected to develop a simulation that focused on communication among neurons, based on spatial and temporal integration. This appeared to be a satisfactory topic because information flow through the system would be important in all simulations of nervous system activity, and because it would allow the introduction of additional topics such as recurrent collateral inhibition and presynaptic inhibition. Clearly, the operation of these principles in communication among neurons was based on iterative procedures, and, through appropriate construction of a model, multiple outcome situations and feedback operations could be easily developed. Thus, this topic satisfied the criteria I had established. The model is given in Figure 1 of the handout developed to accompany the simulation NEURON.

In designing this model and deciding how the model would operate, I was first faced with the problem of specifying the general nature of the questions the student should be asking and the types of answers the students should be seeking. There appeared to be two ways to address this issue. First, the simulation could be used to illustrate a model and seek its ramifications. A set of simulations developed by Bewley (1974) for use in a cognitive psychology course is directed toward this end. Second, the simulation could be used to teach the student something about *what* the model represents. I chose the latter approach and developed the model to focus on the following points. First, the model itself was constructed to illustrate spatial arrangements of neurons clearly, including feedback loops. Second, to examine temporal characteristics, different rates of firing for pairs of neurons were employed. Third, to examine the characteristics of "long-distance" communication in a neural network, different amounts of activity were selected for "starting neurons" in the model system.

It should be clear at this point that, through making a basic decision about what the simulation should accomplish, choices about the types of input that the student can profitably apply have also been made. Specifically, the student may decide where activity starts in this system, the total amount of activity that occurs for these starting neurons, and the rate at which these starting neurons fire. The decision about what outputs to provide follows in a similar manner. Because it was seen as desirable to allow the student to view the *operation* of the system, and because one important criterion for these simulations focused on guaranteeing that the student sees all the ramifications of his input choices, it was decided to output the number of action potentials that occurred for each neuron in the model system.

A more difficult decision in designing NEURON involved the degree of correspondence desirable between operation of the model system and actual operation of the nervous system. A first programming attempt faithfully followed known parameters of nervous system operation. This attempt proved unwieldy in terms of actual programming techniques, the length of time needed to execute the simulation, and the nuances that appeared in the total activity shown for each neuron. Although the latter point, in particular, may have proved interesting to the sophisticated user, it was felt that such outcomes unnecessarily complicated the task desired for the typical undergraduate student. Thus, certain differences were introduced to simplify operation of the program, and are described in the accompanying handout. These differences were seen as important for allowing the simulation to meet the educational objectives specified earlier.

The final decision involved the allocation of teaching responsibilities. In order to integrate the use of the simulations into regular ongoing class activities, it was decided that a full exposition of the principles on which the simulation operates would remain part of the lecture-discussion activities of the class; the simulation would then focus on illustrating and refining the student's understanding of communication among neurons; the accompanying handout was designed to help the student explore the simulation fully. Examination of the handout illustrates how this was done.

It should be reiterated that the points made in this discussion are still theoretical: the final test of the effectiveness of this approach remains to be made when the simulations are actually implemented as part of the daily class activities. Undoubtedly, this experience will suggest some changes in both the actual simulations and the manner in which they are used in the course. It is hoped, nonetheless, that this type of activity will produce some improvement in both teaching effectiveness and the quality of understanding that the student develops in this course.

NOTE

1. For example, when presenting material on the subject of sensory coding, classroom time is devoted to developing examples of how

activity in individual neurons may represent different sensory parameters. Later in the course, a different topic may be presented, such as the role that the hypothalamus plays in the regulation of several different motivational behaviors. To understand this topic, the student must recognize that different neural codes may underlie the regulation of different behaviors. Because coding, however, is simply one of several physiological principles that are important in understanding this topic, little classroom time is available for developing good examples of this phenomenon, particularly because such examples had been presented earlier for other topics. The need to have such examples available is clear from the students' failure to do so independently.

REFERENCES

Bewley, W. L. *Cognitive psychology: A computer-oriented laboratory manual.* Hanover, New Hampshire: Project COMPUTE, 1974.
Inbar, M., and Stoll, C. S. *Simulation and gaming in social science.* New York: Free Press, 1972.

APPENDIX

MANUAL FOR STUDENT USE OF NEURON

This module is designed to illustrate the manner in which neurons communicate. Figure 1 depicts a model system of neurons that will be used in the simulation. This simulation is designed to allow you to observe the effects of activity in any neuron or pair of neurons on others in the model system.

The first step in understanding the transfer of activity from one set of neurons to another involves producing a change in a postsynaptic neuron. The change that occurs is described in terms of either a positive or negative voltage change from the resting potential. A change in the positive direction is called an excitatory postsynaptic potential (EPSP) and a change in the negative direction is called an inhibitory postsynaptic potential (IPSP). Each time an action potential occurs in a presynaptic neuron, one EPSP or one IPSP occurs in the postsynaptic neuron.

EPSPs and IPSPs are graded potentials, and do not result in any further transmission of information. If, however, enough EPSPs are added together (approximately 10), threshold is reached, and an action potential may occur in the postsynaptic neuron, allowing it to affect other neurons in the system. EPSPs and IPSPs sum algebraically: if an EPSP is designated as +1, and an IPSP is designated as −1, simultaneous occurrence of an EPSP and an IPSP results in no change from the resting potential in the postsynaptic neuron [(+1) + (−1) = 0]. If two EPSPs occur simultaneously, the net change is positive [(+1) + (+1) = +2] and the electrical potential of the cell is moved toward threshold.

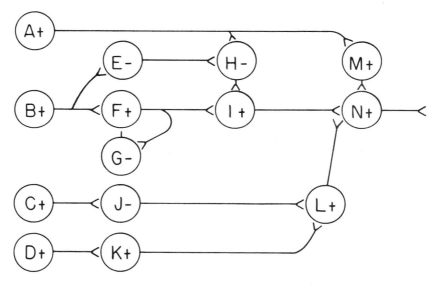

FIGURE 1
A SIMPLE NEURONAL MODEL

EPSPs and IPSPs may add in two ways: over space and over time. The former process is termed spatial summation and results from the addition of effects produced by two or more presynaptic neurons simultaneously affecting the postsynaptic neuron. The latter process is termed temporal summation, and occurs when a single presynaptic neuron fires repeatedly, allowing an adding of the graded potential changes that result from this successive firing. EPSPs and IPSPs last approximately 3-4 msec; thus, if the presynaptic neuron fires every 2 msec, for example, the first EPSP is a building block onto which the second EPSP is added.

In actuality, the potential changes that occur at the postsynaptic neuron are a result of both spatial and temporal summation acting together to determine whether or not threshold is reached and an action potential is produced in the postsynaptic neuron. This is termed spatiotemporal integration. You should use the simulation to examine the effects of all three possibilities: spatial summation alone, temporal summation alone, and spatiotemporal integration.

In the hypothetical "nervous system" employed in this simulation, you can see that neurons are indicated by letters and synaptic effects are indicated by "+" and "−" signs. A "+" means that when an action potential occurs in that neuron, an EPSP will result in the postsynaptic neuron(s), and a "−" means that an IPSP will result in the postsynaptic neuron(s). Although activity in this "nervous system" is conceptually similar to that in a real nervous system, a few differences in actual operation of this system have been introduced in order to simplify the computer operations. As in a real nervous system, EPSPs and IPSPs sum algebraically to produce action potentials in the neurons, but fewer EPSPs are needed to reach threshold in this system. In actuality, an EPSP (or IPSP) produces a 1-2 mv change in the electrical potential of a postsynaptic neuron, resulting in the need for approximately 10 EPSPs to summate before threshold is reached and an action potential occurs; in this simulation, only *four* EPSPs are needed to reach threshold. In actuality, EPSPs and IPSPs have a duration of 3-4 msec before resting potential is reestablished; in this simulation, resting potential is reestablished after 4.5 msec. Also, in actuality, EPSPs and IPSPs show a gradual onset, reach a peak amplitude of 1-2 mv, and then decay gradually back to the resting potential; in this simulation, EPSPs and IPSPs are treated as "all-or-none" events: they reach the "peak amplitude" immediately, remain at this peak for 4.5 msec, and then return immediately to the resting potential. These simplifying differences *do not* significantly alter communication among neurons in the simulation as compared to communication among neurons in an actual nervous system.

In general, the simulation applies the rules of spatial and temporal summation and determines whether or not action potentials result in each neuron in the model nervous system, given certain inputs to the system. After the user provides input to this system, the simulation provides a list of the number of action potentials that subsequently occur in each neuron in the system. Again, for reasons of simplification and to help ensure that the user is able to explore communication among neurons in the simulation in an orderly fashion, certain restrictions have been placed on input characteristics, as described below.

To use the simulation for the first set of questions, which explores spatial and temporal summation and spatiotemporal integration, select one or two starting neurons from one of the following list: *A, B, E,* or *F*. (*Note*: If two starting neurons are employed, the combinations *B* and *E,* and *B* and *F,* are not admissible: Can you see why?) For each starting neuron, select the total number of times that that neuron will fire (2, 4, 8, 16, 32, 64, 128, or 256 times) and the rate at which that neuron will fire (200 or 1000 times a second). As noted earlier, the simulation will list the number of action potentials that results at each neuron in the system. The set of questions provided below should be used to guide your examination of communication among neurons in this system.

FIRST EXERCISE

1. Examine Figure 1 and determine where spatial summation may occur. Use the simulation to determine how much spatial summation occurs when the presynaptic neurons fire a few times and when the presynaptic neurons fire many times.

2. Examine Figure 1 and determine where temporal summation only may occur. Use the simulation to determine the effect of firing the presynaptic neuron at different rates and different number of times.

3. Why is it more reasonable to view neural processes in terms of spatiotemporal integration than simply in terms either of spatial summation or of temporal summation alone?

Suggestion: Pick several different *combinations* of presynaptic neural firing rates, and observe the effect on the postsynaptic neuron.

4. It has been suggested that each neuron in the nervous system is an integrator of information. How can we use EPSPs and IPSPs and the process of spatiotemporal integration to illustrate this point? Is it adequate to look merely at the activity of the immediate postsynaptic neuron to make this point?

5. Under what conditions can information be passed from one neuron, to a second neuron, *and* to a third neuron? How do spatial and temporal factors influence this "long-distance" communication?

6. In what set of neurons do we see connections that allow one neuron to modify its own activity? This configuration is called recurrent collateral inhibition. To what extent does recurrent collateral inhibition depend on the firing rate of the neuron that modifies its own activity? Is this inhibition "complete," that is, can you find a way to get this neuron to turn itself "off"?

7. What happens in this system when activity is started simultaneously at two different neurons? Find two starting points that together result in more distant effects than would be found by starting at either one of the points alone. What effect does having the two starting points fire at different rates have? Find two starting points that *together* block the distant transmission of information that would occur if activity were started at one of these points alone. What is the effect of firing these neurons at different rates?

Second Exercise

One aspect of neural communication that has not yet been examined using this simulation involves presynaptic inhibition. Presynaptic inhibition occurs where an axo-axonic synapse occurs prior to an axo-dendritic or axo-somatic synapse. Remember that this arrangement still produces EPSPs in the postsynaptic neurons of both the axo-axonic synapse and the axo-somatic (or axo-dendritic) synapse; the "inhibition" is merely the production of a smaller EPSP in the axo-somatic postsynaptic neuron than would normally occur. The role played by presynaptic inhibition in the transmission of information through the model nervous system should be investigated by answering the following questions:

1. Presynaptic inhibition is illustrated by the combination of neurons *L*, *I*, and *N*. Use the simulation to demonstrate presynaptic inhibition by comparing the effect of starting activity in neurons *F* and *K* simultaneously with the effect of starting activity in neuron *F* alone and neuron *K* alone.
2. Explore the effect of various amounts of starting activity in neuron *F* and *K*. What does this illustrate about presynaptic inhibition?
3. Explore the effect of various firing rates when starting with neurons *F* and *K*. What does this illustrate about presynaptic inhibition?
4. In what way does spatiotemporal integration affect presynaptic inhibition? How does this compare to the role played by spatiotemporal integration in determining activity in other parts of this system?
5. How does presynaptic inhibition compare with recurrent collateral inhibition? (See question 6, first exercise.) In what ways are these two types of inhibition similar? In what ways are they different?
6. Pick different pairs of starting neurons and compare the effect of these on neuron *N* with the effect produced by starting activity in just one neuron of the pair. Summarize your findings about the role of starting activity in different neurons, at different rates, and with different amounts of starting activity on producing activity in this model "nervous system" through spatiotemporal integration, presynaptic inhibition, and recurrent collateral inhibition. Try to present your summary as a set of generalizations about communication among neurons.

THE MANUAL FOR STUDENT USE OF *PAIN*

This module is designed to allow you to explore fully the Melzack and Casey (1968) model of pain perception. The present model synthesizes information obtained from both clinical observations and basic physiological research and thus attempts to provide a comprehensive account of the factors that determine whether a particular stimulus event will be perceived and reported as painful in a variety of contexts. Although a brief description of this model is provided below, you should read the Melzack and Casey (1968) paper before attempting to provide your parameter inputs to the simulation. The reference is given at the end of this handout.

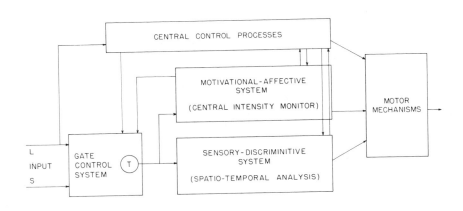

FIGURE 2

The Melzack and Casey model of pain perception (from Melzack, R. and Casey, K. L. Sensory, motivation, and central control determinants of pain: A new conceptual model. In Kenshalo, D. (ed.), The Skin Senses, 1968. Courtesy of Charles C. Thomas, Publisher, Springfield, Illinois.)

The model consists of two basic parts: the gate control system, found in the spinal cord, and the "higher" central nervous system (CNS) components, called central control processes, the motivational-affective system, and the sensory-discriminative system. By looking at Figure 2, you can see that the gate control system provides most of the input to the "higher" CNS components, and in turn may be influenced by them. Thus, this model provides for considerable feedback that modulates incoming stimulus information.

Figure 3 illustrates the mechanisms by which the gate control system operates. The stimulus produces activity in large (*L*) and small (*S*) diameter first-order afferents.

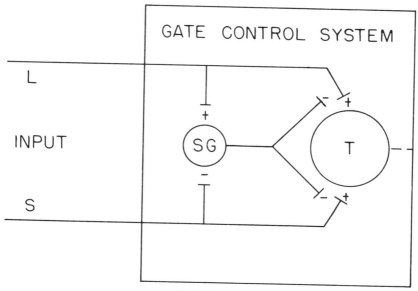

FIGURE 3

The gate control system (from Melzack, R. and Wall, P. D. Pain mechanisms: A new theory. Science, *Vol. 150, Fig. 4, 19 November 1965. Copyright 1965 by the American Association for the Advancement of Science.)*

These fibers synapse on cells in the substantia gelatinosa (SG) and on central transmission (T) cells. These cells are associated with the spinothalamic systems. L and S fibers are both excitatory on T cells, but have opposite effects on SG cells: L fibers are excitatory but S fibers are inhibitory. SG axons exert presynaptic inhibition on T cells and thus provide one mechanism by which T cell output may be reduced. The amount of T cell activity is an important determinant of pain: the more T cell activity that is produced by a particular stimulus, the more likely it is that the stimulus will be perceived as painful.

The gate control system provides an alternative to the specification of a "pain" receptor or "pain" fiber: instead, this model suggests that the ratio of activity in L and S fibers will determine, to a large extent, whether or not a stimulus is painful. If a stimulus produces activity primarily in S fibers, then the SG cells will be inhibited, and nothing will reduce the transmission of the stimulus representation to "higher" CNS areas. On the other hand, if a stimulus produces activity primarily in L fibers, the SG cells will become active and reduce transmission to "higher" CNS areas. Other consequences of the set of mechanisms described for the gate control system will be explored later in this handout, and in the exercises accompanying this simulation.

Activity in the "higher" CNS areas is also important in determining whether a stimulus will be perceived as painful. Essentially, this activity exerts influence in two ways: first, by modulating T cell output directly, and, second, by providing a background to which T cell activity is added. All three components also interact with each other, and the combined effects of their activities result in the response that is produced to a particular stimulus. Thus, this aspect of the model produces yet another departure from the notion of specific "pain" receptors or fibers, in that the balance of activity across these various areas is the final determinant of the pain response.

The central control processes represent cognitive influences on perception. Factors such as context, attention, suggestion, and learning have been shown to be very important in determining the response to a particular stimulus. In this model, these factors are given influence not only through an effect on the motor mechanisms involved in the response to a stimulus, but also through modulation of activity in the gate control system and in the other components of "higher" CNS areas as well.

The sensory-discriminative system provides important analysis of the more "sensory" features of the stimulus. Activity in these areas is important in determining how well the details of the stimulus will be reported: its locus, duration, intensity, etc. The output of these areas primarily affects the response mechanisms and the central control processes.

The motivational-affective system provides information about the noxious quality of the stimulus. These areas comprise the central-intensity monitor: up to a certain point, activity in these areas results in a report of a pleasurable effect: higher levels of activity result in a report of a noxious, or painful, effect. These areas also provide input to the central control processes and gate control system, and thus may regulate response to a stimulus in several ways: through the behavioral responses of approach or avoidance, and through regulation of their own inputs.

The simulation of this model includes a representation of all the relationships shown in Figure 2. Operation of the simulation is based not only on the stimulus input but also on "preset" activity levels in the central control processes and motivational-affective system, thus allowing simulated context and mood to play an important role in operation of this model. As in the hypothetical nervous system employed in Figure 2, operation of this model is based on spatial summation: four input "pulses" are required to produce an action potential at any neuron represented in this model. Because of the complexity of the interactions represented here, however, temporal decay has been ignored: it is assumed that all activity occurs rapidly enough to allow complete temporal integration.

This model may be examined by using the simulation in several different ways. First, you may choose to see the outcome of providing the simulation with stimuli and contexts that have already been specified. Stimuli that in general are considered painful or not painful are both available. Several contexts are also available, and pairs of stimuli may be examined in each context. Thus, a tap on the back (generally not painful) and a hard slap on the back (generally painful) may be examined in the same set of contexts, so that you can see the effect of each context in influencing the response to each stimulus. After you select the stimulus and the context, the simulation will provide the following information: whether or not the stimulus was felt at all, how well the stimulus could be described, and whether or not the stimulus was perceived as painful (or pleasant) in the chosen context. The Appendix provides a specification of the parameter selections that have been made for each stimulus and each context.

This model may also be examined by individual selection of parameters. If you choose to provide the parameters, you may also choose to examine the operation of the gate control system in isolation, or you may examine the whole system in operation. The exercises will focus on both possibilities.

To examine just the gate control system, you will define the stimulus in terms of its duration, the base rate of activity produced in the first-order afferents, the type of stimulus (static or changing), and the ratio of activity produced in L and S fibers. Stimulus intensity is defined in terms of both the base rate and ratio parameters. Remember that, in general, the frequency of firing is a direct function of stimulus intensity: a high-intensity stimulus produces a higher firing rate than a low-intensity stimulus. Thus, if you choose a low base rate (e.g., 1 pulse per unit time) but a high ratio (e.g., L:S=4:1), you will *increase* the base rate on the large diameter fibers by a factor of four, and thus will have defined a higher intensity stimulus than indicated by the base rate alone.

Examine Figure 3 again. The operation of the gate control system is based on physiological principles for the constituent parts. First, remember that L fibers are faster-conducting than S fibers: under some circumstances, you will see that activity occurs earlier in these fibers. Also remember that L fibers are associated with rapidly adapting receptors: thus, you must provide a "changing" stimulus to maintain activity for a sustained period of time in these fibers: adaptation will occur to a "static" stimulus. The SG cell is affected in an opposite manner by L and S fibers, and activity in this cell is determined by summation of the EPSPs and IPSPs produced by the L and S fibers, respectively. Also, because the SG cells exert their influence through presynaptic inhibition, and presynaptic inhibition "lasts" longer than an IPSP, this effect is represented by a sustained SG output once an action potential has been produced here. The T cell activity is then a function of L fiber, S fiber, and SG cell activity.

After you have "defined" the stimulus by your parameter selections, the simulation will provide the total activity that results in the T and SG cells, as well as the pattern of activity that results in the axons of the T and SG cells, and the L and S fibers. Careful examination of this information should allow you to explore fully the mechanisms represented in the gate control system.

If you choose to examine the simulation of the whole system by providing your own parameter inputs, a few parameters in addition to those necessary for gate control operation must be specified. This essentially involves "presetting" the system. First, you will select the type of cognitive influence that is operating: choose either attention factors or suggestion (or placebo) factors, and the manner in which they are to be preset. (You may not preset both simultaneously.) Then you may also preset affective influences. Presetting these influences basically involves providing the simulation with a certain amount of starting activity in these areas that will both affect the output of the gate control system as well as provide a background of activity to which T cell output will be added. When the whole system is examined, the simulation will provide output about whether the stimulus was felt at all, and, if it was felt, output will also include whether it could be described, whether it was painful, and the description of activity occurring in the components of the gate control system.

The exercises described below will help you explore the simulation of this model of pain perception in an orderly fashion. You should be reminded of three things before you begin. First, this model is an abstraction of processes hypothesized to occur in the CNS after reception of a tactile stimulus. In actuality, such an event will undoubtedly influence other parts of the nervous system in subtle ways and these will also interact in some fashion with the areas represented by this model. Thus, a perfect match between the responses provided by a human being to a particular stimulus and the responses provided by the simulation may not be obtained. What is important is how well changes in the factors (such as L:S ratio, context, etc.) represented by the model predict the manner in responses to particular stimuli change. In this regard, the *direction* of the change is more telling of the usefulness of this model than the details of the actual output that results.

Second, the values associated with stimulus features such as duration, intensity, etc., and with the preset "higher" influences, are abstractions and simplifications of the values that might be obtained from actual CNS recording. Thus, only to the extent that a reasonable representation of stimulus encoding in the nervous system has been provided for operation of this simulation may reasonable evaluation of the efficacy of this model be made. In developing a simulation within the limitations of space imposed by the computer available, such simplification must be severe and can significantly affect the quality of such an evaluation.

Third, the simulation is designed to provide information about an abstract "person," one whose experience and/or affective responsivity is idealized and simplified rather than actual and accounted for. The model itself is based on the idea that such individual factors are critically important in determining the response made to a particular stimulus in a particular context. The simulation represents this important notion in only the most general fashion. Some opportunity to explore the effects of general individual differences is provided in the exercises, but the richness of individual experience and the nuances of individual reactions cannot be adequately represented at the present time.

Despite these disclaimers, the simulation of this model of pain perception provides some rather interesting and accurate responses to a variety of inputs. It is expected that through exploration of the model with the simulation, not only will a better understanding of the model be obtained, but ideas concerning the strengths and weaknesses of the model should also be generated.

FIRST EXERCISE: USING THE STIMULI PROVIDED

This exercise will introduce you to the simulation and allow you to see the types of stimuli and contexts that may be specified, and the types of responses that are obtained from the simulation.

1. Select a pair of stimuli (such as choices 1 and 2: a tap on the back and a slap on the back). Obtain output for perception of these stimuli under each of the contexts provided. Develop a few generalizations about the manner in which context affects stimulus perception. State how well you think the simulation's responses match the responses you think that you would have under the same circumstances.
2. To what extent do you think that the present model accurately characterizes the stimuli and contexts it is concerned with? What changes would you make to improve this characterization? Keep a record of these for use in future examination of the simulation.

SECOND EXERCISE: SETTING PARAMETERS FOR THE SIMULATION

I. *The Gate Control System*

To examine the gate control system, the following "fixed" parameter values should be employed for all parameters not being directly examined to answer a question. Using these "fixed" values will simplify your examination of this aspect of the model: Duration=Moderate; Base Rate= Moderate; Stimulus Type=Changing; L:S Ratio=1:1.

1. What effect does changing stimulus duration have on T cell output? On SG cell output?
2. What effect does changing the base firing rate have on T cell output? On SG cell output?
3. What effect does changing stimulus type have on T Cell output? On SG cell output?
4. What effect does changing the L:S ratio have on T cell output? On SG cell output? What types of stimuli might produce each of the L:S ratios provided in this simulation?
5. Examine the various ways that stimulus intensity may be specified by manipulating the base rate and the L:S ratios simultaneously. What does this suggest about limitations on the types of stimuli that may be represented for examination by this simulation?
6. How might "second" pain occur, according to this simulation of the gate control system? List the parameter values that produce a pattern of T cell output that would produce first the "bright" brief, intense sensation, followed by a "quiet" or "no sensation" period, followed by a more persistent, dull "second" pain. Then, describe the types of stimuli that might be expected to produce this type of pain sensation.
7. Summarize your findings about the types of stimulus characteristics that would most likely produce a report of pain, based solely on T cell output. You may want to explore more combinations of parameter values to ascertain that some of your generalizations are correct.

THIRD EXERCISE: SETTING PARAMETERS FOR THE SIMULATION

II. *The Whole System*

The same set of "fixed" parameter values as used in the second exercise should be employed here.

1. The importance of the "higher" areas in the determination of pain can be seen by comparing T cell output produced under the "fixed" parameter values for the gate system alone with that produced when the whole system is examined, even when no preset values are specified. What differences are obvious? What does this suggest about the way "higher" areas influence pain perception?
2. As a follow-up to question 1, derive some generalizations about the

way that stimulus duration, intensity, and type influence T cell output when the whole system is operating.

3. How does presetting the two types of cognitive influence affect the perception of pain? In what ways do these two types of cognitive influence differ?
4. How does presetting the affective influence alone affect the perception of pain?
5. In what manner do the cognitive and affective influences interact, i.e., to what extent can they facilitate pain perception together or cancel each other's influence on pain perception?
6. Summarize your findings about the role of "higher" CNS influences on the perception of pain.

Fourth Exercise: Using the Simulation to Investigate User-Defined Stimuli and Contexts

1. For the first exercise, you were asked to keep a record of the changes you would make in the characterization of the stimuli and contexts you examined. You should now use this list to set new parameter values for these stimuli and contexts, based on the experience you developed in the third exercise. Examine the output you obtain. Do the responses seem more reasonable to you? What does this tell you about the usefulness of this simulation in investigating whether or not pain will result in a certain situation?
2. While the results obtained with your new parameter values in question 1 may be appropriate for you, they may not be appropriate for individuals with experience different from yours, or with different amounts of emotional reactivity. To investigate the potential role played by these factors, you should maintain the same stimulus parameter values used above, but manipulate the "higher" influences to investigate following possibilities:
   a. How would a person with "flat" affect, or a generally unresponsive person, react to these stimuli?
   b. How would a highly emotional, or highly reactive person, react?
   c. How would a person who has been in the same context many times in the past react?
   d. How would a person who is in this context for the first time react?
   e. How would a person who is highly susceptible to suggestion react?
   f. How would a person who is resistant to suggestion react?
3. Many different kinds of stimuli and contexts are described in the references cited at the end of this handout. Select two or three that have documented responses and develop parameter values to represent them. How well does the simulation match the responses that are usually obtained?

REFERENCES

Chaves, J. F., and Barber, T. X. Needles and knives: Behind the mystery of acupuncture and Chinese meridians. *Human Behavior*, 1973, 19-24.

Melzack, R. The perception of pain. *Scientific American*, 1961, *204*, 41-49.

Melzack, R., and Casey, K. L. Sensory, motivational, and central control determinants of pain: A new conceptual model. In Kenshalo, D. (Ed.), *The skin senses*, Springfield, Illinois: Charles Thomas, 1968, 423-439.

Timmermans, G., and Sternbach, R. A. Factors of human chronic pain: An analysis of personality and pain reaction variables. *Science*, 1974, *184*, 806-808.

17

SIMULATION GAMES IN PSYCHOLOGY

RITA E. SNYDER

ABSTRACT

Simulation games offer an alternative to traditional classroom teaching techniques that have been shown to be advantageous in several ways. The present paper discusses problems that are encountered in selecting games for use in psychology classes, and describes a technique that may be useful for evaluating currently available games. A list of games appropriate for use in psychology classes at the undergraduate level is included.

I. *Games as an Educational Vehicle*

A simulation game is an activity that combines the properties of simulation, or the execution of a model, with a game, which focuses on competitive activity among players. Coleman (1967) describes six general characteristics of a simulation game: it is comprised essentially of players striving toward a goal; usually a small, fixed number of players are involved; the players' activities are defined by the rules of the simulation game; the rules also structure these activities temporally; specific constraints on the range of activities and the time in which activities must be completed are specified, and rules of the game demand that the players substitute the rule-defined temporal and spatial constraints on activity for their normal activities while involved in the game. He suggests that the creation of an alternative environment through a simulation game can be educationally useful and, further, can provide the student with learning experiences not readily obtained in a more traditional classroom setting.

The suggestion that simulation games offer unique educational opportunities is widely made. Before examining this claim in more detail, it would be useful to contrast gaming and "traditional methods" as learning devices. An excellent exposition has been provided by a report from The Johns Hopkins Center for Social Organizatisn of Schools. In this report, it suggested that, in the traditional approach, learning occurs in the following sequence: "1. Reception of information . . . 2. Understanding the general principle . . . 3. Particularizing . . . 4. Acting." On the other hand, the type of experiential learning typified by simulation games occurs in nearly the opposite order: "1. Acting . . . 2. Understanding the particular case . . . 3. Generalizing . . . 4. Acting in a new circumstance." In addition, these approaches differ in the amount of time that is needed for exposition of the ideas under study: that simulation games are much more time-consuming is a commonly noted feature. Although traditional methods depend almost exclusively on the use of a verbal, symbolic means of communicating ideas, games do not, and thus may prove especially beneficial when teaching individuals with poorly developed verbal skills. This point may also prove useful to the instructor for better evaluating a student's progress in learning to deal with the concepts under study. While students with poorly developed verbal skills may have actually made progress in mastering class material, this may not be reflected in performance on a written examination, whereas it could be obvious in their actions in a simulation activity. A major problem observed in traditional settings often involves making the final step to application of the principles mastered by the student; simulations have an advantage in this regard because the activities involved in executing the simulation provide a guide for action in other similar situations. Finally, it is pointed out that motivation for learning in the traditional setting is intrinsic to the learning situation and must be provided by artificial means, such as grades, whereas motivation is intrinsic to the simulation activity.

Generally, then, it is quite evident that simulation games provide a fundamentally different vehicle for learning than is provided through a more traditional classroom approach. In what contexts might this approach provide a better learning experience for the student, and how might an instructor go about implementing simulation games in the classroom? These two questions will be addressed next.

II.   *Implementing Games in the Psychology Classroom*

Livingston and Stoll (1973) have surveyed a large number of studies focused on evaluating the learning effectiveness of simulation games and have offered several generalizations. Those pertinent to psychology courses are summarized below. First, there does not appear to be any difference in effectiveness between games and traditional methods for teaching mere factual material. Second, attitude changes in a positive direction about individuals whose roles are played are often evident, accompanied by a more realistic appraisal of the situations in which such individuals operate. Third, although they suggest that students usually express preferences for simualtion games over traditional classroom activities, it should be noted that many of the studies they surveyed included grammar and high school students. Finally, it was noted that, for students with lower ability or achievement, more progress is evident in learning how to play games than in learning general principles from games and applying these principles to actual situations. Although Livingston and Stoll conclude that more research is needed before a definite statement can be made on the particular manner in which simulation games can enhance the learning shown in the classroom, they suggest indirectly that attempts in this direction may be worthwhile, but currently instructors must rely on their own experience and judgment and their colleagues' advice.

To some extent, particularly in psychology, the decision to use simulation games in the classroom is already restricted by the small number of areas for which good simulations have been developed. Through a personal search for available games and through consultation with colleagues, it readily became apparent that, although a great number of simulation games exist in this area, the number of games that appear to be of sufficient quality to be useful in a college class is quite small. One may easily become dismayed wading through page after page of superficial and poorly presented materials! It is clear that some careful editing would be most useful to those interested in searching for good simulation games. To this end, some of my colleagues have helped prepare the list of simulation games addended to this paper. (See Appendix 1.)

By examining the areas of psychology represented by the games included in this list, another potential restriction in the use of simulation games becomes apparent: such games have been developed for very few areas of psychology, mainly in social psychology, and actually for very few topics within social psychology! Thus, if one becomes interested in the potential uses of this educational approach, it is likely that a commitment to develop the necessary materials will also be required. Some excellent guidance on development and design of simulation games for classroom use may be found in Inbar and Stoll (1972), particularly Chapter 13, and in Stadskelv (1974).

To aid in the selection of simulation games currently available, I have found the format suggested by Gillespie (1972) to be particularly helpful. By attempting to analyze games that appear interesting in this manner, it soon becomes apparent whether a game will suit the purposes of the instructor. Essentially, this format demands complete specification of the game's central problem, objectives, manner of play, rules, and organization, as well as planning of the summary activities that will be employed in the more intellectual analysis of the principles illustrated by the game. An analysis of a simulation, "Hung Jury," is included at the end of this paper to illustrate this format. (See Appendix 2.)

In conclusion, it appears that simulation games offer an alternative teaching method that may have advantages over more traditional methods, although the exact nature of these advantages is not clear at the present time. One of the most difficult problems likely to be encountered in attempting to incorporate simulation games into classroom activities is that of finding simulations that suit one's perceived needs. It is clear that the potential for developing good simulation games for college teaching has not yet been realized, and what is needed at this time is more careful, thoughtful planning of such activities to replace the apparently nondirected proliferation of materials that has been so characteristic of many of the efforts in this area.

ACKNOWLEDGMENT

I would like to acknowledge gratefully the advice and suggestions of Allen Parchem and Gordon Hammerle, Denison University, in preparing the materials that accompany this paper.

REFERENCES

Coleman, J. S. Academic games and learning. Educational Testing Service: *Proceedings of the 1967 Invitational Conference on Testing Problems, 1968.* In R. Stadskelv (ed.), *Handbook of simulation gaming in social education (Part I: Textbook),* University of Alabama: Institute of Higher Education Research and Services, 1974, 15-25.

Gillespie, J. A. Evaluating materials: Analyzing and evaluating classroom games. *Social Education,* 1972, 33-42.

Inbar, M., and Stoll, C. S. *Simulation and gaming in social science.* New York: Free Press, 1972.

Johns Hopkins University, Center for Social Organization of Schools, Report No. 155. In R. Stadskelv (ed.), *Handbook of simulation gaming in social education (Part I: Textbook),* University of Alabama: Institute of Higher Education Research and Services, 1974, 26-32.

Livingston, S. A., and Stoll, C. S. *Simulation games: An introduction for the social studies teacher.* New York: Free Press, 1973.

Stadskelv, R. *Handbook of simulation gaming in social education (Part I: Textbook).* University of Alabama: Institute of Higher Education Research and Services, 1974.

APPENDIX 1

SOME SIMULATIONS/GAMES FOR PSYCHOLOGY

More complete information about each simulation/game can be found in the source indicated for each brief description.

REFERENCES:

Denison Simulation Center Catalogue, Denison University, 1975-76.

Pfeiffer, J. W., and Jones, J. E. *A handbook of structured experiences for human relations training*, La Jolla, Calif: University Associates, Vol. I, 1974; Vol. II, 1974; Vol. III, 1974; Vol. IV, 1973; Vol. V., 1975.

Pfeiffer, J. W., and Jones, J. E. *The annual handbook for group facilitators*, La Jolla, Calif: University Associates, 1972, 1973, 1974.

Stadsklev, R. *Handbook of simulation gaming in social education*, (Part II) Institute of Higher Education Research and Services, The University of Alabama, 1975.

SIMULATIONS/GAMES:

Ball game (Who can talk)—Social/Interpersonal Communication

"To explore the dynamics of assuming leadership in a group; to increase awareness of the power held by the member of a group who is speaking at a given time; to diagnose communicaiton patterns in a group." Discussion of a topic is determined by who holds the ball at any given time.

Pfeiffer and Jones, Vol. IV, 27

Catalyzer—Social/Influence

"To demonstrate how people act and feel as they assume positions of power, oppression, and change. The polarities involved in the social model have been exaggerated to build impact into the simulation experience."

Stadslev, Part II, 54

Committee Meeting—Social/Leadership

"To illustrate the effects of hidden agendas on task accomplishment in a work group." A committee meeting is simulated, with participants taking prescribed roles.

Pfeiffer and Jones, Vol. I, 36

The Desert Survival Situation—Social/Group Problem-Solving

"The Desert Survival Situation simulates a crash landing in the Sonaro Desert. The members of a team are told they were able to salvage 15 items from the aircraft before it burned. Their task is to rank order the items individually and as a team according to their importance to the team's survival—To improve the effectiveness of both group and individual decision making processes."

Fork-Labyrinth—Social/Leadership

"To diagnose the behavior of leaders and followers in a small group performing a complex competitive task: to teach on-line feedback and coaching on leadership behavior; to practice different leadership behaviors."

Pfeiffer and Jones, Vol. V, 53

Hang-up—Social/Attitudes

"Designed to catch people in racial stereotyping and to increase empathy for the problems of prejudice. The stress situations and the "hang-ups" bring out ordinary dormant racism, especially in people who still associate racism with slavery and the deep South while refusing to see prejudice which may exist in their own lives."

Denison Simulation Catalogue, Section I, 23

Hung Jury—Social/Group Problem-Solving

Decision-making processes are examined after simulating a jury deliberation of a criminal case. Materials for two cases are provided.

Kerner Report—Social/Group Problem-Solving

"To compare the results of individual decision-making with the results of group decision-making; to generate data to discuss decision-making patterns in task groups; to diagnose the level of development in a task group." The simulation uses a form based on the Kerner Report (U.S. Riot Commission Report).

Pfeiffer and Jones, Vol. III, 64

Leadership Characteristics—Social/Leadership

> "To compare the results of individual decision-making and group decision-making; to explore values underlying leadership characteristics; to examine effects of value judgments on personnel selection."

Pfeiffer and Jones, 1974, 13

Lutts and Mipps—Social/Group Problem-Solving

> "To study the sharing of information in a task-oriented group; to focus on cooperation in group problem-solving; to observe the emergence of leadership behavior in group problem-solving." A set of cards, some containing questions and some containing answers, is distributed randomly to participants. A single problem is described that demands that people combine their individual information cards to achieve a solution.

Pfeiffer and Jones, Vol. II, 24

The Picture Game—Social

> "To demonstrate the unthinking trust and confidence in the "rules" of society which, in this case, perpetuate the status quo by stigmatizing those who deviate from the group norm."

Stadsklev, Part II, 196

Pins and Straws—Social/Leadership

> "To dramatize three general styles of leadership: autocratic, laissez-faire and democratic; to increase awareness of how different styles of leadership can affect the performance of subordinates; to study the phenomenon of competition among groups." Three different groups construct sculptures with pins and straws, each one under a different leadership style. Observers note specific aspects of the leader's and the group's behaviors.

Pfeiffer and Jones, Vol. V, 78

Plea Bargaining—Criminal Justice
E. Katsh, R. M. Pipkin, B. S. Katsh

> "A game of criminal justice. This is a simulation of the process of nonadjudicative convictions. Its purpose is to aid the non-lawyer in understanding how the criminal justice system works and why it works that way."

Denison Simulation Catalogue, Section I, 39

A Problem-Solving Program—Social/Organizational

> "For defining a problem and planning action. The workbook is designed to help in analyzing a problem in organization management, or human relations—any problem which involves people working or living together."

Denison Simulation Catalogue, Section I, 42

Process Observation: A Guide—Social/Group Processes

> "To provide feedback to a group concerning its process; to provide experience for group members in observing process variables in group meetings." A report form is provided for observers to structure their task and aid in discussion.

Pfeiffer and Jones, Vol. I, 45

Project Planning Problem—Social/Group Decision-Making

> "To improve the effectiveness of group decision-making—For this activity, participants are divided into teams, each representing a task force which has just taken over a secret project presently being handled by research and development."

Stadsklev, Part II, 211

The Propaganda Game—Social/Attitudes
R. W. Allen, L. Greene

> "Students learn techniques aimed at influencing public opinion: 'bandwagon' appeals, faulty analogy, out-of-context quotes, rationalization, technical jargon, emotional appeals, and many more."

Denison Simulation Catalogue, Section I, 42

Psych City: 1975—A Simulated Community—Social/Community Dynamics
R. Cohen, J. McManus, D. Fox, C. Kastelnik

> "This is a series of complementary learning activities which enable the student to acquire and integrate cognitive, affective, and behavioral understanding of community dynamics. Students assume the roles of representative figures of a hypothetical community meeting in a town meeting format for an extended period, and attempt to resolve a community problem which the class has selected from ten problems described in the textbook."

Denison Simulation Catalogue, Section I, 42

Queries 'N Theories—Scientific Method
L. E. Allen, J. Ross, P. Kugel

"The Wff 'n Proof game of science and language. Through inductive reasoning, players learn scientific method of inquiring and gain skill in organizing, analyzing, and synthesizing data while engaged in a game of linguistics."

Denison Simulation Catalogue, Section I, 43

The Red and Blue Game—Social/Competition and Cooperation

"To demonstrate the difficulty of getting a group of people to be cooperative and develop a win-win situation rather than a win-lose situation—*The Red and Blue Game* illustrates the dominance and submissiveness of people in social situations and the way that this contributes to competitiveness and lack of cooperation among people and groups."

Stadsklev, Part II, 219

Residence Halls—Social/Group Problem-Solving

"To study the degree to which members of a group agree on certain values; to assess the decision-making norms of the group; to identify the 'natural leadership' functioning in the group." Residence halls ranking sheet provided and individual and group rankings are compared.

Pfeiffer and Jones, Vol. I, 72

Rumor Clinic—Social/Interpersonal Communication

"To illustrate distortions which may occur in transmission of information from an original source through several individuals to a final destination."

Pfeiffer and Jones, Vol. II, 12

The Seven-Minute Day—Social/Group Problem-Solving

"Provides a context in which the participants can experience the problems and possibilities of making decisions and bringing about change within an institution/community with which they are familiar."

Denison Simulation Catalogue, Section I, 47

Shoe Store—Social/Group Problem-Solving

"To observe communication patterns in group problem-solving; to explore interpersonal influence in problem-solving." A so-called mathematical problem is posed about making change in a shoe store. A group decision about the correct answers must be reached.

Pfeiffer and Jones, Vol. IV, 5

Status-Interaction Study—Social/Interpersonal Communication

"To explore effects of status differences on interaction among group members."

Pfeiffer and Jones, Vol. II, 85

Strategies of Changing—Social/Group Problem-Solving

"To acquaint people with three different interpersonal strategies for trying to effect change in human systems." Roles are assigned to individuals involved in trying to change conditions in a hospital pediatrics ward.

Pfeiffer and Jones, 1973, 32

Styles of Leadership—Social/Leadership

"To explore the impact that leaders have on decision making in groups; to demonstrate the effects of hidden agendas." Prescribed roles are given to participants. A specific debriefing sheet pointing out features of each role is provided.

Pfeiffer and Jones, Vol. V, 19

Testing: Intergroup Competition—Social/Competition

"To explore the impact of the lack of communication in competitive situations; to demonstrate the need for collaboration and interdependence." Testing score sheets, question blanks, and answer blanks are provided.

Pfeiffer and Jones, Vol. V, 91

Twelve Angry Men—Social/Group Problem-Solving

"To compare the accuracy of predictions based on group consensus-seeking to those made by individuals; to generate data for a discussion of the merits of attempting consensus." The movie *Twelve Angry Men* is employed as the vehicle for discussion in groups. Prediction sheets are provided for the task.

Pfeiffer and Jones, 1972, 13

ANALYSIS OF THE *HUNG JURY* SIMULATION

(Hung Jury Simulation, From J. W. Pfeiffer and J. E. Jones, *The 1974 annual handbook for group facilitators,* La Jolla, Calif.: University Associates, 1974)

	Central problem presented in the simulation	*To study decision-making processes in groups*
Objectives		1. To examine the emergence of leadership and characteristics of leaders. 2. To examine consensus-reaching behaviors. 3. To examine pressures for conformity. 4. To contrast the simulation situation as a tool for learning about group processes to its use as a research device.
Game play		1. The "jury" is instructed and information about the case is provided. 2. Jurors discuss the case and try to reach a verdict. 3. Group decision-making is discussed.
Game rules		1. Maximum of 30 minutes in jury deliberation. 2. Jury may elect a foreman by majority vote. 3. Jury may take an unlimited number of votes; if no consensus is reached, a final vote must be taken at the end of the 30-minute deliberation period.
Debriefing activities		1. Discussion of foreman selection: How, who, why? This will focus on the general topic of leader selection and characteristics. 2. Analysis of voting behavior: when was first vote taken; how did group decide when to take a vote? This will focus on consensus-reaching behaviors and other decision-making behaviors of the group. 3. Discussion of vote-changing by individual jurors: why, when did jurors change their positions? This will focus on conformity in groups. 4. Discussion of what was learned about group decision-making processes through participation in this simulation; discussion of alternative uses for this simulation, focusing on degree of structural reality as a dependent variable when using simulations as a research tool.

Part XII

EVALUATING THE TEACHING EFFECTIVENESS OF SIMULATIONS

The last five papers of this volume cover a broad range of problems and concerns related to asking the question "Does using simulation in the classroom allow me to fulfill the objectives I have set for its use?"

The first essay, by Bewley, overviews briefly some assumptions and some problems involved in considering whether computer simulations serve satisfactorily or to what degree of satisfaction they serve, as part of an educational curriculum. Because a major part of Bewley's research has been directed at creating and evaluating such simulations, his comments are especially important for those of us who have been working with the complexities of educational evaluation for a shorter time.

The second evaluation paper, written by economist King, involves an elaborate experimental study comparing the teaching of macroeconomics with the aid of computer simulations to the same kind of course without the simulations. King compared both how much the students liked the two courses and how much improvement they showed in a standardized test on macroeconomic phenomena. Further, he performed a cost analysis on both the control and experimental sections, thus allowing some generalizations to be made about what he terms "learning achievements per dollar per student."

The third evaluational paper is also a study comparing relative learning outcomes for self-paced materials and simulation-gaming techniques, both of which covered the same material covered in a course called "Curriculum and the Social Order." Written by education professor Gallant, the paper deals with some of the problems encountered in educational research when the number of students enrolled in the target courses is typically small, and when there are slight shifts in the background statistics on the students. Although his results did not show simulation to be a more effective technique, the value in Gallant's paper lies in the way in which he carefully structured the study so as to treat reasonably the numerous confounding problems that the situation surrounding the course prescribed.

The fourth paper, by psychologist Thios, outlines a concept we believe to be crucial to useful evaluation of the teaching effectiveness of simulation. This is the notion that there are unified clusters of behaviors that individuals typically show to perceiving and operating in their worlds (henceforth called "cognitive styles") and that differing clusters may predict to various ways that students learn best. For example, a person who tends to learn much about his environment by watching and listening to those around him may react very favorably to a gaming-simulation, while a person who learns best by reading by himself may derive little or no value from participating in a simulation. Thios outlines the argument that knowledge of cognitive styles is important for any kind of educational evaluation, reviews some of the cognitive style work created at Oakland Community College in Detroit, and then reports on a study carried out by himself and two students at Denison. The study provides one of the first steps toward correlating style measures with affect for simulation, and, it is hoped, will serve as a stimulus for additional such studies.

The last paper, also written by a psychologist, reviews much of the work done in educational evaluation related to simulation. The author, Morris, points out that few studies have shown any form of simulation to be more effective than more traditional means of instruction, and proceeds to ask why. Is it because simulation is simply *not* more effective? In view of educational research, Morris concludes that he thinks not, and goes on to make a number of suggestions about how to make more sensitive the studies aimed at comparing the learning outcomes of simulation techniques. Interestingly, most of the preceding four evaluation projects have followed the suggested techniques and, except for Gallant's work, all have found positive effects. This fact, together with Morris's argument from the general educational research literature, provides strong support for Morris's contentions.

18

EVALUATING
THE EFFECTIVENESS
OF INSTRUCTIONAL COMPUTING

WILLIAM L. BEWLEY

ABSTRACT

This paper is essentially a summary of remarks made during a presentation at the 1976 Denison Simulation Workshop. It is based on my experience during the early part of 1976 trying to develop a design for a study of the impact of educational computing under a contract from the National Institute of Education (NIE). Comments made here are based on a fairly thorough examination of the literature and on conversations with several consultants. The comments are, of course, my own and do not necessarily represent the position of NIE or of the consultants.

Although the design for NIE is much broader in scope, I would like to focus on problems with evaluating the effectiveness of individual computer-based instructional applications, e.g., simulations, in the area of cognitive outcomes. The question is: Do students learn more from the computer-based application? The question is admittedly a bit vague, especially with regard to the word "more," but more about that later (no pun).

Virtually all studies that have attempted to answer this question have used an experimental-versus-control group design, where the experimental group receives the computer-based instruction and the control group receives "traditional" instruction. These studies are plagued by several problems:

1. *"Traditional" is often undefined.*
What exactly is the traditional instruction? What are the objectives?

What methods and media are used? What are the characteristics of teachers and students? How does the traditional treatment differ from the computer-based treatment? These questions are usually not answered. When they are answered, there are, perhaps inevitably in an educational setting, numerous confounding variables.

2. *The computer-based instruction is undefined.*
   The application itself may be defined, but its use is usually not. How does it fit into the course? Does it change the course? Does it change the role of the instructor? These are all powerful confounding variables.

3. *The computer-based instruction is usually an "add on."*
   The experimental group often gets traditional instruction (whatever that is) *plus* the computer-based instruction (assuming that the traditional part of the course is unchanged—which is usually unknown). Any difference could be attributed to more instruction rather than to the specific computer-based application. This, of course, assumes that the objectives of traditional and computer-based instruction are the same; they often are not—see number 5 below.

4. *The computer-based instruction has been systematically developed.*
   Much curriculum development time and effort have usually been expended on the computer-based application. This is not true for traditional instruction. Evaluators wonder what would happen if the same time and effort had been devoted to improving the traditional part of the curriculum.

5. *Computer-based and traditional instruction often have different objectives.*
   Many suggest that this is not only often the case, but should be the case. I tend to agree. If this is true, however, comparisons are invalid.

I think that we need to look at the effectiveness of computer-based instruction from a value-added point of view. Some of the problems listed above may be avoided if we represent the relationship of traditional to computer-based instruction as shown in the Venn diagram. This diagram shows that traditional and computer-based instruction each have some unique objectives and some that are shared with the other mode. An experimental-versus-control group comparison is appropriate only for the shared objectives. For the objectives unique to computer-based instruction, we can only determine the extent to which they are achieved—no comparison with traditional instruction is possible. If they are achieved, they (the objectives) must be evaluated by users. Are they worth achieving? Does the value added by their achievement balance the cost of their achievement?

The new objectives must, by the way, be truly unique to the computer-based application. It must be clear that those objectives could not be achieved without the computer. As Arthur Luerhmann of Dartmouth has pointed out, the computer must be used to do something new, not to do old things better.

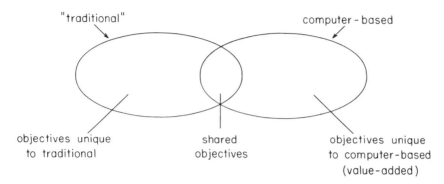

Do students learn *more* from the computer-based application? The value-added representation suggests that there are two senses of the word "more": (1) with reference to the shared objectives, we can ask if students using the computer-based applications achieve these objectives at a higher level—more within objectives; (2) for the unique objectives, we can ask if students achieve new objectives when they use the computer-based application—more objectives.

I think that the value-added approach can help us avoid problems 3 through 5 above, because they become problems only when experimental-versus-control group comparisons are attempted.

The value-added approach will not help us avoid problems 1 and 2. These problems are caused by sloppy research, not by experimental-versus-control group comparisons. The educational situation is admittedly complex. It is impossible to control all potentially relevant variables, but we can at least attempt to identify them.

19

COMPUTER TECHNOLOGY AND THE TEACHING OF MACROECONOMICS: AN EVALUATION

PAUL G. KING

ABSTRACT

One of the prime difficulties in teaching economic theory courses that emphasize policy applications lies in finding the proper tradeoff between real-world model sophistication and excessive mathematical complexity. This paper attempts to address that question by exploring the learning differences between two groups of students, one of which (27 students) learns macroeconomic theory and policy by means of fairly complex computer simulation models and computer-assisted instruction lessons, while the second group (35 students) uses only the more traditional lecture-discussion pedagogy. The goal is to enhance the learning of the one group of students by the use of the computer technology, which permits the sophistication of the economic models to be carried further without introducing the complication of complex mathematical solutions for the students.

The level of preparation and the match between the two groups was examined in terms of a variety of background evidence relating to both basic ability and acquired cognitive skills. An evaluative instrument, the "Test of Understanding of College Economics," was used as both a pre- and a posttest. It indicates changes in student performance in terms of both economic concepts and their applications. In addition, each student was required to keep and submit a detailed weekly record of time spent on course-related activities. This was used as part of the examination of the cost effectiveness of the two instructional methodologies.

The results of the experiment indicate that, both in terms of standardized test performance and in terms of final grades, there is some significant difference favoring the group using the experimental methodology. In addition, regression analysis, using all of the background information among its independent variables, indicates that membership in the experimental group is causally responsible for a portion of the learning differences that emerge.

Finally, evaluating the learning improvements relative to the cost of the experiment indicates that the computer methodology is cost effective relative to the traditional pedagogy—that is, learning achievements per dollar per student are greater with the experimental methodology.

The Problem

One of the recurring problems in the teaching of undergraduate economics courses that have a policy orientation is that of developing in the students an intuitive understanding of the complexities of real-world policy making without getting many of them hopelessly entangled in the mathematics of complex economic models. To cope with this problem, the present experiment used simulation as a fundamental element. By using relatively sophisticated and mathematically complex computer simulation models of the aggregate economy, it was hypothesized that students could come to grips with the policy implications of such models, while allowing the computer algorithm to take care of the mathematical manipulations and solutions.

In addition to the use of the simulation models, the author was searching for some ways to open up more classroom time for discussion of policy matters. Much of the material taught in intermediate macro theory, particularly in the first third of the course, is strictly descriptive, not analytic. Clearly, some time must be spent teaching and reinforcing an understanding of these ideas, but they certainly do not represent the analytic heart of macro theory. A reasonable solution seemed to be the development of some computer-assisted lessons that could be used to teach and drill students on the descriptive material. Classroom time formerly devoted to this material would then be free for much more concentration on both policy and analysis.

Some Hypotheses

The potential benefits from these alternative pedagogical approaches were grouped in two categories: cognitive improvements in understanding about macro theory and policy, and cost—a lower cost per unit of cognitive achievement.

A review of the literature about teaching and learning experiments in economics does not lead one to the expectation that significant cognitive benefits will occur (see especially Soper, 1974). In addition, most educational experiments do not take any account of the time-input differentials for different teaching and learning methodologies. That is, they implicitly treat both faculty and student time as being essentially costless.

In order to examine the benefits flowing from this particular set of alternative methodologies, an experiment was set up to test the following two hypotheses:

a. That there will be no significant differences in cognitive learning outcomes for students using the simulation-CAI methods as opposed to traditional lecture-discussion formats.
b. That the cost per unit of cognitive achievement will be less for the simulation-CAI format than for traditional pedagogy.

The Experimental Framework

The experiment was designed for the first semester of the academic year 1975-1976. During that semester, the author was responsible for teaching two sections of intermediate macroeconomic theory. After student registration had been completed, one of the sections was designated as experimental (simulation-CAI) and the other as control. The two sections used essentially the same course outline and textbook (Shapiro, 1974) were given the same tests, and were generally treated the same in all respects, except that the experimental group substituted CAI lessons and the running of simulation models for about 8 to 9 regular class hours. In its turn, the control group had some limited reading outside the textbook to cover more effectively the policy material that the experimental group was learning with the simulation models. Although the individual members of the two groups were not randomly selected and no pair matching was attempted, they were in fact reasonably well matched in terms of certain background variables.

Table 1 summarizes this information.

All of the students were, at the beginning of the semester, given the Test of Understanding of College Economics (TUCE), part I (macro). At the end of the semester, the students again took the TUCE test. The TUCE test and the students' overall performance (grades) in the course were used to test the cognition hypothesis.

During the semester, the students had to turn in a time sheet each week, showing the hours devoted to various activities related to the course. This was used to test the cost and time-commitment hypothesis.

Methodology

a. Cognitive Measurement

The first task was to determine what cognitive improvement, if any, took place during the semester. The students in each group were given the macroeconomic part of the TUCE test at the beginning and at the end of the semester. The test consists of 26 multiple-choice questions and has two forms. The questions are divided into three taxonomic subsets: simple concepts, simple applications, and complex applications. The percentage improvement in performance on the test from the beginning to the end of the semester was then compared for each of the two groups of students, for both the total score and the taxonomic subsets of the test. Both significant improvement and significant differences in improvement were tested for, using the student's t-test.

Isolating the causative factors that contributed most to the learning that did take place was the next task. That is, what factors were most useful in explaining the improvement in the TUCE scores (both aggregate and component) for each student? Linear regression techniques were used here, with the following general formulation:

$$TUCEDIF_{in} = f(X_{jn}),\qquad\qquad(1)$$

where

> $TUCEDIF_{in}$ is the improvement measure for the ith component of the TUCE test for student n ($i=1,\ 4;\ i=1$ for total score component),
> X_{jn} is the value of the jth potential explanatory variable for student n ($j=1,\ 10$).

Finally, overall performance in the course was examined in terms of the final arithmetic average for each student. Because the students were given a set of objectives at the beginning of the semester, and because the course examinations were designed to measure performance vis-à-vis those objectives, it was felt that final arithmetic class averages were acceptable measures of cognitive achievement, even though there was no pretest to allow measurement of the size of the cognitive gain.

These performance data were used first to examine the differences between the control and experimental groups by means of a t-test. Then performance per student was examined in a linear regression format, using the following general form:

$$F_n = g\ (X_{jn}),\qquad\qquad(2)$$

where

> F_n is the final arithmetic class average for student n,
> X_{jn} is the value of the jth potential explanatory variable for student n.
> For both equations 1 and 2, the potential explanatory variables, X_{jn}, are

X_{1n} age of student (as of 9/75, in years)   (AG)
X_{2n} total credits earned (9/75)   (CR)
X_{3n} economics credits earned (9/75)   (MA)
X_{4n} mathematics credits earned (9/75)   (SM)
X_{5n} SAT score—mathematics   (SM)
X_{6n} SAT score—verbal   (SV)
X_{7n} GPA in Economics (9/75)   (GPAE)
X_{8n} Overall GPA (9/75)   (GPA)
X_{9n} dummy for sex (0 = male, 1 = female)   (SC)
X_{10n} dummy for section (0 = control, 1 = experimental)   (SEC)

The abbreviations in parentheses at the right-hand margin are the source name codes for the variables in the regression analysis.

b. Cost Effectiveness Measurement

Each student was required, each week, to turn in a time sheet indicating total hours spent in each of the following activities:

1. in class
2. reading textbook
3. reading other course materials
4. studying notes
5. working at computer terminal
6. discussion with other students

These time inputs were then aggregated to get total student time input for each section. A dollar value can then be placed on these time inputs with the following procedure:

Assume that the average student in the control group pays 25 percent of one semester's tuition for this course, while the experimental group students pay that amount multiplied by the ratio

$$T_1/T_0,$$

where

T_1 average student time input—experimental group,
T_0 average student time input—control group.

This approach asserts that, if, for example, experimental-group students spend less time on the course, on the average, that frees their time for other courses or activities and reduces the real cost of this course to them.

A dollar value is placed on the time input of the faculty member by using approximately one-sixth of faculty salary for each course. Again, this should be adjusted up or down for the experimental course to reflect different uses of faculty time as a result of the experimental course.

Finally, there are developmental costs involved in creating and using the experimental materials. These include faculty summer salary, computer time, student assistant time, and equipment cost. These costs should not, however, simply be added to the time costs described above. There must be a discounting mechanism reflecting the fact that total development costs must be spread over the useful life of the methodology and materials if the experiment is successful enough to be repeated. In this case, we assumed that the materials could be used for 6-10 semesters and that 10 percent was the appropriate rate of discount.

This time and cost information can be used to find the cost/unit of any significant positive changes or achievements in the cognitive domain resulting from student participation in the course. Thus, raw improvement can be tempered with cost, allowing us to learn something about the cost effectiveness of various teaching methodologies. That is, $A_1/cost_1$ can be compared with $A_2/cost_2$, where A_1 and A_2 represent some achievements with teaching methodology 1 and teaching methodology 2, respectively.

Analysis of Results

a. COGNITIVE OUTCOMES

The mean values of the cognitive variables are shown in Table 2.

1. *Cognitive Improvement—TUCE*

In order to determine whether significant learning took place during the semester, a t-test was applied to measures i, j, k, and l from Table 2. All of these TUCEDIF (improvement) measures were significant at at least the .005 level for both the control and experimental groups (Table 3).

2. *Learning Differences—TUCE*

The next question concerns whether either the control or experimental groups learned significantly more. Because the TUCE test forms A and B as used here are slightly different in terms of number of questions in each taxonomic subset, some modification of the raw data was necessary to ensure comparability between the two groups. The following example illustrates the modification. For the control group, the overall percentage of TUCE questions correct in September was 49.46. This means that potential improvement was 50.54 percentage points. The actual improvement was 13.62 percentage points, or 26.95 percent of the potential. The comparable figures for the experimental group are 51.86 percent correct, 48.14 percentage points potential improvement, 15.94 percentage points actual improvement, or 33.11 percent of the potential. A t-test was used to compare this 33.11 percent with the 26.95 percent for the control group. It showed a significant difference between the two groups at the 1 percent level.

Therefore, it can be concluded that, measured in terms of the overall TUCE scores, the experimental group achieved significantly more in cognitive terms than did the control group.

A similar approach was used for the components of the TUCE test. Table 4 summarizes the results. As can be seen from the table, the difference in improvement for the simple applications questions was highly significant, indicating that the experimental group had a higher degree of improvement in this area than did the control group. Although this is contrary to the initial hypothesis, it is not unreasonable, because any differences that do occur should be in the applications area, reflecting the more intensive exposure to model manipulation and application on the part of the experimental group. The lack of a significant difference in improvement for the complex applications questions reflects, it is hoped, a lack of sufficient complexity and sophistication in the simulation models. If that is true, then further development and use of the models and methodology should lead to even greater improvement for students using the new method.

3. *Learning Differences—Final Grades*

During the semester there were four hour exams, including a final exam. Each of these counted for 25 percent of the total grade. Both sections took the same tests, which were designed to measure student ability to satisfy the learning objectives of the course. In Table 2, the experimental group is shown to have done better than the control group by approximately 15 total points, which translates to about 3.8 percent, significant at the 10 percent level. Translated into letter grades, this means that the average student in the control group got a grade of C+, while the average student in the experimental group got a grade of B/B−. Insofar as these results are valid, they indicate a greater ability to fulfill the learning objectives of the course on the part of the experimental group, which translates into an ability to get a higher grade from the course.

4. *Source of Differences—Regression Analysis*

Several different regression analyses were tried in an effort to explain the cognitive changes that had taken place, i.e., what caused the significant changes and differences that have been presented in Tables 3 and 4 and in the discussion of final grades. Can these differences be explained solely by some of the background variables, or does the choice of section (and hence teacher-learning methodology) play an important role?

Using ordinary least squares multiple regression analysis, the best results (in terms of R^2) for TUCE tests came with models in which the dependent variable was the TUCE improvement relative to potential for improvement (see Table 4). The independent variables for these models include all of those described in section IV-*a*, plus the initial overall and component TUCE percentage scores.

Because even a casual observation of the set of explanatory variables shows the very real possibility of multicollinearity, a stepwise procedure for adding variables was used. The "best" versions of each model were then the ones for which the marginal additions to R^2 were just significant. The resulting regression equations are:

TUCEOVER= $-19.67 \ - \ .81 \ \text{TUCE} + \ \ .09 \ \text{SV} + 12.47 \ \text{SEC} + \ \ .08 \ \text{SM}$ (3)
                         (-4.42) (2.17) (2.38) $1.83)$
                $R^2 = .3516 \ \ F = 7.728 \ \ \text{Degrees of freedom} = 57$

TUCESIMP= $39.94 \ -2.19 \ \text{TUCE1} + \ 1.55 \ \text{TUCE} + \ .17 \ \text{SM} - 21.04 \ \text{GPA}$ (4)
                         (-5.30) (3.03) (2.31) (-1.72)
                $R^2 = .4348 \ \ F = 10.962 \ \ \text{Degrees of freedom} = 57$

TUCEAPPL= $200.71 - 1.73 \ \text{TUCE2} + \ .73 \ \text{TUCE1} + 21.64 \ \text{GPAE} + 21.89 \ \text{SEC}$
                         (-5.63) (2.11) (2.28) (1.82)
                $-10.53 \ \text{AG}$ (5)
                (-1.72)
                $R^2 = .4354 \ \ F = 8.639 \ \ \text{Degrees of freedom} = 56$

TUCECOMPL= $38.92 \ -1.83 \ \text{TUCE3} + \ .17 \ \text{SV} + 1.07 \ \text{TUCE}$ (6)
                         (-5.47) (2.54) (2.40)
                $R^2 = .3779 \ \ F = 11.742 \ \ \text{Degrees of freedom} = 58$

FINAL= $155.62 + 20.94 \ \text{GPA} + 14.29 \ \text{SEC} + 23.27 \ \text{GPAE} + 1.03 \ \text{MA}$
                         (1.92) (2.10) (3.17) (2.12) (7)
                $+ .27 \ \text{CR} \ - \ .56 \ \text{TUCE3} + \ .62 \ \text{TUCE}$
                (1.91) (-2.37) (1.89)
                $R^2 = .5920 \ \ F = 11.19 \ \ \text{Degrees of freedom} = 54$

(The numbers in parentheses under each equation are t-values.)

TUCE   = beginning percentage TUCE score—overall (o)
TUCE 1   = beginning percentage TUCE score—simple concepts (sc)
TUCE 2   = beginning percentage TUCE score—simple applications (sa)
TUCE 3   = beginning percentage TUCE score—complex applications (ca)
TUCEOVER = change in percentage TUCE score relative to potential (o)

TUCESIMP = change in percentage TUCE score relative to potential (sc)
TUCEAPPL = change in percentage TUCE score relative to potential (sa)
TUCECOMP = change in percentage TUCE score relative to potential (ca)
FINAL   = final arithmetic grade

In the cases of overall TUCE improvement, simple applications TUCE improvement, and final grades, the dummy variable SEC is clearly significant and indicates that membership in the experimental group adds significantly to cognitive achievement.

For equations 3-6, the corresponding TUCE score has a negative coefficient, indicating that students with high initial TUCE scores and thus limited potential for improvement do not improve as much as other students relative to potential.

5. *Summary of Cognitive Outcomes*

In general, it is clear that some significant learning took place in both sections of this course. In addition, there is evidence of a differential learning advantage accruing to the students in the experimental section. That is, the teaching and learning methodology of the experiment appears to be, in at least some areas, cognitively superior to the traditional methodology used in the control group.

b. TIME AND COST EFFECTIVENESS

1. *Time and Cost Inputs*

The students in the control group put in a total of 5,183 hours of time during the semester. For the 35 students in the control group, this averaged out to 148.1 hours per student. For the experimental group, there were 3,677 hours input for 27 students, or an average of 136.2 hours per student. Assuming a tuition of $3,200 per year, the control group tuition cost per student would be $400. Because the experimental group time commitment is only 92 percent of that for the control group (136.2/148.1), their real cost is reduced by 8 percent, and thus it becomes $368 per student.

Faculty time input was just about exactly 5 percent greater in the experimental group than in the control group. This was due to some grading and counseling work, which more than compensated for the reduced classroom time resulting from the experiment. This does not include time spent on program repair and reformulation, a process that is included in and part of the capital input for the methodology. The value of the faculty time input for the control group should be one-sixth of faculty salary, or approximately $3,000. Because the commitment to the experimental group is approximately 5 percent greater, its faculty cost should be $3,150.

The capital cost for the experimental group includes summer faculty salary ($1,800), a part of a computer terminal ($300), student assistant support ($400), computer time ($100), and materials purchases ($125). Total capital input is thus $2,725. Assuming a useful life of 8 semesters and a discount rate of .10, the capital cost per semester is about $420.

Added to these costs, we have computer use by the students during the semester, which amounted to about $115 for the first semester's experiment.

The faculty, capital, and computer time costs for the experimental group total $3,685, or $136.50 per student per semester, making total cost per student $504.50. For the control group, the $3,000 of faculty cost translates into $85.70 per student per semester, making total cost per student $485.70 for the control group.

2. Cost per Cognitive Achievement

The cognitive achievements measures in this experiment include percentage improvement in TUCE component score relative to potential. For the overall TUCE measure, this percentage is 26.95 for the control group and 33.11 for the experimental group. Dividing by the respective costs shows us that, for every dollar spent per student in the control group, overall TUCE score went up .055 percent relative to potential. For the experimental group, the achievement was .066 percent per dollar spent per student. The other measures of cognitive achievement per dollar are summarized in Table 5.

As the table shows, in almost all instances, the achievement per dollar per student is greater in the experimental group than in the control group, indicating that the new teaching methodology is cost effective in cognitive terms.

Conclusions and Proposals

On the basis of all the evidence presented here, it would seem that the development of the experimental simulation-CAI teaching methodology has met with some success and that further development and testing is desirable. It is particularly interesting that there is such strong evidence of cognitive achievement differentials favorable to the experimental group. This, of course, refutes the initial hypothesis that no such differences would occur.

There is a clear time advantage accruing to the experimental group. They spent 8 percent less time on the course than did the control group. The cost-effectiveness measures almost all seem to favor the experimental group, too. This is encouraging, because it argues that even relatively costly educational experiments can yield educational returns that more than compensate for the increased cost.

Finally, there is a clear scope for changing the internal construction of this course in a way that allows the introduction of more interesting and current policy matters without sacrificing the quality of the material that has traditionally formed the core of macroeconomic analysis at the undergraduate level.

In terms of further experimentation, I am currently conducting a repeat of this experiment using the same evaluative instruments and adding to them some primitive efforts at cognitive style mapping to see if there may be any discernible relationships between student cognitive styles and the degree of learning with the alternative pedagogic methods. Significant outcomes here might lead to some very real benefits to students in choosing among alternative teaching and learning methodologies.

TABLE 1

BACKGROUND DATA FOR SIMULATION-CAI EXPERIMENT

| | *Average Values* | |
Variable	*Control*	*Experimental*
Age	19.6	20.1
Percent Male	85.7	85.2
Total Credits	54.7	69.3
Econ Credits	7.5	10.4
Math Credits	7.4	6.6
SAT-Math	592	598
SAT-Verbal	519	522
Econ GPA (4.0 = A, 3.0 = B, etc.)	3.19	3.03
Overall GPA	2.90	3.03
No. of Students	35	27

TABLE 2

MEAN VALUES OF COGNITIVE VARIABLES

| | | *Mean Values* | |
	Cognitive Measure	*Control*	*Experimental*
a)	TUCE (Sept.)	49.46%	51.86%
b)	TUCE—simple (Sept.)	57.42%	65.52%
c)	TUCE—simple appl. (Sept.)	44.36%	52.00%
d)	TUCE—complex appl. (Sept.)	43.43%	40.37%
e)	TUCE (Dec.)	63.08%	67.80%
f)	TUCE—simple (Dec.)	74.66%	78.32%
g)	TUCE—simple appl. (Dec.)	52.67%	64.56%
h)	TUCE—complex appl. (Dec.)	61.14%	61.85%
i)	TUCEDIF (Dec.-Sept.)	13.62%	15.94%
j)	TUCEDIF—simple (Dec.-Sept.)	17.24%	12.80%
k)	TUCEDIF—simple appl. (Dec.-Sept.)	8.31%	12.56%
l)	TUCEDIF—complex appl. (Dec.-Sept.)	17.71%	21.48%
m)	FINAL grade	304.86	319.56

TABLE 3
T-TEST FOR AGGREGATE LEARNING
TUCE IMPROVEMENT

	Control		Experimental	
Variable	Average	t-value	Average	t-value
TUCEDIF	13.62	5.92 (P<.001)	15.94	6.13 (P<.001)
TUCEDIF—simple	17.24	7.84 (P<.001)	12.80	5.33 (P<.001)
TUECDIF—simple appl.	8.31	3.61 (P<.005)	12.56	4.83 (P<.001)
TUCEDIF—complex appl.	17.71	7.70 (P<.001)	21.48	11.31 (P<.001)

TABLE 4
LEARNING DIFFERENCES, TUCE COMPONENTS

Group Scores	Overall TUCE	Simple TUCE	Simple Appl. TUCE	Complex Appl. TUCE
Control				
(1) Sept. Score	49.46	57.42	44.36	43.43
(2) Improve Potential	50.54	42.58	55.64	56.57
(3) Improve Actual	13.62	17.24	8.31	17.71
(4) (3)/(2)	26.95	40.49	14.61	31.31
Experimental				
(5) Sept. Score	51.86	65.52	52.00	40.37
(6) Improve Potential	48.14	34.48	48.00	59.63
(7) Improve Actual	15.94	12.80	12.56	21.48
(8) (7)/(6)	33.11	37.12	26.17	36.02
t-value for (8)-(4)	2.68 (p<.01)	−0.75 (not signif.)	3.07 (p<.005)	1.23 (not signif.)

TABLE 5
COGNITIVE ACHIEVEMENTS PER DOLLAR
PER STUDENT

	Control		Experimental	
Cognitive Measure	Average	Per dollar Per student	Average	Per dollar Per student
TUCEDIF—overall	26.95	.055	33.11	.066
TUCEDIF—simple	40.49	.083	37.12	.074
TUCEDIF—simple applications	14.61	.030	26.17	.052

TUCEDIF—complex				
applications	31.31	.065	36.02	.071
FINAL Grade	304.86	.628	319.56	.633

REFERENCES

Fels, R. Multiple choice questions in elementary economics. In K. G. Lumsden (Ed.), *Recent research in economics education.* Englewood Cliffs, New Jersey: Prentice-Hall, Inc. 1970.

Shapiro, E. A. *Macroeconomic analysis.* 3rd ed. New York: Harcourt Brace Jovanovich, Inc., 1974.

Soper, John C. Computer assisted instruction in economics: a survey. *Journal of Economic Education,* Fall, 1974, *6.*

Treyz, George I. Active programming and computer simulations by intermediate macroeconomic theory students. *Economic Education Experience of Enterprising Teachers,* Vol. 8. New York: Joint Council on Economic Education, 1971.

20

A COMPARATIVE STUDY OF THREE INSTRUCTIONAL APPROACHES: SELF-PACED LEARNING MATERIALS PACKAGES, SIMULATION GAMING, AND COMPETENCY-BASED BEHAVIORAL TASKS

Thomas F. Gallant

ABSTRACT

This study compared and evaluated the use of three instructional approaches in the professional education sequence of a teacher-education program. These are self-paced study of Learning Materials Packages ("LMP" group), simulation gaming ("SIM" group), and self-paced, individualized study of behavioral objectives in a special Internship program ("INT" group).

Student attitudes toward the course work were assessed through opinionaires given to INT and SIM. Comparisons of cognitive achievement by INT and SIM were made with the use of the Education Test marketed by the Educational Testing Service. LMP and SIM were compared cognitively by use of an instructor-made multiple-choice test. SAT Verbal scores were used as a control measure for all three groups.

Student reaction to the simulation games was positive. Clarity of game objectives and the contribution the games made to learning the subject matter ranked high as strengths. The lowest, but still positive ranking, related to the value of the games in helping students understand the complexity of the particular systems involved.

INT students also were positive in their attitudes toward the instructional approach used in that program, with relevancy of materials and assignments receiving the lowest rating, and availability of materials and instructor rated highest. Additionally, students were quite positive toward the individually paced nature of the work and the general format of the course.

Statistically, no significant differences in achievement between INT and SIM on material common to both groups were revealed by the Education Test, though the two groups differed significantly (.02) on the SAT-Verbal. Therefore, it might only be conjectured that SIM gained some slight advantage on topics related to philosophy of education and curriculum, and lost a similar advantage in the areas of sociology of education, aims of education, and organization and administration.

Similarly, the instructor-made multiple-choice test showed no statistically significant differences in total test scores between LMP and SIM and no significant differences between these groups in the twelve separate categories of the test, except one. The lone exception was "Professional Organizations," and this might suggest a benefit was derived by SIM in the use of a simulation game called "Collective Negotiations." Though not statistically warranted, test results also indicated that simulations may have contributed to SIM's advantage in the study of "Curriculum," "Finance," and "Governance," while Learning Materials Packages may have been more beneficial in the study of "Accountability" and "Alternative Education."

Purpose of the Study

The purpose of this study is to evaluate and compare three instructional approaches in the professional education sequence of the teacher-education program at Denison. These approaches are (1) self-paced study of twelve Learning Materials Packages (LMPs), (2) simulation gaming, and (3) self-paced, individualized study organized around forty-three behavioral objectives.

Summary of Instructional Approaches

Education 213, "Curriculum and the Social Order," is taken by students in concentrated fashion during the four weeks preceding student teaching. During the '74-'75 academic year the students who studied LMPs constituted one class each semester. These students studied twelve self-paced Learning Materials Packages, each of which was devoted to one of the following topics: Accountability, Alternative Education, Curriculum, Finance, Flexible Scheduling, Governance, Grouping for Instruction, History, "The New," Professional Organizations, Team Teaching, and Urban Education. Each package contained an assortment of Xeroxed materials or references to be read and a list of questions or behavioral objectives to guide the student's study. Achievement on eight packages was evaluated through written tests; for the other four, individual conferences with the instructor were scheduled. This work was supplemented by an independent project, three field trips, a simulation game, a speaker, and one optional film. The field trips were to a vocational school, a nongraded high school, and an alternative high school. The simulation game was a 90-minute culminating exercise that dealt with relationships among the public, a school board, administrators, and teachers. The speaker dealt with the topic of school financing, and the film, *And No Bells Ring*, highlighted recent educational innovations such as team teaching, variable grouping for instruction, and independent study. The classes did not meet as groups except for the special activities named above.

The students who learned primarily through simulations during the school year '75-'76 constituted one class each semester. The course format featured five simulation games supplemented by an independent project, the same field trips experienced by those who used LMPs, and three of the same packages (History, "The New," and Urban Education) studied by those students. Simulation games dealt with curriculum, school financing, professional negotiations, alternative schools, and performance contracting. In addition, several of the games included aspects of school governance. Preparation for the games required the completion of some of the same readings that were incorporated in corresponding LMPs. Short tests were administered after the completion and debriefings of simulation games and/or field trips.

The Internship is an alternative route to the completion of professional education requirements. In 1975-76, one small group was enrolled each semester. The "Society, School, and Curriculum" block of the Internship semester contained most of the material and experiences which would have their counterparts in Education 213 of the standard program. The material was organized into forty-three rather specific "behavioral tasks" under the following topics: Accountability, Curriculum, Governance and Support, Individual Teacher Concerns, School Organization, and School-Society Relationships. Students could acquire proficiency on these tasks in a variety of optional but equivalent ways: tapes, readings, filmstrips, interviews, school resources, field trips, etc. Depending on the task, proficiency was demonstrated by written assignments, short tests, or individual oral tests given by the instructor. The tasks could be done in any order, but had to be completed during the first six weeks of the semester. Students could redo any of the tasks as many times as necessary to achieve full proficiency. They also participated in the three field trips in which the other two groups engaged. Intern students were required to be at their assigned schools for the entire semester, including the time they were working on "Society, School, and Curriculum." Many of the behavioral tasks for the work related to the student's school setting or required the resources of the school for completion.

Procedures

All three approaches will be evaluated through measures of student cognitive achievement, and the latter two also will be evaluated by the use of student opinionaires.

Three groups of students were involved separately in the three approaches:

1. 1974-75 classes in Education 213, which employed self-paced study of LMPs (designated "LMP" group); 21 students
2. 1975-76 classes in Education 213, which employed simulation gaming (designated "SIM" group); 17 students[1]
3. 1975-76 Interns in Education 417, which employed the use of behavioral objectives (designated "INT" group); 9 students

Comparisons in cognitive achievement will be made between SIM and INT and between LMP and SIM. No comparative study of student attitudes can be made because common instruments were not utilized, but student reactions to two of the teaching approaches were collected with the use of two sets of instruments. Because this study was not anticipated in 1974-75, no student feedback was elicited for LMP group. The instruments were designed only to evaluate each approach independent of the other, because it would not be valid for students to make comparisons when they experienced only one format.

SIM was asked to complete anonymously, after each simulation game debriefing, an evaluation form supplied by the Simulations Office. Eight questions were asked, each of which could be answered with "yes" or "no." Students, however, often supplemented or elaborated on their answers in such a way as to qualify them. In reporting the results of these students' evaluations, an attempt has been made to reflect these qualified responses. The first question on the questionnaire asked if the student had participated previously in simulations activities. Because the response was overwhelmingly "yes," and because the question had little or no relationship to the evaluation of each simulation, it was not included in this study. The substance of each of the additional questions is as follows: (2) Objective clear? (3) Helped understand complexity of the system? (4) Helped examine value questions and issues? (5) Opportunity to practice decision-making? (6) Helped learn about subject matter? (7) Interesting and motivating? (8) Recommend re-use?

Interns were given a set of three questionnaires during the last week of their respective semesters. One dealt with reactions to the Internship experience in general, another with the teaching methodology component, and the third with the "Society, School, and Curriculum" work. This study will report on only the latter questionnaire. It contained nine questions, with responses to be made on a descending scale of 10 through 0. Each question was to be viewed with this basic goal of the component in mind: "To integrate the academic study of the 'institution' of education into an experience in a particular school and community, thereby making this study as meaningful and realistic as possible." Questions are condensed and paraphrased here for convenience: (1) Relationship between tasks and school resources and experiences? (2) Feeling toward individually paced nature of work? (3) Clarity of the statements of the behavioral tasks? (4) Relevancy of the tasks to an understanding of educational issues and topics? (5) Appropriateness of the learning resources to the tasks? (6) Appropriateness of the means of evaluation of the tasks? (7) Availability of learning resources? (8) Accessibility of the instructor for oral tests? (9) Overall feeling toward the format of the work?

When Education 213 was first organized into a self-paced LMP course, an objective test was developed that consisted of 88 multiple-choice questions. This test was used both as a pretest and a posttest for LMP and SIM, although students were not permitted to see the test during the final three weeks of the four-week course. Questions were formulated around each of the twelve topics of the course. Numbers in parentheses indicate the allocation of questions to these topics: Accountability (5), Alternative Education (7), Curriculum (9), Finance (9), Flexible Scheduling (4), Governance (11), Grouping for Instruction (8), History (10), "The New" (7), Professional Organizations (5), Team Teaching (7), Urban Education (6). The use of these pretest and posttest scores permits comparisons to be made between LMP and SIM on the means of total test scores and the increases in scores on each of the twelve course topics.

On the dates of May 8 and 9, 1976, and in four separate administrations the following week to accommodate student conflicts, the Education Test of the Undergraduate Program, Educational Testing Service, was administered to Denison teacher-education students. The Education Test is a two-hour standardized test consisting of 150 multiple-choice questions. The designers of the test have grouped the questions into the following categories, with each question being assigned to two categories. Numbers in parentheses indicate total questions in that category: History (20), Psychology (46), Philosophy (31), Sociology (32), Theory-Research Based on Technology (21), Aims of Education (30), Curriculum (32), Organization and Administration (19), and Teaching-Learning (69).

It is possible that any significant differences in achievement under the three instructional approaches could result from other variables, one of which is student aptitude for learning. Therefore, to provide some measure of this general aptitude, SAT scores were acquired for all students included in the study.

Results

Tables 1-5 contain summaries of student evaluations of each of the five simulation games played by SIM. Games were played in the same order as the tables are numbered. "Curriculum Development" received the most favorable overall rating from the students, with "yes" responses to the questions constituting 81% of the total and "no" responses constituting only 5%. The game rated lowest was "Collective Negotiations," with the percentages being 54% and 15%, respectively, with a sizable percentage (31%) of qualified responses.

Table 6 summarizes the responses to each question from the simulations collectively. On the basis of total "yes" responses to each question, students rated the clarity of the game objectives, Question 2, the highest (94%), and helpfulness in understanding the complexity of the system, Question 3, lowest (41%). In addition, Question 2 also had the lowest percentage of "no" responses (5%), but Question 3 had fewer such negative responses than did Questions 4, 5, and 7, for which there were slightly higher percentages of positive responses. Questions 4 and 6, which pertained to values and subject matter, respectively, received more favorable ratings than might have been anticipated, because these are areas in which simulation learning is often questioned.

Table 7 summarizes the responses of the Interns to the "Society, School, and Curriculum" portion of the Internship semester. Although the medians of the responses to the questions ranged only from 7 to 9, indicating overall positive reaction to the program, considerable scattering of responses will be noted for most of the individual questions. This is especially true of Question 1, which pertained to the relationship between the behavioral tasks and the Intern's own school resources and experiences. Closely allied to this issue is Question 4, which asked for a judgment of the relevancy of the tasks to an understanding of educational issues and topics. Here, too, considerable spread in student responses is noted.

The mean scores of INT and SIM on the Education Test differed by 42 points, with the former scoring highest (See Table 8). However, a two-tailed t-test revealed that this difference was significant only at a level of confidence slightly over .10. Even had there been a greater likelihood that this difference did not occur by chance, there is the possibility that INT and SIM differed in their learning potential, and that the mode of instruction was not the fundamental factor in the ultimate cognitive achievement of the students. Therefore, SAT scores were used to supply a control measure to test this hypothesis. The rank-difference method was used to correlate these SAT scores with those of the Education Test. For the combined groups, correlations of .760 for the SAT-Verbal and .363 for the SAT-Math were discovered. In light of this finding, only SAT-Verbal scores were used for control purposes. Table 8 reveals that the mean of INT (586) surpassed that of SIM (514) on the SAT-Verbal by 72 points, a difference that could have occurred by chance only two times out of 100 (.02 confidence level). Such data give support to the hypothesis that the difference in Education Test averages may have been more a function of learning aptitude than instructional approach. Indeed, one could conjecture that the gap in the Education Test scores of the two groups that might have been predicted from SATs was narrowed somewhat by SIM. Another way of stating this is that, on the SAT, the mean score of INT surpassed that of SIM by 14%, but, on the Education Test, the means differed by only 10%.

This difference in achievement favoring INT held true not only for the Education Test as a whole, but also for each of the nine subdivisions of the test. Table 9 gives this comparative data. Because none of the t values (two-tailed) is significant at less than the .20 level of confidence, it is quite possible that the differences between the two groups in all categories could have occurred by chance. Yet it might be worthwhile to examine the categories individually or in groups to hypothesize about possible differences in the scores, even if such scores were not significantly different. Here again, it is important to remember that the mean score of INT on the SAT-Verbal was 14% higher than that of SIM.

Students in both groups had a common instructional experience only in Education 217, "Child and Adolescent Development," because all teacher candidates take this course. The difference in percentage of correct responses that occurred on the related Education Test area, Educational Psychology, might have been predicted on the basis of learning aptitude (SAT-Verbal). No formal instruction was given in Theory and Research, so any differences in scoring that occurred there could not be attributed to teaching techniques.

The anticipated differences between the two groups were narrowed somewhat by SIM in Philosophy of Education and Curriculum, suggesting the possibility of more effective approaches for that group in those areas. Similarly, the gap was widened by INT in Sociology of Education, Aims of Education, and Organization and Administration, suggesting a similar hypothesis for that group in those categories. Differences in History of Education and Teaching-Learning were of a magnitude consistent with SAT differences. Simulation games used in SIM group related to curriculum, aims of education, and organization and administration.

Mean scores for LMP and SIM on the 88-question test when used both as a pretest and a posttest were quite similar (see Table 10), and their differences were not statistically significant. Again, to provide a control measure, these two groups were compared using the means of their SAT-Verbal scores. The mean for LMP was 549 and for SIM 514. The difference of 35 points was not significant at the .10 level. It would be possible to hypothesize that the heavy emphasis on simulation activity by SIM prevented that group from falling below LMP in cognitive achievement as measured by the posttest, but such a hypothesis would be very tenuous indeed. A more productive exploration would be to compare the two groups on each of the twelve topical areas of the test and relate these findings to the instructional approach(es) used to teach each topic. Table 11 records these findings.

It may be noted from Table 11 that, on the basis of mean increases in the number of questions answered correctly on the posttest compared with the pretest, LMP surpassed SIM in Accountability, Alternative Education, Flexible Scheduling, and Team Teaching. SIM excelled in the other eight categories. Only in Professional Organizations, however, did the difference between means approach statistical significance (.05 level of confidence). Confidence levels for all others ranged between .1 and .7. Two-tailed t-tests were used for all comparisons. Simulations were used in SIM to teach Accountability, Alternative Education, Curriculum, Finance, Governance, and Professional Organizations, while LMP utilized learning materials packages to study these and the remaining six topics. As mentioned previously, almost identical learning materials packages were used by both groups to study History of Education, "The New," and Urban Education. As might be anticipated, increases in scores were similar for both groups in these "control" topics.

Summary and Conclusions

Taken as a group, the simulation games were reasonably well received by students. The clarity of game objectives and the contribution of the games toward learning the subject matter content ranked high as strengths. The extent to which the games facilitated an examination of certain value-laden issues was greater than might have been anticipated, because the games were relatively straight-forward and of short duration. Perhaps it is these characteristics, however, that caused only 53% of the respondents to feel that the simulations unqualifiedly helped them understand the complexity of the systems portrayed. This may also have been a factor in students' only mildly favorable assessments of the decision-making potential of the games.

"Curriculum Development" received the best composite rating of the simulations employed. Interestingly enough, it was the longest simulation (approximately 11 hours), consisted of two separate parts, and, because groups were developing their own high school curricula, probably provided the greatest latitude for decision-making. It had high "scores" on the five points mentioned above. Similarly, "Collective Negotiations," which had the lowest composite rating, also had the least favorable ratings on most of those same points. It would appear that students value especially the opportunity to make decisions, grapple with values, and gain insights into the complexities of social, economic, and educational systems. Perhaps it was these factors that were largely responsible for the degree of student motivation and interest that the games engendered (Question 7).

Internship students revealed positive feelings toward the "Society, School, and Curriculum" component of that program. They were not wholly convinced of the oneness between theory and practice, or at least concrete examples of some of the theory were not immediately evident to them in their school settings. There was much more consensus on Questions 7 and 8, relating to the availability of materials and the accessibility of the instructor. In summary, however, students seemed favorably disposed toward the individually paced work (Question 2) and the general format of the course (Question 9).

Results of measures of student cognitive achievement in the three groups are more difficult to evaluate. Statistically, there was not a significant difference in achievement, as measured by the Education Test, on material common to both SIM and INT. This was true in spite of the fact that INT revealed a statistically significant (.02 level of confidence) higher aptitude for learning, if one is to place any value in SAT-Verbal scores. With very little certainty of factors operating other than chance, it could be said only that SIM may have gained some slight ground on topics related to philosophy of education and curriculum, and lost similar amounts in the areas of sociology of education, aims of education, and organization and administration. If this is true, the simulation "Curriculum Development" had both good and not so good results, for it included topics related not only to curriculum but also to educational aims, organization, and administration. In addition, all of the simulations contained, to some extent, topics and issues related to organization and administration. Again, the reader must be mindful that such conjecture has little or no statistically significant support.

Similarly, a comparison between LMP and SIM on the instructor-made multiple-choice test revealed no significant differences on total post-test scores or in the percent of improvement over pretest scores. An analysis of student improvement on posttest scores in each of the twelve categories of the test revealed that SIM may have profited considerably by use of a simulation game in the study of professional organizations, because its mean increase in correct answers differed significantly from that of LMP. In fact, though such a statement is not warranted on the basis of statistically significant differences, simulations may also have contributed (to a lesser extent) to SIM's greater improvement in Curriculum, Finance, and Governance. Similarly, learning materials packages may have had a more beneficial effect than simulations in Accountability and Alternative Education, because LMP displayed greater comparative increases in scores in those areas.

The relatively small number of students included in this study mitigated against the discovery of statistically significant differences between groups. Future studies should attempt to utilize more students or add to the number included here. In many cases, doubling the number of students would have produced quantitative results where confidence levels would have ranged between .05 and .01. For example, on the pre-test and post-test analysis made in the final part of this study, if the groups had numbered 42 and 34 (instead of 21 and 17) students, and assuming the distribution of scores had remained the same, the level of confidence reached in the comparisons in the Flexible Scheduling category of questions would have been between .02 and .01 (instead of .1)!

Another acknowledged problem with this study was the "contamination" of the SIM teaching approach by the use of some of the same reading materials as were included in the LMPs. In other words, the two approaches (SIM and LMP) were not entirely discrete or separate from each other. This same phenomenon operated to a lesser extent in INT and SIM, because of the fact that both groups took the same three field trips. They, too, had some common experiences that constituted or supplemented their study of certain topics. Nevertheless, some insights may have been gained about the comparative advantages of certain instructional emphases or combination of materials and activities.

NOTE

---

1. Three of these students did not take the Education Test and, therefore, are not included in the SIM/INT comparison (see below).

TABLE 1
SUMMARY OF STUDENT EVALUATIONS OF
"CURRICULUM DEVELOPMENT"

Questions	Responses		
	Yes	Qual.	No
2. Objectives clear?	16	0	0
3. Helped understand complexity of the system?	12	4	0
4. Helped examine value questions and issues?	13	2	1
5. Opportunity to practice decision-making?	11	1	4
6. Helped learn about subject matter?	13	1	1
7. Interesting and motivating?	14	3	0
8. Recommend re-use?	12	4	0
Total Responses	91	15	6
Percent of Total	81	14	5

TABLE 2
SUMMARY OF STUDENT EVALUATIONS OF
PURSE STRINGS

Questions	*Responses*		
	Yes	*Qual.*	*No*
2. Objectives clear?	15	0	2
3. Helped understand complexity of the system?	10	4	3
4. Helped examine value questions and issues?	11	4	2
5. Opportunity to pratice decision-making?	11	1	5
6. Helped learn about subject matter?	16	0	1
7. Interesting and motivating?	10	4	3
8. Recommend re-use?	13	3	1
Total Responses	86	16	17
Percent of Total	72	14	14

TABLE 3
SUMMARY OF STUDENT EVALUATIONS OF
"COLLECTIVE NEGOTIATIONS"

Questions	*Responses*		
	Yes	*Qual.*	*No*
2. Objectives clear?	15	0	2
3. Helped understand complexity of the system?	5	10	2
4. Helped examine value questions and issues?	7	7	3
5. Opportunity to practice decision-making?	7	5	5
6. Helped learn about subject matter?	12	4	1
7. Interesting and motivating?	8	5	3
8. Recommend re-use?	10	5	2
Total Responses	64	36	18
Percent of Total	54	31	15

TABLE 4
SUMMARY OF STUDENT EVALUATIONS OF
"ALTERNATIVES"

Questions	*Responses*		
	Yes	*Qual.*	*No*
2. Objectives clear?	11	0	0
3. Helped understand complexity of the system?	3	5	3
4. Helped examine value questions and issues?	8	1	2
5. Opportunity to practice decision-making?	5	3	3
6. Helped learn about subject matter?	10	0	1
7. Interesting and motivating?	7	1	3
8. Recommend re-use?	8	0	3
Total Responses	52	10	15
Percent of Total	68	13	19

TABLE 5

SUMMARY OF STUDENT EVALUATIONS OF
"PERFCON"

Questions	Responses		
	Yes	Qual.	No
2. Objectives clear?	15	1	0
3. Helped understand complexity of the system?	11	2	4
4. Helped examine value questions and issues?	12	0	5
5. Opportunity to practice decision-making?	13	0	3
6. Helped learn about subject matter?	15	1	1
7. Interesting and motivating?	10	3	4
8. Recommend re-use?	12	2	3
Total Responses	87	9	20
Percent of Total	75	8	17

TABLE 6

SUMMARY OF STUDENT RESPONSES BY QUESTION
FOR ALL SIMULATION GAMES

Questions	Yes		Qual.		No	
	No.	%	No.	%	No.	%
2. Objectives clear?	73	94	1	1	4	5
3. Helped understand complexity of the system?	41	53	26	32	12	15
4. Helped examine value questions and issues?	51	65	14	18	13	17
5. Opportunity to practice decision-making?	47	61	10	13	20	26
6. Helped learn about subject matter?	66	86	6	8	5	6
7. Interesting and motivating?	49	63	16	20	13	17
8. Recommend re-use	55	71	14	18	9	11

TABLE 7

SUMMARY OF STUDENT EVALUATIONS OF
"SOCIETY, SCHOOL, AND CURRICULUM"

Question	Scale Strong⟶Weak											Total	Median
	10	9	8	7	6	5	4	3	2	1	0		
1. Relationship between tasks and school resources and experiences?	1	1	2	2	2	1	1	0	0	0	0	10	7
2. Feeling toward individually paced nature of work?	2	1	4	2	1	0	0	0	0	0	0	10	8
3. Clarity of the statements of the behavioral tasks?	3	3	1	2	0	0	1	0	0	0	0	10	9
4. Relevancy of the tasks to an understanding of educational issues and topics?	1	1	4	1	1	1	1	0	0	0	0	10	8

5. Appropriateness of the learning resources to the tasks?

   0 5 1 1 1 0 0 0 0 0 0   8   9

6. Appropriateness of the means of evaluation of the tasks?

   1 4 1 2 0 5 0 0 0 0 0   9   9

7. Availability of learning resources?

   4 3 2 0 1 0 0 0 0 0 0   10   9

8. Accessibility of the instructor for oral tests?

   3 3 2 2 0 0 0 0 0 0 0   10   9

9. Overall feeling toward the format of the work?

   4 2 2 0 1 1 0 0 0 0 0   10   9

TABLE 8

GROUP MEAN SCORES ON THE EDUCATION TEST
AND THE SCHOLASTIC APTITUDE TEST (VERBAL)

| | Ed Test | | SAT | |
GROUP	Mean	SD	Mean	SD
INT	483	30	586	51
SIM	441	99	514	79

TABLE 9

PERCENTAGE OF CORRECT RESPONSES
BY INT AND SIM STUDENTS
ON NINE CATEGORIES OF QUESTIONS IN THE EDUCATION TEST

Category	INT	SIM	% of Difference	SE_{Diff}	t Value
History of Education	34	29	17	20.60	.243
Educational Psychology	68	62	10	19.77	.303
Philosophy of Education	51	49	4	20.61	.097
Sociology of Education	63	50	26	25.53	.633
Theory and Research	53	50	6	20.61	.146
Aims of Education	59	49	20	20.59	.486
Curriculum	43	42	2	20.37	.049
Organization and Administration	50	40	25	20.45	.489
Teaching-Learning	64	58	10	20.19	.297

TABLE 10
MEAN SCORES OF LMP AND SIM
ON PRETEST AND POSTTEST

Group	Pretest	Posttest
LMP	35.19	60.95
SIM	32.41	60.24

TABLE 11
COMPARISON OF LMP AND SIM STUDENTS
ON GAINS OF POST-TEST SCORES OVER PRE-TEST SCORES
IN TWELVE CATEGORIES OF QUESTIONS

Category	LMP Mean Increase in Correct Answers	SIM Mean Increase in Correct Answers	$^{SE}Diff$	t Value
Accountability	2.19	2.06	.46	.283
Alternative Education	2.71	1.82	.62	1.369
Curriculum	1.90	2.71	.62	1.306
Finance	3.33	3.65	.63	.508
Flexible Scheduling	1.67	1.00	.41	1.634
Governance	1.76	2.76	.68	1.471
Grouping for Instruction	2.05	2.35	.58	.517
History of Education	2.29	2.59	.65	.462
"The New"	1.90	2.12	.62	.355
Professional Organizations	2.29	3.18	.41	2.171*
Team Teaching	1.90	1.29	.49	1.245
Urban Education	1.76	2.18	.51	.824

* significant at the .05 level of confidence

21
COGNITIVE STYLES
AND STUDENT RESPONSE
TO SIMULATIONS

SAMUEL J. THIOS

ABSTRACT

This paper first defines cognitive style and then argues for the importance of the concept in the process of evaluating the teaching effectiveness of simulation. Finally it describes an experiment that correlated several style measures with the amount of positive affect students reported about simulation gaming.

In recent years, a great deal of research activity has focused on the area of cognitive styles. As defined by Biggs, (1968) a cognitive style is "a qualitatively consistent and characteristic approach to a problem, or to encoding the world, that is mostly independent of the quantitative or 'power,' aspect of intelligence" (p. 120). In short, cognitive style has come to mean the personal style of functioning that we all, as individuals, employ in our daily lives.

Recently, several investigators from different disciplines have hypothesized that cognitive styles may play an exceedingly important role in the educational field. Witkin (1973) noted that "perhaps the most promising and exciting prospects for a cognitive-style approach lie in the field of education. While relatively little research has been done, compared to what is possible and needed, it is already clear that cognitive style is a potent variable in students' academic choices and vocational preferences; in students' academic development through their school career; in how students learn and teachers teach, and in how students and teachers interact in the classroom" (p. 1).

From the above discussion and from other evidence reviewed by Witkin (1973) and Cross (1976) it seems clear that the learning process is importantly influenced by teachers' teaching styles and students' learning styles. An excellent example that demonstrates the potential of this approach to education is provided by the program at Oakland Community College. Dr. Joseph Hill, President of Oakland Community College, offers the following description of their program:

> An individual's cognitive style is determined by the way he takes note of his total surroundings—how he seeks meaning, how he becomes informed. Is he a listener or a reader? Is he concerned only with his own viewpoint or is he influenced in decision-making by his family or associates? Does he reason in categories as a mathematician does or in relationships as social scientists do?
>
> These are a few examples of the facets of human makeup that are included in a student's cognitive style. Family background, talent, life experiences, and personal goals make each of us unique. Each map, like each student, is different. A cognitive map provides a complete picture of the diverse ways in which an individual acquires meaning. It identifies his strengths and weaknesses as the basis upon which to build an individualized program of education. (Hill, 1973)

Hill has deveolped a set of tests and inventories designed to determine an individual's cognitive style (Hill, 1973). The results of these tests are printed in the form of a cognitive style map, which describes the ways in which the individual seeks meaning from his or her environment. This map describes three basic sets of elements. The first set of elements refers to a person's tendency to use certain types of symbolic information. For example, Theoretical Auditory Linguistic refers to one's ability to find meaning from words one hears, whereas Theoretical Visual Linguistics refers to one's ability to find meaning from words one sees.

The second set, Cultural Determinants, refers to those influences that help an individual interpret information. A person may be highly individualistic in his interpretations or he may rely on discussions with associates or discussions with family members.

The third set refers to the manner in which an individual typically reasons. That is, does he or she tend to reason in terms of categorical relationships, or think in terms of differences or similarities, or some combination of all three?

A recent exploratory investigation by Preston, Hudson, and Thios (1976) studied educational cognitive styles of college students as a factor in learning through simulation. This study was designed primarily to investigate only two specific cognitive style dimensions. One of these dimensions, Qualitative Code Empathetic Q (CEM), refers to one's "sensitivity to the feelings of others; (the) ability to put yourself in another person's place and see things from his point of view" (Hill, 1973). It was hypothesized that those students who enjoy simulations and feel that they learn well from such simulations are better able to see things from another's point of view and thus would score higher on the empathetic stylistic dimension.

The second dimension under specific investigation was the Associates (A) cultural determinant, which characterizes "an individual who understands that which is under consideration, but explains or discusses these matters mainly in the words of his associates who may be involved with him in the situation" (Hill, 1973). Here it was hypothesized that those students who enjoy simulations and feel that they learn well from these simulations would prefer a style that emphasizes discussion with associates involved in the simulation, and thus would score higher on the Associates (A) stylistic dimension.

Twenty Denison University undergraduates participated in the experiment. They were selected from class lists of students who had been in simulations. Students who had been in computer simulations were not used as subjects. On the basis of answers to a questionnaire, the twenty students were divided into two groups of ten subjects each. Students in one group said they not only liked simulations, but felt that they also learned well from them, while those in the second group indicated that they disliked simulations and felt that they did not learn well from them. All students were administered Hill's "Cognitive Style Mapping Interest Inventory" (Hill, 1973).

The results of the study showed that those who indicated that they liked simulations and felt that they learned well from them clearly ranked higher on the Empathetic dimension, $t(18) = 5.12$, p<.01, and thus are presumably better able to put themselves in another's place and see things from his point of view. This result seems to support the intuition that willingness to empathize might be quite important in group simulations, especially those involving extensive interpersonal communication or role-playing.

With respect to the second hypothesis, however, the two groups did not differ on the Associates (A) dimension. The initial assessment of the task requirements involved in simulations suggested that the two groups would differ on the Associates (A) dimension. In an attempt to better understand this result, the questions on the Cognitive Style Test designed to assess the Associates Stylistic dimension were reviewed. Several of those questions measured the influence of one's associates in situations where such activities as shopping for clothes and taking a new job were involved. Thus, it was decided that a new questionnaire would be formed where the questions were more directly related to classroom/academic activities. Examples of the new questions included:

I enjoy classes in which professors stimulate class participation.
I like to hear the ideas of others in group discussions.

I learn a subject better when I can discuss it with others.

I usually take an active role in group discussions.

The new questionnaire was administered to five subjects in each of the original two groups. The results, although certainly preliminary, were clear in indicating that those who were positive toward simulations also emphasized the importance of their associates in group interaction.

The above study directly investigated hypotheses regarding only two specific cognitive style dimensions—Empathetic and Associates. The cognitive style test that was administered, however, also provided measures of all other stylistic dimensions. Out of the remaining twenty-five stylistic dimensions, the original two groups of subjects differed statistically on eleven of them. No specific hypotheses had been offered for those dimensions, and these data, consequently, should be viewed as tentative. The data do, however, suggest potentially important differences that need additional exploration. For example, the two groups differed on the Transactional dimension, which is defined as the "ability to maintain a positive communicative interaction which significantly influences the goals of the person involved in that interaction" (Hill, 1973). As might have been expected, those persons who were most favorable toward simulations in the present study ranked much higher on the Transactional dimension.

It should be emphasized that the Preston *et al.* (1976) study investigated only affective responses, that is, how one felt toward simulations. It certainly is possible that one might actually learn a great deal from a simulation and still feel uncomfortable or unfavorable toward the process. Thus, research has begun that is designed to investigate the role of cognitive style in determining cognitive gains from participation in simulations.

DeNike (1976) reported results relevant to this latter point in a recent study using simulation games with fifth-grade children. DeNike investigated the question "Are certain educational cognitive style elements held in common by students who achieve with regard to cognitive learning when simulation games are employed as an instructional strategy?" (De-Nike, 1976). This question was answered affirmatively and, most relevant to the Preston *et al.* (1976) study, both the Empathetic and Associates dimensions were found among those elements common to the group that showed greatest cognitive learning.

It should be pointed out again that the above results refer only to non-computerized simulations, especially those concerned with gaming and role-playing. It is quite possible, indeed probable, that a somewhat different set of cognitive style dimensions will emerge as important ones to consider for work with computerized simulations where the group interaction component might be minimized.

Current research has only begun to investigate systematically the role of educational cognitive style in learning through simulation. Although it is clear that a great deal of research remains to be done, it is apparent that some students enjoy and learn better from simulations than others and that educational cogntive style may help identify those learner characteristics that are most important in determining both the success and satisfaction of those students who derive maximal benefit from simulation activities.

REFERENCES

Biggs, J. B. *Information in human learning.* Glenview, Illinois: Scott, Foresman & Company, 1971.

Cross, K. P. *Accent on learning.* San Francisco: Jossey-Bass, 1976, Ch. 5.

DeNike, L. An exploratory study of the relationship of educational cognitive style to learning from simulation games. *Simulation and Games,* 1976, 7, 65-74.

Hill, J. E. *The educational sciences.* Bloomfield Hills, Michigan: Oakland Community College Press, 1973.

Preston, N. E., Hudson, B. L., and Thios, S. J. Educational cognitive style as a factor in learning through simulation. Paper presented at the meeting of the North American Simulation and Gaming Association, Raleigh, October, 1976.

Witkin, H. A. The role of cognitive style in academic performance and in teacher-student relations (ETS RB 73-11). Princeton, New Jersey: Educational Testing Service, 1973.

22

SIMULATION EVALUATION DESIGNS[1]

CHARLES J. MORRIS

ABSTRACT

This paper briefly overviews some of the research that has been aimed at evaluating the teaching effectiveness of simulation, asking why the research has tended so often to show no positive results. The answer, it is argued, revolves around the fact that much of the research methodology used to evaluate simulation has itself biased against finding significant effects. Four major suggestions are made for remedying the methodological problems, including suggestions about the administrative context in which the target simulations are used, the learning environment that surrounds them, the way they fit into the motivational structure of the courses involved, and how they affect the cognitive processes of those using them.

Evaluators are the natural enemies of educational and social reformers, very often for good reasons. Advocates for change may well fear "reality testing," as Campbell (1969) suggested, but it is also true historically that the seemingly inevitable outcome of an evaluation was a negative result or, at best, a weak positive effect. Why, then, should proponents of a program look forward to a process that will very likely rob them of precious funds or undermine the credibility of their arguments for innovation? For in spite of admonitions to the contrary, an unrejected null hypothesis is taken, by funding agencies and colleagues, to mean that a program has failed, and thus the absence of a positive impact can have devastating consequences for a program. It is for this reason, as indicated most recently by Ross and Cronbach (1976), that the antipathy toward evaluation by reformers is simply a pragmatic response to the myriad circumstances—political and otherwise—surrounding an evaluation. These writers go on to make the important point that the strategies involved in program evaluation are rarely adequate tests of the hypothesis that initiated the program in the first place. But it is a rare occasion when the absence of positive results gets interpreted as a failure of the evaluation rather than the program. This concern has been echoed by Bronfenbrenner (1976), who, in making a strong case for a more "ecological" orientation in education research, has argued that the failure of intervention efforts ". . . reflects not the ineffectiveness of our schools but the inadequacy of our research models." The message of these and other writers seems quite clear: *Current evaluation strategies may be inappropriate for the evaluation of many educational programs.*

I begin my discussion of simulation evaluation designs with the above comments because they appear to have direct relevance to how one interprets the less than impressive results of most of the research on the educational benefits of simulation. Are the generally negative results of these studies an indication that, contrary to what the proponents claim, simulation is not an effective teaching device, or are they to be attributed to faulty research design and measurement? I shall return to this question in a moment. Before doing so, however, it is necessary to provide some context for the views I will express.

When asked to explore the literature on the educational effects of simulation, an area with which I was largely unfamiliar, I began with the hope that I could perform what Gene Glass (1976) in last year's presidential address (American Educational Research Association) called a "meta-analysis" (an analysis of analyses) on simulation research. Much as he went about assessing the effectiveness of psychotherapy, I intended to collect all of the research studies available, describe the "effect size" for each measure in standard deviation units, and then make a number of comparisons as a function of a host of simulation variables—for example, type of simulation, duration, experience of user, age of subjects, extent of role-playing, etc. The rationale seemed simple enough and I was initially optimistic enough to believe that I could make as much sense out of the simulation literature as Glass and his colleagues did out of the almost 400 studies of psychotherapy they analyzed. That I failed to do so, or even perform the analysis hoped for, serves as the basis for much of what I have to say about simulation research designs. It became clear rather quickly that, with the exception of showing that simulation is better than nothing (i.e., no treatment control groups), my analysis would reveal no significant effects of simulation compared with conventional teaching methods. As an agnostic with regard to the virtues of simulation, the absence of a strong impact did not disturb me personally. But, as a methodologist, I could not convince myself that simulation had really been given a chance. Poor research designs or implementation strategies seem to be equally likely explanations of the lack of a strong impact, and thus I came to the conclusion that the kind of summative evaluation I had in mind was premature. There was, moreover, the tremendous enthusiasm for simulation by people for whom I had a great deal of respect that dissuaded me from putting too much faith in the literature. I therefore decided to focus my attention upon future directions for simulation research rather than commenting on the apparent inadequacy of the research up to this point in time.

Before moving on to specific recommendations, I should mention that my conclusions about the literature on simulation are shared even by the strongest advocates of simulation techniques, conclusions that, incidentally, have remained unchanged after a decade of research. For example, Livingston and Stoll (1973), after reviewing the literature, suggest that the choice to use simulation must be based upon the advice of colleagues or personal experience, a view reminiscent of the "acceptance on faith" phase of simulation history described by Boocock and Schild (1968). Implicit agreement with this conclusion is indicated by a call for more research by all the reviewers I consulted. My own concern, however, is whether more of the same kind of research will substantively change this conclusion in the future. Perhaps a new approach must be taken if the educational benefits of simulation are to be fully realized. It will be argued here that, although there is definite room for improvement in the methodological aspects of simulation research (appropriate controls, better measurement, etc.), *the real problem is that most of the research on simulation has been biased against finding significant effects.* If this is the case, some of the most ardent supporters of simulation, or at least those confident enough to test their presuppositions empirically, find themselves in the ironic position of undermining faith in an instructional method the effectiveness of which they had hoped to demonstrate. It is in this sense that my initial comments about the inappropriateness of evaluation strategies become relevant to simulation research. I turn now to a more detailed treatment of this issue.

Claims and Conditions

Most of us are probably aware of the excessive claims that have been made for simulation, ranging from the facilitation of factual learning to forms of personal growth that would put even the most effective psychotherapist to shame. Even taking into consideration the inevitable oversell that accompanies the introduction of innovative methods, the marked discrepancy between claims and research outcomes makes things look worse than they actually are. For example, one reasonably consistent effect of simulation relates to what Goodman (1973) has called the "consummatory side" of simulation activities, i.e., the interest and enjoyment generated among students, which presumably has a motivational impact. But this important effect looks small indeed compared with the full list of claims that have been made.

An even more striking discrepancy, however, is to be found between the expectations for a given simulation and its actual implementation in the classroom. This issue has received very little attention in the literature but its significance cannot be overemphasized. It seems to me, for instance, that the way in which many simulations have been incorporated into the ongoing process of instruction has virtually guaranteed a minimal impact.

Consider for a moment a slightly exaggerated but not too atypical setting for far too many simulation experiments. The first thing one notices is that participation in the simulation is rarely contingent upon prior preparation by students. A brief description is offered, materials (if any) provided, and the exercise begins. Second, the duration of the simulation is usually very brief, lasting anywhere from a few hours to perhaps a few days. A third feature of many simulations is that successful completion of the exercise does not require the learning of anything new. In fact, one usually has no way of knowing the level of participation by a given student. Fourth, the simulation activities are generally independent of the ongoing reward structure of the course and even of the course content in some cases. Fifth, debriefing sessions appear to be relatively short in many instances and absent in others. Finally, the activities engaged in during the simulation are typically not reinforced by subsequent events taking place in the classroom.

Put in its simplest terms, the simulation often bears only a superficial relationship to the overall structure of the course, is in direct conflict with the motivational constraints imposed in the course—as well as those in courses taken concurrently—and makes no provisions for the subsequent strengthening of the processes activated during the exercise. Given these conditions, an outsider like myself wonders, not why measurable effects of simulation have been hard to come by, but why we should expect anything more than a transitory effect in the first place! Have we so convinced ourselves of the virtues of simulation that we need not be concerned about the context in which a particular simulation takes place? Quite frankly, I have the impression that an appropriate analogy for many simulations is the "school recess," a brief time out from more serious pursuits, enjoyable, to be sure, but hardly expected to modify significantly the cognitive and affective structure of the individual. This is not the way to test what many believe to be a serious challenger to traditional practices.

If we have learned anything from the past fifty years of educational research, it is that tinkering with the instructional process within a conventional format will not differentially affect student performance. Dubin and Taveggia (1968), in their important review of college teaching, make this point very clear. Their comparative study of roughly four decades of research on college teaching revealed no differential effect of lecture, discussion, and independent study formats. I submit that much of the simulation research falls within the tinkering category, the consequence being inconsistent and sometimes contradictory results. A fair test of the potential benefits to be derived from simulation demands much more, the issue to which I now turn. The suggestions offered should be taken as working hypotheses with little and sometimes no empirical support. Several of the ideas presented, however, have been deduced from simulation experiments in which positive effects have been found. My tactic was to use these experiments as the basis for developing some hypotheses about the components necessary for a successful simulation exercise.

1. *The Simulation Context.* The ideal experiment, I think, would take place in an environment in which administrators, colleagues, and students view simulation activities as legitimate learning experiences. This is what Bronfenbrenner (1976) calls the "phenomenological validity" of the experiment—whether the participants perceive the experience in a manner consistent with that of the instructor. A requirement of this kind is probably difficult to establish in many instances, but it is absolutely essential in the case of simulation because of the "gamelike" nature of many exercises. Of course, the way in which the simulation is actually incorporated into the course will determine to a large extent how participants perceive the exercise (as indicated below), but the broader context can also play a significant role. In either event, a measure of phenomenological validity should become part of future simulation research.

2. *The Learning Context.* Although relevant details are often missing in the reports, one gets the impression that in many experiments the dominant mode of instruction is actually quite conventional, with the exception of the typically brief simulation exercise. In my mind, this amounts to an extreme form of the tinkering mentioned earlier and should not be expected to have much impact. (One might also wonder about the phenomenological validity of such experiments.) There is, moreover, or so it seems, a tendency to treat all simulations as essentially the same in terms of their presumed effects, in spite of the fact that enormous differences may exist among exercises. Finally, more often than not there is no attempt to conceptualize the simulation within the total context of the course or to relate it to course objectives. This brings me to what I believe is the heart of the problem in simulation research: *How are we to conceptualize and implement the simulation into the overall course structure and relate it to specific course objectives?* This point needs some elaboration. The way in which one goes about accomplishing this task can also be problematic, so I have listed below a few options that might be considered, along with additional comments aimed at clarification of my point.

a. *Simulation as an Advance Organizer.* One way to conceptualize a simulation, especially certain games, is as an advance organizer, which, according to Ausubel (1963), provides a general overview of material prior to a more detailed consideration and serves an organizational function. Research on the ability of advance organizers to facilitate learning has been mixed (Barnes and Clawson, 1975), but the role of simulation in serving this purpose has not been investigated. My concern at this point, however, is to emphasize that, by conceptualizing simulation in these terms, we see immediately where to introduce the exercise into the classroom and what aspects of performance to assess. All too often this is not the case. Instead, we find claims being made independently of the actual implementation of the exercise, along with assessment of a host of potential outcomes, only a few of which (if any) should be expected to be found. It is this so-called "shotgun" approach to simulation research that must be resisted. A clear specification of the relationship between the simulation and course structure, along with a set of limited, rationally derived objectives, would provide a much better test.

  b. *Simulation as a Course Integrator.* A good argument can be made for the view that many simulations are ideally suited for some kind of culminating learning experience within a course. In fact, one can imagine a situation in which all prior course activities are conceived as preludes to the final act of the course—the "putting it all together" in the simulation exercise. This would be a particularly strong test of the effectiveness of simulation, because it becomes the focal point of the course, all other activities being subordinate, and hence assumes the status of the most important component of the course. If simulation is indeed an important mode of instruction, I would expect strong effects to emerge under these circumstances.

  I recently had the opportunity to observe a simulation conceptualized as a course integrator at the University of Michigan. The simulation, called the Middle East Conflict game and developed by Len Suransky, was carefully embedded into a course on the Israeli-Arab conflict. Much of the students' work during the semester was geared toward ultimate participation in the game, which consisted of assuming the role of a given personage and becoming involved in negotiations for a settlement. Although not subjected to an experimental evaluation, a videotape provided by Suransky suggests enormous effects of the game. The motivational consequences, both before and after the play of the game, were most obvious. Some hints that the game served an integrative function are available, especially for the principles involved in the negotiations, but any strong conclusions must await a more rigorous analysis. Nonetheless, the model provided by Suransky's monumental effort is one that should be emulated in future simulation research. It is a striking example of creating a fundamentally different and integrated learning environment through simulation.

  c. *Simulation as a Reinforcer of Ongoing Learning.* A third way to conceptualize simulation exercises is to think of them much as we do laboratory experiences, concrete "hands-on" activities that are meant both to strengthen and extend learning via the conventional mode. Although the implication strategy suggested by this model is less clearly specified than those mentioned above, the basic idea is to introduce the simulation exercises at appropriate points throughout the semester. Computer simulations would be a good example.

One of my colleagues at Denison University, Paul King, an economist, has recently completed an analysis that demonstrates a successful application of this approach. Students in a macroeconomics class spent considerable time working with computer simulations of the aggregate economy, in addition to studying the text and attending lectures. Compared to an equivalent control class that was treated essentially the same, with the exception of the simulation exercises (but added reading materials), the students were found to perform significantly better on a set of questions requiring the application of macroeconomic principles. Presumably, the opportunity to participate in the simulation exercises allowed the students to sharpen their problem-solving skills. Whatever the case, the important point is that care was taken to incorporate the exercises within the total context of the course, both establishing their phenomenological validity and building upon prior learning, as was also the case in the Suransky simulation of the Middle East conflict.

3. *The Motivational Context.* Incorporation of simulation activities into the overall course structure necessarily includes motivational variables. However, perhaps because of the presumed "autotelic" (self-directed) nature of simulation exercises, it is indeed a rare occurrence when performance in the simulation is part of the classroom reward structure. Students simply are not held accountable for their level of performance on the exercise, the net effect of which is likely to be something less than total involvement and questionable legitimacy of the exercise as a learning experience in the eyes of students. Some will no doubt recoil at the thought of imposing additional constraints on what seems to be an inherently interesting activity, but we must keep in mind other demands that are placed upon student time. They must be pragmatic in how they invest their limited time and energies, and this usually means devoting oneself to those activities most closely related to course success (i.e., grades).

One obvious way to establish a motivational context for simulation is to reward level of performance in the exercise differentially, or, even better, make completion of a successful exercise contingent upon the acquisition of certain cognitive skills, which in turn serve as a basis for evaluation in the course. This was an inherent feature of the computer simulations used by King (1976) and in Suransky's Middle East Conflict game. An even clearer example is provided by DeVries's (1976) research on the so-called "Teams-Games-Tournaments" gaming technique. Although relevant primarily to nonsimulation exercises (which were, incidentally, found to be highly effective), DeVries has suggested a learning and motivational structure that may have implications for the design, play, and evaluation of simulation activities. The essential feature of this approach involves the simultaneous use of both the information-processing and experiential modes, along with a supporting motivational context. This is basically what is being suggested here as a model for a fairer test of what simulation can and cannot do in the classroom.

4. *Process Validation.* Efforts to embed simulation within a total learning and motivational environment will unquestionably lead to a better assessment of simulation as an instructional tool, but none of the suggestions offered really takes us far enough. Eventually, we must come to an understanding of the cognitive processes activated during a given simulation exercise.

Consider, for example, that in the King study cited earlier the computer simulations facilitated performance on simple application questions but not on those of a more complex nature. Why was this the case? More generally, why are some simulations successful whereas others are not? When we can answer this question, we have understood the processes that must be activated in order to produce a particular learning outcome. Getting back to my first question, King has made the not unreasonable argument that the complex questions on his exam were more sophisticated than any of the simulation models utilized by the students. This is an interesting point because it suggests a direct link between the cognitive processes evoked during the exercises and subsequent performance. In other words, he is implying a rationale for predicting the conditions under which a simulation will or will not be effective: If these processes are activated (and presumedly practiced), they will be enhanced; if not they will remain unchanged. This is, of course, nothing more than a version of the view that learning requires active and constructive processes. But the presence of these processes has too often been taken for granted in simulation exercises, when, in fact, they may not exist in many instances. Clearly, an analysis of simulation at this level must be considered the ultimate goal of our research efforts, because it will lead eventually to causal statements about the processes activated during simulation and instructional effects. Note also that it will provide a rational basis for measuring learning outcomes, thus eliminating the "shotgun" approaches that have guided most research efforts. The obvious first step in achieving this goal is much more precision in describing what students do during a simulation exercise. A similar (but more fully developed) point has recently been made by Esther Thorson (1977), Denison's Simulation Director, who, in addition to making a cogent argument for conceptualizing simulation as a rather pure form of problem-solving activity, has questioned the extent to which many simulations meet the criteria for inclusion in this category.

Conclusion

In response to allegations that compensatory education was a failure, many critics claimed that it had not really been tried. My own analysis of the literature suggests that a similar conclusion is appropriate for the research on the educational effectiveness of simulation. We have not really arranged the kinds of environments under which simulation would be expected to have its greatest impact, and thus we do not know if the claims made for simulation are valid. And, while the call for better research designs and measurement should be heeded, it is doubtful whether more studies along the lines of those already conducted will provide the answers we need. Incorporation of simulation into the total learning environment and the identification of the cognitive and affective processes activated by simulation exercises are viewed as the key elements of an adequate research program.

Implicit in the foregoing comments is the belief that the research literature provides a reasonably accurate picture of the effects of simulation as it is currently utilized in many classrooms. Past research tells us that significant changes in student behavior do not come easily, and a brief simulation exercise within the conventional mode simply is not a major restructuring of the learning environment. Significant changes should not be expected, and, consistent with this argument, they have rarely been found. We must, therefore, redirect our efforts to create fundamentally different learning environments via simulation activities. Only then will we discover if simulation is indeed an effective technique for achieving our educational goals.

NOTE

1. This paper was presented at the Annual Meeting of the American Educational Research Association, New York, April 4-8, 1977.

REFERENCES

Ausubel, D. P. *The psychology of meaningful verbal learning.* New York: Grune & Stratton, 1963.

Barnes, B. R., and Clawson, E. U. Do advance organizers facilitate learning? Recommendations for further research based on an analysis of 32 studies. *Review of Educational Research,* 1975, *45,* 637-659.

Boocock, S. S., and Schild, E. O. (Eds.). *Simulation games in learning.* Beverly Hills, California: Sage Publications, 1968, 15-18.

Bronfenbrenner, U. The experimental ecology of education. *Teachers College Record,* 1976, *78,* 157-204.

Campbell, D. T. Reforms as experiments. *American Psychologist,* 1969, *24,* 409-429.

DeVries, D. L. Teams-games-tournament: A gaming technique that fosters learning. *Simulation and Games,* 1976, *7,* 21-33.

Dubin, R., and Taveggia, T. C. *The teaching-learning paradox.* Eugene, Oregon: University of Oregon Press, 1968.

Glass, G. V. Primary, secondary, and meta-analysis of research. Paper presented at the Annual Meeting of the American Educational Research Association, San Francisco, April 21, 1976.

Goodman, F. L. Gaming and simulation. In R. M. W. Travers (Ed.), *Second handbook of research on teaching.* Chicago: Rand McNally, 1973, 926-939.

King, P. G. The use of computer simulation models in the teaching of economics: An evaluation of their cost and their effectiveness. Report from the Denison Simulation Center, Denison University, Granville, Ohio, 1976.

Livingston, S. A., and Stoll, C. S. *Simulation games: An introduction for the social studies teacher.* New York: Free Press, 1973, 31-38.

Ross, L., and Cronbach, L. J. (Eds.). *Handbook of evaluation research.* Essay review by a task force of the Stanford Evaluation Consortium. *Educational Researcher,* 1976, *5,* 9-19.

Suransky, Leonard. The Middle East conflict simulation game. Videotape presentation, University of Michigan, February, 1977.

Thorson, E. Gaming and computer simulation as problem-solving vehicles in higher education. *Liberal Education,* 1977, LXIII, No. 2, 284-300.

ABOUT THE AUTHORS

CHRISTINE E. AMSLER graduated from Denison in 1974. She received an M.B.A. in finance from the Amos Tuck School of Business Administration at Dartmouth in 1976, and is now working toward her Ph.D. in the Graduate Group in Economics at the University of Pennsylvania. Together with Denison faculty member Robin L. Bartlett, she has authored a number of articles in economics and educational evaluation.

ROBERT J. AUGE is Assistant Professor of Psychology and at Denison since 1972. His primary academic interest is behavior theory, especially conditioned reinforcement, stimulus control, and schedule-induced and schedule-dependent phenomena. Recently, however, he has been doing research in the area of sex role development and is currently writing a book on that topic.

ROBIN L. BARTLETT is Assistant Professor of Economics, and at Denison since 1973. She received her Ph.D. in economics from Michigan State University. She is particularly interested in money and banking and domestic financial institutions. Her experience as an economist for the Board of Governors in Washington gives her firsthand knowledge of the inner workings of the Federal Reserve. In addition, Dr. Bartlett has presented several papers at professional meetings on the topic of women as workers, and has authored a number of papers on simulation in economics.

BRUCE E. BIGELOW is Associate Professor of History. At Denison since 1971, he received his Ph.D. from the University of Chicago. Bigelow is a specialist in Russian, Balkan, and Middle Eastern history. He has been the recipient of NDEA foreign language and Fulbright-Hays foreign study fellowships. Dr. Bigelow served as assistant director of the GLCA urban studies seminar in Yugoslavia during the summers of 1970 and 1972 and directed Colgate University's Yugoslav study program in 1975. He has been active in the Simulation Project since its inception, and will be the Project Director in 1977-1978.

SUSAN R. BOWLING, at Denison since 1973, is Associate Dean of Students. Her Ed.D. is from the University of Tennessee; her research centered upon leadership development and management. She is currently Vice-President for Commissions of the American College Personnel Association. Bowling has actively used gaming-simulations for a number of years, forming her course "Organizational Development and Leadership" around a series of twenty-eight such simulations.

Louis F. Brakeman, Provost, and former Dean at Denison, has been at the college since 1962. His Ph.D. is from Tufts University. He also currently heads the Dean's Council of the Great Lakes Colleges Association. Trained as a political scientist, Brakeman has made extensive use of simulation-gaming both in his teaching and in his administrative work.

Daniel O. Fletcher, Professional of Economics with a Ph.D. from the University of Michigan, has been at Denison since 1966. His primary research interest is government and business relations. He has taught his subject on four campuses and worked in Washington, D.C., acquiring practical experience. Fletcher is the author of articles dealing with American economic history, as well as several in computer simulations in economics.

Thomas F. Gallant, Professor of Education with an Ed.D. from Case Western Reserve University, has been at Denison since 1965. Gallant has published several articles exploring the Progressive Education movement of the 1920s-40s and its parallels in higher education. He has been involved with simulation projects in his courses since 1974.

George L. Gilbert is a Professor of Chemistry. At Denison since 1964, he received his Ph.D. from Michigan State University. His research interests range from synthesis of potential anticancer drugs to development of new instructional techniques, one of which has been simulation.

Amy G. Gordon is Assistant Professor of History, with a Ph.D. from the University of Chicago. At Denison since 1975, and for two nonconsecutive years prior, Gordon offers courses in Early Modern Europe and Tudor-Stuart England. Her current interest is in French historical thought and the contact between European and non-European cultures in the Early Modern period.

Michael D. Gordon is Associate Professor of History with a Ph.D. from the University of Chicago. At Denison since 1968, Gordon offers courses in Medieval and Early Modern European history. His particular specialties are Spanish history and Renaissance political thought. He is currently developing an interest in comparative European legal history.

Zaven A. Karian, Associate Professor of Mathematics, with a Ph.D. from The Ohio State University, has been at Denison since 1964. With a specialty in number theory and statistics, Karian has, for several years, been interested in mathematical models or simulations in the social sciences. He teaches an upper division course in Modeling and Simulation, attended by both students and Denison faculty.

PAUL G. KING, Associate Professor of Economics, and at Denison since 1967, received his Ph.D. from the University of Illinois. King is a specialist in economic policy and economic development. His current research interests involve the development of computer-assisted instruction in economics and the building of simulation models that relate the economic system to environmental quality.

LARRY K. LAIRD was Assistant Professor of History at Denison from 1974-1976. His primary academic interest is Latin American economic development, especially its agricultural aspects. He left Denison to take a position with the U.S. Government.

LARRY C. LEDEBUR, at Denison from 1967-1976, was Associate Professor of Economics. Ledebur served as Associate Dean of Students for three years before returning to full-time teaching in the fall of 1973. He is co-author of two books: *Economic Disparity* and *Urban Economic Problems and Prospects,* and has written a number of articles. His current research interests are leadership dynamics, creative critical thinking, "future" studies, and urban and regional economics. He served as Director of the Denison Program on Learning Through Simulations in 1974-1975. He is now a senior economist for the White House Conference on Balanced National Growth and Economic Development in Washington, D.C.

ANTHONY J. LISSKA received his Ph.D. from The Ohio State University. He is Associate Professor of Philosophy, and has been at Denison since 1969. His principal academic interests revolve around those issues found in medieval philosophy that have significance for contemporary philosophy. A recipient of grants from the Ford Foundation and the National Endowment for the Humanities, he is presently working on projects in the structural history of philosophy centering on issues in perceptual theory and ethical naturalism exemplified in the writings of medieval philosopher Thomas Aquinas. Lisska's interests in simulation have revolved around questions of ethics and values clarification.

DAVID L. POTTER, Associate Professor of Sociology and Anthropology, and at Denison since 1972, received his Ph.D. from Syracuse University. Potter specializes in urbanization, social change, Southeast Asia (particularly the Philippines), and structural theory. He has received a Wenner-Gren Foundation award for anthropological research for the 1974-1975 academic year, when he was on leave as the visiting faculty member for the GLCA Philadelphia Urban Semester program.

RITA E. SNYDER, at Denison since 1973, and currently Assistant Professor of Psychology, received her Ph.D. from the University of Indiana. Her research interests include tactile pattern perception and tactile memory. She has developed a simulation for tactile pattern perception, is working on a computer simulation of models for physiological psychology, and has adapted currently available simulations for a Statistics and Design course.

DAVID S. SORENSON, Assistant Professor of Political Science, has his Ph.D. from the University of Denver. Sorenson's academic interests are in the areas of international policy, American foreign and defense policy, public policy analysis, and political China. He currently coordinates the international relations concentration of the Model U.N. program at Denison.

ERIC STRAUMANIS is presently Director of Denison's January Term. His Ph.D. is from the University of Maryland, and his areas of specialization are philosophy of education, curriculum development, and values education.

JOAN STRAUMANIS received her Ph.D. from the University of Maryland. At Denison since 1971, she is now Associate Professor of Philosophy. Her research interests center upon women's studies, the philosophy of science and mathematics, logic, and the philosophy of mind, in addition to working on a computer simulation in logic and continuing interest in abortion and the ethical and philosophical problems of the Women's Movement.

SAMUEL J. THIOS, at Denison since 1972 and Associate Professor of Psychology, received his Ph.D. from the University of Virginia. A specialist in human learning, memory, and other cognitive processes, Thios has worked with computer simulations of cognition and with the use of cognitive styles as a device for educational measurement.

ESTHER THORSON, at Denison since 1971, and Associate Professor of Psychology, received her Ph.D. from the University of Minnesota. Thorson's areas of research are in the development of politically socialized behaviors in children and in perceptual-processing differences in good and poor readers. She is also interested in the possibilities for mathematical or other types of formal modeling and simulation in the social sciences, and has been the Simulation Project Director since 1975.

In addition to the Denison faculty, three individuals who had worked as consultants in the 1976 workshop are part of this volume. William L. Bewley is a Research and Development specialist at the Minnesota Educational Computing Consortium. Robert E. Nunley is a professor in the Geology Department at the University of Kansas. And Robert Wismer, formerly at Denison, is an Assistant Professor at Millersville State College, Millersville, Pennsylvania.

WILLIAM L. BEWLEY is the author of numerous papers on simulation in psychology and its use in teaching. He is presently a research and development specialist at the Minnesota Educational Computing Consortium.

ROBERT E. NUNLEY is Professor of Geography at the University of Kansas. He specializes in the study of demographic trends, especially in Latin America. He has published more than twenty-five books and articles, among which *The Distribution of Population in Costa Rica* and *Living Maps of the Field Plotter: Analog Simulation of Selected Geographic Phenomena* are best known. For the past several years he has directed a large NSF program for the development of a hybrid analog-digital computer system that simulates geographic and historical phenomena.

ROBERT K. WISMER, formerly at Denison, is now Assistant Professor of Chemistry at Millersville State College, Millersville, Pennsylvania. His interests include teaching general physical and analytical chemistry, chemical educational simulations, and X-ray crystallography.